'Peter and Catherine have created a timely and essential guide in *Team of Teams Coaching*. This book is a masterclass in addressing the complexity of today's interconnected challenges through systemic collaboration. By blending deep insights with actionable frameworks, the authors equip leaders, coaches and organizations to foster sustainable, large-scale cooperation. It's a transformative read for anyone committed to creating collective impact in a world that desperately needs it.'
Marshall Goldsmith, Thinkers50 #1 Executive Coach and *New York Times* bestselling author of *The Earned Life, Triggers* and *What Got You Here Won't Get You There*

'From the earlier models on the 5 Cs of Systemic Coaching and 7 Eyes of Supervision, Peter and Catherine have created a far more powerful systemic team approach and models of STOTA and STOTC. As a practicing systemic leadership team coach with an organization that focuses on spiritual intelligence, I see great coherence and convergence. I resonate with the call for action *If not now, when? If not us, who? If not working together, how?* spiritually.'
Ram Ramanathan, Self-Development Coach

'This book challenges us to consider how a more connected way of working is an evolved and efficient way to tackle the complexities of our modern day. It prompts us to reconsider how we work together at a critical juncture in history, urging us to choose a more connected and effective approach. We are called to action to fully appreciate, investigate and nurture deeper understanding of the interconnections between individuals, teams and their wider ecosystems. Readers might be initially drawn to this book to improve team performance, but will leave inspired to foster a more sustainable and interconnected future.'
Alana Weiss, Director, People Development, Google

'Peter Hawkins and Catherine Carr have created a compelling read in *Team of Teams Coaching*. No, I would go further - they have created an *essential* read. Essential for coaches, leaders and humanity. The authors bring together ecological issues with systems thinking and team working to create a master-piece of a book that redefines our thinking around team leadership, team collaboration and system wide working.'

Professor Jonathan Passmore, Henley Business School and Senior
Vice President, EZRA Coaching

'In a world driven by competition and national interests, Peter and Catherine invite readers to rethink the very nature of human collaboration. We welcome this timely and important book which defines Systemic Team of Teams Coaching (STOTC) and explores practical ways to work with teams in a deeply inspired, radical and interconnected way. We are confident that this book will help shape the future of how each of us leads, coaches and contributes to teams, organizations and wider society.'

Lucy Widdowson and Paul J Barbour, Executive and Team Coaches,
Co-authors of *Building Top Performing Teams*

Team of Teams Coaching

Using a teaming approach
to increase business impact

Peter Hawkins and Catherine Carr

KoganPage

First published in Great Britain and the United States in 2025 by Kogan Page Limited

Kogan Page
Kogan Page Ltd, 2nd Floor, 45 Gee Street, London EC1V 3RS, United Kingdom
Kogan Page Inc, 8 W 38th Street, Suite 90, New York, NY 10018, USA
www.koganpage.com

EU Representative (GPSR)
Authorised Rep Compliance Ltd, Ground Floor, 71 Baggot Street Lower, Dublin D02 P593, Ireland
www.arccompliance.com

Kogan Page books are printed on paper from sustainable forests.

ISBNs

Hardback   978 1 3986 1397 3
Paperback   978 1 3986 1395 9
Ebook   978 1 3986 1396 6

British Library Cataloguing-in-Publication Data

A CIP record for this book is available from the British Library.

Library of Congress Cataloging in Publication Data

A CIP record for this book is available from the Library of Congress.

Typeset by Integra Software Services, Pondicherry
Print production managed by Jellyfish
Printed and bound by CPI Group (UK) Ltd, Croydon CR0 4YY

To all the future leaders, coaches, and consultants striving to create value-driven, net-positive, and future-fit teams and organizations.

CONTENTS

PART FIVE
Going forward together

The future role of STOTA in bringing together the different
    development professions 261
The emerging agenda for team coaches and team of teams
    coaches 261
The emerging agenda for the professions 263
The emerging agenda for training organizations 263
Going forward 265

LIST OF FIGURES AND TABLES

ACKNOWLEDGEMENTS

This book is a product of a team of teams, and although it is our names on the cover, we would like to thank all the other teams and team members who have made it possible.

The book began in a research partnership between Professor Peter Hawkins and Renewal Associates, and Professor Salome Van Coller and Stellenbosch University. We would like to thank Salome for the important groundwork she did, before sadly having to withdraw through illness. Her passion for the work still echoes in these pages. Also thank you to Vlad Duțescu from Romania, who followed Salome as the Renewal Foundation scholar in residence and co-wrote Chapter 13 on ethical dilemmas.

Dr Catherine Carr then assumed the role of co-author and research lead, and together we assembled a large research partnership comprising our most experienced Systemic Team Coaching associates and senior-level practitioners we have trained from around the world. This esteemed team has been invaluable as co-learning partners. They have engaged their client and employee organizations, distributed our questionnaires around the world, conducted interviews, co-written case studies and vignettes with key organizational partners, and provided feedback on various chapters.

We also extend our gratitude to the organizations and their leaders – their CEOs, HR teams and other key stakeholders – who generously contributed to this research by completing questionnaires, participating in interviews and co-authoring case vignettes. As we hoped, the interviews proved mutually beneficial, sparking new insights and inspiring the next stage of team and team of teams work.

Much of the material on which this book is based has been developed over the last 50 years or more, through work in and with organizations and teams. The over 100 organizations we have worked with around the world have been great teachers, providing us with new important challenges and opportunities that have taken our work to a new learning edge.

We would like to acknowledge and thank all our teachers, those who trained, coached, mentored and supervised us in our work as leaders, organizational consultants, systemic team coaches, systemic team coach supervisors and trainers of systemic team coaches.

We would also like to express our gratitude to everyone we have coached, mentored, consulted, supervised and trained through the courses we have developed at Renewal Associates and in partnership with the Academy of Executive Coaching and Coaching.com. Whether in Systemic Team Coaching, Systemic Team of Teams Coaching (STOTC), or organizational leadership and transformation, they have been our constant teachers, helping us refine our craft. Their fresh challenges and encouraging feedback continue to inspire and shape our work.

This book builds on the earlier books, I, Peter, wrote and edited on Systemic Team Coaching with Kogan Page: *Leadership Team Coaching* (2011, 2014, 2017, 2021) and *Leadership Team Coaching in Practice* (2014, 2018 and 2022). It has been a delight to see these works become foundational texts and be translated into many languages. Working with Lucy Carter and Joe Ferner-Reeves at Kogan Page has been a true pleasure. Special thanks to Joe for providing detailed feedback and suggestions on the early versions of this work and for ensuring we get it over the finish line.

In the USA 'Team of Teams' is a registered trademark of McChrystal Group. The use of this trademark in connection with this book is with the kind permission of McChrystal Group, for which we are very grateful.

In analysing the research data, Naysan Firoozmand, COO of Renewal Associates, played a pivotal role in transcribing interviews, preparing text and managing the complex research process and contributions from numerous partners. We received tremendous support from the core administration team at Renewal Associates, particularly Jo Ellis, along with help from Dan Hawkins, Natalie Bearman and Julie Jeffery. We also extend our gratitude to the Renewal Foundation for its financial sponsorship of several key elements.

I, Catherine, would like to express my profound gratitude to Peter for his remarkable thought leadership and enduring legacy, which have greatly influenced and enriched my professional journey. I am also deeply thankful to my family for their unwavering love and inspiration to live and work with purpose and joy.

Finally, I, Peter, would once more like to thank my wife and partner Judy Ryde for her love, patience, colleagueship, support (including editing many chapters) and her many important contributions to my thinking.

Professor Peter Hawkins (Bath, UK) and Dr Catherine Carr (Victoria, Canada)

Renewal Associates

WELCOME

Our story starts six million years ago. This may seem to many of you as a very long time in the past, but it is a relatively recent episode in the evolution of life on this planet, and a very short moment in the evolution of creation in our cosmos. Six million years ago, early Hominoids left the forest and were living on the African savanna, which offered far less protection from hunting mammals that were faster and stronger than they were. To survive, our human ancestors had to find a capability that would make them no longer easy prey. The capacity they developed was teamwork, the ability to collaborate so that the group was stronger than the sum of its members.

Many other forms of life, such as ants, wolves and amphibians, have developed a great collaborative capacity. What was developed by humans went further, the capacity to become a 'Team of teams'. Whereas ants collaborate at much greater numbers, they do so with far less differentiation than humans. Where wolves have great teamwork as a pack, which is probably greater than most human teams, they mostly operate in isolated packs.

Many have argued (Boehm, 1999; Lent, 2021; Rushkoff, 2019) that it is this capacity, which evolved in and through humans, that has led us to become the dominant species on this planet. Humans have developed the ability to collaborate with differentiated roles and contributions, not just in small packs or tribes, and not just in large numbers, but in large groups with differentiated sub-groups – a complex adaptive team of teams. They have evolved the capacity to have separate, semi-autonomous teams, each focussing on different specialities, aligning to achieve extraordinary achievements well beyond an individual team or tribe.

However, the strength of any individual, group or species can also become its weakness. This human collaborative capacity has allowed our species to flourish in almost every type of ecological niche on the planet, from tropical forest to arctic tundra, and from mountainous glacial terrains to arid deserts. In each ecosystem human beings have learnt how to flourish and dominate other species. Human team of teams capacity has led, in recent years, to our species more than trebling its population in one generation, while our species is the main contributor to the accelerating decrease in population of nearly all other mammalian species, including amphibians, fish, birds and many insects. We are now in the sixth great mass extinction of life on this planet, the first to be caused by one species – humans. This is a time when the few species that are growing in population and ecological niches that are flourishing, have become dependent on human activity (Whybrow et al, 2023).

As with many human organizations that become super-successful, they fall in love with their own success, believe they are indestructible and become arrogant and human centric. They forget or ignore the evolutionary truth and warning that: *the species that destroys its ecological niche destroys itself* (Bateson, 1972; Hawkins, 2021, 2025; Hawkins and Turner, 2020; Whybrow et al, 2023).

For many years, both of us have been coaching teams in a wide variety of organizations around the world. These teams range from front-line teams in charitable organizations to boards of highly successful global businesses, and from government departments to sports teams. In every case, we focus on helping the team become more than the sum of its parts, by aligning to its clear collective purpose, and focussing on how it can co-create greater value with and for all of its stakeholders.

We have become increasingly concerned with the word stakeholder, for like the word mission, it carries military, colonial, acquisitional and exploitative cultural nuance and implicit references. The word has echoes of colonialists moving into other lands and planting their stake deep into the earth and claiming it as their own. Other echoes include having a financial stake in a gambling game, which metaphorically underscores the prominence given to company investors, who gamble in shares on the global casino of stock markets.

We have explored alternative words, that might more fully represent the collective group of individuals, groups and systems that the team or organization need to work with to be successful. We believe that, at a minimum, this group includes: customers or clients; suppliers or partner organizations; employees; investors or funders; the communities within which the organization operates, and which provide all the necessary infrastructure, without which the organization could not operate; and the 'more-than-human' world of the wider ecology. Unless the team, or organization, is co-creating value with and for all these groupings, we believe that it is not sustainable in the long term.

In our previous books and papers, we have termed this collective group the stakeholder ecosystem. We have tried various alternatives and at times in this book have used the alternative term, 'ecosystem partner'. However, we have decided, for two reasons, that we cannot fully adopt this term. One is that we want to avoid confusion and show the link with both our own earlier writing and the wider literature on organizational and team development. However, the more important reason is that we want to differentiate stakeholders who have a remote interest in the business, from those who want to truly partner to co-create greater beneficial value for their joint worlds and the wider world they share. The former may be only interested in what they can get from the organization and are certainly not interested in partnering. These might include customers who just want the best deal, and suppliers or employees who just want the highest price for their contribution, or investors who want the highest short-term return on their investment. None of these can be described as true partners.

Perhaps, in the future, we will also discover a better term for stakeholders, while still being able to distinguish between transactional and transformational engagements, and we welcome any suggestions.

In our work and research, we have discovered that there is a long continuum between self-interested exploitative stakeholders at one end, and full ecosystem partners at the other end. Ecosystem partners, in whatever role, wish to co-create a win-win-win partnership, that not only benefits both immediate partners, but also delivers partnership benefit to the wider communities they share and separately serve.

Ecosystem partnerships require a systemic perspective that takes us beyond transactional win-win relationships of two-way mutual benefit. It is important to discover the beneficial value for the wider ecosystem that the parties can co-create together that they cannot do apart. We have worked with many teams and organizations who have become very stressed by trying to meet all the different competing needs of their wide variety of stakeholders. To do this they disaggregate their organization, with different functions focussed on different stakeholder groups: the finance department focussed on better returns for the shareholders, funders or tax payers; the sales department on customer needs; and the HR department on the employees etc.

Only when a team or organization develops a wider systemic perspective can they see the interconnections between all these different groups and create a virtuous and synergistic cycle and engage all the stakeholders as ecosystem partners. This requires a perspective that can see: the interplay between wholes and parts; the connections and relationships as having a life of their own; and how individuals, teams and organisms are complex adaptive systems, continually changing and adapting. We need to understand that teams and organizations are both self-creating – autopoietic (Maturana and Varela, 1980) through all the relational engagements within themselves, and ontopoietic (Mathews, 2009) adapting to all the continual changes within their ecosystem context.

We have also increasingly become less happy with the term 'complex adaptive systems'. Although the work in this field that uses this perspective has been very beneficial (Boulton, 2024; Prigogine, 1980, 1997; Prigogine and Stengers,1984; Stacey, 2001, 2010), it still uses language that locks us into outdated thinking. The term 'adaptive' emphasizes a reactive adaptation of the organism to its context and does not carry the sense that the organism is also part of, and has agency within, the wider ecosystems it is nested within. It plays into the common assumption that the context is 'out there'. When we talk about 'The organization'; 'The community' or 'The environment', we configure them as bounded systems, which are external to us, and can forget that every systemic level we are part of, is also part of us. It stops us from realizing that the organization, family, community and ecology are us. We are an inextricable part of these wider wholes, which in part, live, breathe and transform through us, our relationships and connections. The whole is transformed by the parts, at the same time as the parts are contained and transformed by the wholes. Thus, evolution is always co-evolution, and autopoiesis and ontopoiesis are united in an 'interpoiesis' (Hawkins, 2025). Thus, in this book, we have changed our language to use the term 'complex systemic co-evolution' to emphasize the horizontal and vertical inter-subjectivity of co-abiding and inter-being (Hanh,1987; Hawkins, 2018).

To achieve transformational partnership with wider ecosystemic levels, requires leaders and team members across any organization to move from atomistic and transactional thinking, to multi-layered systemic; perceiving, thinking, doing and being. In our work we have increasingly become aware that traditional forms of team development and team coaching have been constrained by outdated and unhelpful language and assumptions, which focus on the team as a bounded system and on its own performance and success (Hawkins, 2020a, 2020b, 2021, 2022b). In the same way, we have argued that we must move away from seeing the individual as the unit of learning, development, survival and flourishing (Hawkins, 2025; Hawkins and Turner, 2020). We need to move beyond seeing the development and coaching of a team as an end in itself.

This requires seeing all teams through a larger team of teams perspective, which focusses on how the team collectively teams with all the other teams up, down and across the organization. The team of teams perspective also perceives the team as needing to partner with all its stakeholders, in service of the wider whole, so they truly become 'ecosystem partners'.

In this book we start in Chapter 1, exploring more fully why our world needs a team of teams approach in addressing the metacrisis of the many interconnected challenges of our time. Then in Chapter 2 we move from the WHY to the WHAT and describe both a Systemic Team of Teams Approach (which throughout the book we abbreviate as STOTA) and define what is Systemic Team of Teams Coaching (STOTC).

In Chapter 3, we propose that addressing the challenges outlined in Chapter 1 requires an integrated approach that brings together the disciplines of coaching, leadership development, organizational development, organizational transformation, strategy and human resources (HR). Each of these fields shares a collective purpose: to develop individuals, teams, organizations and communities to be 'future-fit' in an ever-evolving world. We suggest that STOTC should not become yet another siloed discipline and methodology, but an approach that helps integrate all the various development disciplines creating future-fitness across all levels.

Then in Part 2, comprising Chapters 4 to 6, we look at the HOW of STOTC and how it integrates various coaching and development approaches in helping organizations develop and transform. In Chapter 4, based on our research, we propose a model of an iterative phase approach to using Systemic Team of Teams Coaching to organizational development. This leads to exploring the life-cycle transitions of organizations in Chapter 5, and the different team of teams approach they require. This provides the platform for a more integrated approach to organizational transformation, through a 'Team of teams' lens in Chapter 6.

In Chapter 7, we look at how all such approaches need to constantly be learning and evolving through continually evaluating what is working and what is less effective than what is required. In Chapter 8, we summarize the key findings of our global research, looking at the current state and best practice in Systemic Team of Teams Coaching (STOTC).

In Part 3, we explore the broader implications of STOTA for other levels of development such as individuals, teams and relationships. Chapter 9 begins by presenting an approach centred on coaching and developing the connections rather than focussing solely on the parts. This includes not only the connections between individuals, teams, organizations and stakeholders but also the connections across systemic levels – such as from individual to team, team to team of teams, team of teams to organizations, and from organizations to the complex world of all ecosystem partners. Furthermore, it emphasizes the critical connections between the human world and the 'more-than-human' world of the wider ecology.

We then in Chapter 10 examine how STOTA can significantly enhance Systemic Team Coaching by recognizing that 'every team is a team of teams', as each member brings connections from their various teams into the current one Following this, in Chapter 11 we explore how coaching and development at the individual level can be more impactful when individuals are guided to recognize, include and align their own internal team of teams.

In Part four, we begin by acknowledging the urgent need for more individuals capable of leading and facilitating deep, transformative change across all systemic levels. This includes not only leading or coaching individuals, teams and teams of teams but also addressing organizational, cultural, societal, global and ecological transformations. In Chapter 12, we delve into how to effectively train and supervise such individuals.

In Chapter 13, Peter has co-authored a chapter on ethical dilemmas in coaching the team of teams in partnership with Vlad Duțescu, who is president of EMCC in Romania. Chapter 14 then provides a summary of some of the most powerful tools and methods we have identified – drawn both from our extensive experience in this field and from our research.

Without dedicated training, support and development for a greater number of such individuals, the very collaborative capacity that has historically served humanity so well could become our undoing. It is imperative that we advance to the next level of transformation and evolution, one that fosters a collaborative capacity that transcends self-centred and human-centric perspectives. Instead, we must prioritize co-creating beneficial value across all systemic levels.

In the final chapter, 'Going forward and looking back', we demonstrate that only by achieving this shift can we begin to heal the divide between the human world and the 'more-than-human' world of the broader ecology. Without this, not only our species, but much of life on this planet, which we have made dependent on us, will become extinct.

We hope this book inspires and supports you in deepening your contribution to this great work, just as writing it has enriched and expanded our own. We acknowledge that there is still much to learn; for us as individuals, for those in the development professions, and for humanity as a whole. As a relatively young species, we have only begun to understand our place within the intricate web of life.

The First Nations people of the Americas remind us that we are the youngest sibling in the one Earth family of organisms (Kimmerer, 2020). They call on us to set aside our arrogance and embrace the wisdom of our older brothers and sisters – all forms of life that have existed long before us. It is time for us humans to learn humbly and deeply from the natural world, as its lessons hold the key to our collective survival and flourishing.

PART ONE

The 'why' and 'what' of Systemic Team of Teams Coaching

01

Why do we need a Systemic Team of Teams Approach?

The challenge of our times

We are living in unprecedented times, where our species and our planet Earth are facing what many refer to as a *polycrisis* wherein multiple crises interact simultaneously, amplifying their impact (Lawrence et al, 2024; Morin, 1999; Tooze, 2022). Throughout history, Earth has faced numerous significant challenges, such as the Ice Age, various mass extinctions and pandemics like the Black Death. However, we are now entering a new geological epoch – the Anthropocene – marked by a mass extinction of biodiversity. For the first time in Earth's history, this extinction is driven by a single species: Homo sapiens, which is us. This new epoch is termed the Anthropocene because humans have fundamentally altered the planet's lithosphere – the geology of the land we live on, as well as the atmosphere and hydrosphere that support all life on this planet.

These enormous challenges represent the shadow side of what is usually celebrated as the success of the human species. The world's population has more than tripled within the lifetime of the authors and has quadrupled since 1930, now surpassing 8 billion people. In 1830, the global population reached 1 billion for the first time. Around 2058 it is predicted the human population of the world will be around 10 billion. Despite global declines in birth rates, the population continues to grow due to advancements in human medical science, which have drastically reduced child mortality and extended life expectancy.

In my (Peter) recent book (Hawkins, 2025), I show how the most significant challenges facing our planet and species are deeply interdependent and cannot be resolved in isolation. These interconnected challenges form a metacrisis, which goes beyond polycrisis, to show how all the crises are rooted in the failure of human consciousness to evolve at the rate we humans have changed the world.

The interwoven impacts of climate change, economic inequality and political instability not only strain societal systems but also amplify anxiety, powerlessness and social fragmentation.

In Hawkins (2025), I passionately advocate for an urgent transformation in human consciousness, warning that without this shift, these challenges will only intensify, with increasingly severe consequences.

Scientists worldwide are sounding a louder and louder alarm that time is running out to prevent irreversible damage to our planet, as we face a rapidly escalating climate crisis, severe biodiversity loss, topsoil erosion and the pervasive pollution of land, sea and air (IPCC, 2021; Whybrow et al, 2023). In his classic study of paradigm shifts in human consciousness, Thomas Kuhn (1962) suggested that such shifts can take centuries. However, ecological science tells us we do not have that kind of time. A radical paradigm shift in human consciousness must occur within the next 30 years or less!

In the words of Cooperrider and Godwin (2022: 29), 'the clock is ticking, future generations are counting on us, and "history has its eyes on us". How will you choose to lead? How will history remember you?'

The challenge to collaborate globally and extend empathy

The great challenges are now Earth-sized and require a level of global collaboration and collaborative intelligence, that we humans have not yet learnt. There is an urgent need to discover how to create global forms of co-creative dialogue that will lead to collaborative and collective action. This requires a new paradigm, that includes our beliefs, values and practices that shape how we view and interact with the world and what we consider to be true, important and possible.

Since the scientific and industrial revolutions in the West during the late 18th and 19th centuries, along with the rise of modernity, our dominant para-digm has viewed nature and evolution through the lens of competition and 'survival of the fittest'. This perspective has deeply influenced our societal structures, leading to the idolization of wealth and success and driving compa-nies to prioritize profit and dominance over cooperation and collaboration.

To address the interconnected crises of our time, we need to shift away from this competitive paradigm and embrace a new one that values collaboration, sustainability and collective well-being. Only by changing the way we understand and engage with the world can we hope to create the global collaboration necessary to tackle these Earth-sized challenges.

Support for this shifting paradigm comes from those rethinking evolution. Contrary to popularized Neo-Darwinism, evolution is as much about cooperation and collaboration as it is about competition (De Waal, 2019; Raihani, 2021; Rifkin, 2009; Rushkoff, 2019). The success of Homo sapiens was not due to superior strength, speed or combat abilities compared to other mammals, but rather our unparalleled capacity for collaboration. For example, hunting a buffalo – an animal larger, stronger and faster than humans – required a coordinated effort from a large team of teams, each team and each member contributing different skills and roles, all aligned with a shared purpose.

Several scholars have argued that what sets humans apart from other species is not attributes like communication, tool use or even brain size - particularly the neocortex – since these characteristics can also be found in other animals. Instead, they suggest that the most distinctive feature of Homo sapiens is our remarkable ability to create and sustain large-scale collaboration across extensive communities. Harari (2018) expands on this idea by building on the evolutionary insights of the sociobiologist E. O. Wilson (2012): 'Humans dominate the planet today not because an individual human is smarter or more dexterous than an individual chimpanzee or wolf, but because Homo sapiens is the only species capable of cooperating flexibly in large numbers.'

While bees cooperate in large numbers, their cooperation lacks flexibility. Wolves, on the other hand, collaborate flexibly, but only in small groups. Humans, however, have mastered the art of flexible collaboration on a large scale, which requires a shared purpose and a unified identity. Maintaining a coherent identity and collective purpose over time and across generations necessitates a shared culture, one that can be passed down and assimilated by new members and incoming generations.

Harnessing our innate capacity for cooperation is crucial. On a global scale, the Covid-19 pandemic has taught us valuable lessons. We witnessed entire societies pivot to remote work, adopt public health guidelines and come together to collectively combat disease. These are the kinds of tipping points we urgently need to address the metacrisis that we are in – and they must happen soon.

We can't solve these issues without bringing everyone along. When our basic material needs are unmet, our circle of moral concern tends to shrink, focussing more narrowly on those closest to us (Raihani, 2021). As leaders, coaches and consultants in this field, we are wise to attend to and remember the socio-economic realties of others, and cultivate wide-angled empathy.

Our evolutionary inheritance had given us the ability to empathize naturally and unconsciously with others through 'bodily synchrony' (De Waal, 2019: 21, 28, 52), our own bodies sensing through resonance what the other person is experiencing. This we share with many mammalian species, which many will have experienced who have had dogs or cats as pets, or worked with horses or cattle. Mammalian empathy is the basis of collective bonding and what is often called the 'herd instinct', looking after each other as part of collective survival.

De Waal (2019: 205) writes:

> The greatest problem today, with so many different groups rubbing shoulders on a crowded planet, is excessive loyalty to one's own nation, group, or religion. Humans are capable of deep disdain for anyone who looks different or thinks another way, even between neighbouring groups with almost identical DNA, such as the Israelis and Palestinians. Nations think they are superior to their neighbours, and religions think they own the truth. When push comes to shove, they are ready to thwart or even eliminate one another.

Excessive loyalty or 'local cooperation' (with one's team) is also a major challenge for organizations. Raihani argues that 'global or societal cooperation is always under threat from more local cooperation, which affects our collective welfare. The big challenge for us is to find ways to cooperate to generate larger societal benefits and not just local benefits'. (Raihani, 2021; Suttie, 2021). We develop group-mindedness, microcultures and other ways of identifying and belonging. This has many benefits, but also causes many problems when it leads to negatively competing and making those 'not part of us' into 'other'.

We have both worked for organizations where the competition was seen to be the other regional teams or functions, with an internal competition for the best people and the most resources. I, Peter, worked in one organization where they talked about the 'back page of the diary people'. Being curious I asked who these were? 'These are the team members you are wanting to offload, as they are a drag on the team performance, so rather than firing them, you have the details in the back of your book, ready for the moment when a colleague is looking for extra resource!'

We humans still have a strong tendency to turn those we do not identify with into 'other', even to the extent of dehumanizing and demonizing them. News broadcasts still spend much longer on the death of two or three children in our own country, than on thousands dying from a natural disaster that is 'far from our home', and we give more to charities for pets and children in our own countries, than relief of suffering abroad. We have increasingly 'othered' those who are different from us, viewing them as enemies. This mindset convinces us that they pose a threat to our survival, causing our empathy to diminish rapidly. However, we know we are capable of empathizing with the suffering of individuals who are very foreign to us. Pictures of starving children in Africa or abandoned orphans in Romania can evoke a shared sense of grief and suffering across the world.

De Waal (2019: 204) suggests that 'empathy for "other people" is the one commodity the world is lacking'. While Goleman (2006: 63) shows how, 'in the growing global economy, empathy is a critical skill for both getting along with diverse workmates and doing business with people from other cultures'. Every organization today is a global organization. Even if you are a small local corner store, your supplies may be shipped from many far-flung countries, and your customers may be migrants from many different cultures.

Eco-empathy: expanding empathy beyond our species

To address the challenges of our time, our empathy must extend beyond our own species to embrace the 'more-than-human' world, the wider ecology of which we are merely a small and completely dependent part. In the Anthropocene, we have not only triggered the sixth mass extinction of biodiversity on this planet, which is the first caused by a single species, but we have also created a world where many species can only survive through human intervention. In Hawkins (2025), I build on the work of Albert Schweitzer (1987, 2009) and Arne Naess (1987, 2011), advocating for a deep reverence for all life on Earth. Schweitzer and Naess both argue that we must move beyond our ingrained separation between humans and nature, recognizing ourselves as an inseparable and entirely dependent part of the broader ecosystem.

Only by viewing ecology not as something 'out there', but as something that flows through us – with every breath we take, every drink and meal we consume, and every microorganism that inhabits our bodies, can we begin to see the entirety of nature as our kin. In doing so, we naturally develop care and concern for all life, just as we do for our family and human community.

In his insightful book *The Empathic Civilization* (2009), Jeremy Rifkin explores how civilizations thrive by developing new forms of empathic collaboration and ultimately decline when they fail to adapt to the unintended entropic consequences of their success. He concludes with a prophetic warning, highlighting that our current civilization is approaching a new and more perilous tipping point:

> Climate change is forcing us, as never before, to recognise our shared humanity and our common plight… We are truly all in this life and on this planet together, and there is simply nowhere any longer for any of us to escape or to hide, because the entropic bill our species has created has now enveloped the earth and threatens our mass extinction. (Rifkin, 2009: 614)

Later on that page he continues:

> At some critical point, the realisation will set in that we share a common planet, that we are all affected, and that our neighbours' suffering is not unlike our own… Only by concerned action that establishes a collective sense of affiliation with the entire biosphere will we have a chance to ensure our future. This will require a biosphere consciousness.

Biosphere consciousness requires us individually and collectively to extend our empathy to embrace all the interconnected life on this beautiful planet. He ends his whole book with the question: 'Can we reach biosphere consciousness and global empathy in time to avert planetary collapse?' (Rifkin, 2009: 614).

The role of organizations

Global companies have been major players in developing and spreading the benefits of the industrial and technological revolutions and they need to be part of addressing the enormous challenges those benefits have brought in their wake and the growing 'technological ingenuity versus wisdom gap'. As Indra Nooyi, former president of PepsiCo, said at the Davos World Economic Forum in 2008:

> It is critically important that we use corporations as a productive player in addressing some of the big issues facing the world. And I think all of those companies want to be the good companies, not just both from a commercial sense but from a moral sense. We want to do our job to make society better.

For corporations and organizations of all types, whether local or global, commercial or non-profit, need to effectively address the challenges of our time, they must transform into laboratories for pioneering new forms of collaboration and collective leadership. The Chinese symbol for crisis famously combines both danger and opportunity, reflecting the dual nature of challenges. In Hawkins (1986), I wrote: 'Crisis creates the heat in which new learning is forged.' The metacrisis provides the heat and the opportunity for transformation, but the transformation must be at, and between, all levels of the system – the individual, teams and families, organizations and communities, the global human species and the biosphere. No level can flourish alone.

There is growing evidence that shared leadership at the highest levels of organizations, along with enhanced teamwork throughout the organization and collaboration with stakeholders, can significantly improve company value creation and overall well-being. This was highlighted in 2009 when Katsuaki Watanabe, who was then president of Toyota, in an interview with *Time* magazine, emphasized the company's strong teamwork culture, stating that 'everyone at Toyota works as a team, including their suppliers, who are considered partners in their mission to produce what is needed' (Gumbel, 2009).

The changing nature of organizations

Ismail, Malone and Van Geest (2014) describe the 21st-century surge in organizational design innovations as a 'Cambrian explosion', highlighting the rapid and diverse evolution of new organizational models. In recent years, we have witnessed the emergence of adaptive concepts like 'holacracy', which introduces new forms of governance (Robertson, 2015), 'teal organizations' that emphasize self-managing teams (Laloux, 2014), organizations inspired by 'biomimicry' (Hutchins, 2012), 'shared value' companies that integrate social responsibility into their core business strategies (Porter and Kramer, 2011), 'net-positive companies' (Polman and Winston, 2021) that thrive by giving more than they take, and those adopting the 'circular economy' model to minimize waste and maximize resource efficiency (Hutchins, 2016).

Additionally, the rise of agile organizations has transformed project management with its flexible and iterative approaches, B Corporations have gained global recognition for balancing profit with social and environmental impact, and platform ecosystems like those of Amazon and Airbnb have revolutionized how industries operate by connecting producers and consumers through digital platforms. Digitalization has increasingly transformed how organizations function and how they do business, and AI (Artificial Intelligence) is predicted to exponentially accelerate the speed of this transformation.

Josh Bersin predicted that 'organizational design' would be the biggest global challenge for human resource departments in 2017. He stated: 'The solution is often easy to understand but hard to implement. We should break our functional groups into teams – teams focussed on product releases, customers, markets, or geographies. These teams should be smaller, flatter, and more empowered' (Bersin, quoted in Sustainable Solutions, 2017).

As organizations strive to remain successful and sustainable in an increasingly complex world, embracing this shift is not just a strategy, but a necessity. The ability to adapt and reorganize swiftly is becoming a critical differentiator in the marketplace.

In his more recent work, Bersin (2021), has emphasized that organizations must now focus on building 'adaptive, network-based structures' where the employee experience and well-being are central to sustained performance. This shift requires HR to play a pivotal role in fostering a culture that supports resilience, continuous learning and agility.

In studying these different developments and examining numerous case studies, we have discerned that all these approaches share eight key patterns:

1 A move from fixed, siloed structures to more emergent and fluid organizing principles.

2 Being less hierarchical, with accountability flowing in multiple directions.

3 Driven and aligned by a clear, transformational purpose.

4 Adoption of guiding values and principles that anchor the organization's purpose.

5 Creation of more porous, boundaryless organizations, with greater involvement of customers, suppliers, partner organizations, investors and the 'crowd' in organizational investment, innovation, production, recruitment, marketing and sales.

6 Strategic use of AI and the world wide web for innovation, stakeholder engagement, reputation management and most aspects of the organization.

7 Building a 'Team of Teams culture', where local teams are empowered to create their own aligned purpose, objectives and targets, becoming much more self-managing, and interconnecting.

8 Prioritization of employee experience and well-being as critical components of organizational success, ensuring that workers are engaged, supported and aligned with the organization's goals.

From fixed structured teams to fluid networking

In today's fast-paced environment, organizational adaptability requires teams to form, disband, reform and continuously evolve in both purpose and membership. Unlike traditional teams, networks offer a more flexible and inclusive framework, allowing a broader group of individuals with varied expertise to collaborate on different challenges. In some cases, a focussed network can be more effective than a small, static team.

Bill Drayton, founder and CEO of Ashoka, underscores the importance of moving away from outdated institutions where 'a few people tell everyone else how to work together efficiently', and a 'limited and vertical nervous system and by walls'. Instead, he advocates for 'networks – an open, fluid team of teams and continuous change-making' (Elkington and Braun, 2014: 38).

The ability to quickly assemble, disband and reconfigure teams based on current needs is critical. The future belongs to organizations that can leverage diverse networks of talent, allowing them to be agile and responsive to change, rather than relying solely on traditional, static team structures (Hawkins, 2021; Katzenbach and Smith, 2019).

While coaching siloed teams can be valuable, it often relies on the assumption of fixed teams acting alone. In contrast, a Systemic Team of Teams Approach (STOTA), works alongside an organization as a partner in its whole development, being vigilant to emerging challenges and ready to disrupt the assumption that every issue must be addressed by the board, executive team or a pre-existing management team. Instead, we should be asking:

- What is the real challenge, and how can the right commission be created to address it?
- What criteria will be used to judge success, and what would a successful response to this challenge be like?
- What diverse mix of people do we need to bring together to tackle this issue, including those with the necessary expertise, connectivity, influence, leadership and teaming skills?

- Who needs to be networked in from our wider stakeholder group (customers, partners, suppliers, other divisions), and how can we engage them?
- How might we engage the broader 'crowd'?
- Given these considerations, who should be in the core team and the wider network?
- Who should lead and who should coach this team?
- What internal and external team coaching resources could help this team succeed quickly?

Coaching networks also goes beyond the organizational boundary. Rifkin (2009: 541) suggests that the whole nature of commerce and exchange is transforming, even more fundamentally than it did in the Industrial Revolution. Then the transformation was: 'From proprietary obligation on the feudal commons to property exchange in a market economy.' Today 'the transition from property exchanging markets, to access relationships in networks, is again changing the assumptions about human nature'.

Many recent organizations including the world wide web, are created by and for global networks. Companies like: Visa, Airbnb, TaskRabbit, Uber and Lift, Instacart, GitHub and many others, make their money by networking and providing access to many suppliers and services. The ability to network and connect between organizations and their stakeholders is becoming more powerful than standalone companies.

It is not personal!

Barry Oshry (1999, 2007) famously explains that the first law of organizations is that 'stuff happens'. Every email, phone call or meeting is just an event – part of the day-to-day flow of organizational life. Even when something doesn't happen as expected, such as when an email goes unanswered, Oshry refers to this as 'negative stuff'. He elaborates that when things happen, we often take them personally and then create a narrative around them. Typically, these stories cast either the other person or us as incompetent, malicious or bad, leading us into a cycle of blame and grumbling. However, Oshry emphasizes that nearly everything that happens in organizations is not personal, we just take it personally.

Elias Amidon (2015: 51) in a similar vein, discusses how we are constantly creating what he calls 'extra'. He recounts a person coming home carrying two heavy bags of groceries. As they approach the door, they slip on a freshly polished step, causing both themself and the groceries to tumble to the ground. While the physical mess might take 15–20 minutes to clean up, the real burden comes from the 'extra' stories that immediately begin to run through our mind: 'Did the neighbours see me and think I looked foolish?' 'Who polished this step without warning me?' 'Why am I always the one doing the shopping?' 'I should have been more careful and carried one bag at a time.'

This pattern is not limited to individuals; it also plays out in teams. Too often, when difficulties arise, we instinctively locate the cause in a boss, another team or department, a stakeholder, or a specific team member, rather than pausing to explore the broader systemic factors that may be contributing to the issue. This tendency to place blame on individuals rather than examining the wider context can prevent teams from addressing the true sources of conflict.

In one of the first team development trainings Peter participated in as a team leader in the 1970s, called 'Task-Oriented Team Development' (Rubin et al, 1978), the importance of understanding the hierarchy of conflict was emphasized. While conflict may be experienced personally and enacted interpersonally, effective teams need to be trained to explore and address the wider systemic roots of these conflicts, rather than simply reacting to the surface-level issues.

Noel Tichy extensively researched team conflicts emphasizing their cascading nature (Pritchett, Tichy and Cohen, 1998; Tichy, 1983, 2002). His research built on the earlier work of Beckhard (1972) revealing a distinct pattern where conflicts predominantly originate from higher systemic levels. Tichy's findings can be summarized as follows:

- 80 per cent of team conflicts are due to unclear or misaligned goals.
- Of the remaining conflicts, 80 per cent arise from unclear roles.
- Subsequently, 80 per cent of the residual conflicts stem from unclear processes.
- Ultimately, only about 1 per cent of conflicts are related to interpersonal relationship issues.
- This sequence demonstrates how ambiguities at one organizational level create a domino effect, influencing subsequent levels. Typically, issues that surface at lower levels are often manifestations of unresolved conflicts at higher organizational levels.

- Unclear organizational vision, purpose and goals often lead to uncertainties in team and individual roles, creating confusion about responsibilities and accountabilities.
- Ambiguity in roles can then escalate conflicts within team processes, complicating workflow and communication.
- If processes are not clearly defined, these accumulated unresolved issues tend to surface as interpersonal conflicts.

Attending to all systemic levels

We often emphasize with the Systemic Team Coaches we train that while it's crucial to stretch our awareness to recognize the systemic nature of conflicts, individual responsibility remains equally important. While systemic work always starts by focussing 'outside-in' and 'future-back', change begins in the now, with the individuals and teams in the room stepping up to take responsibility for what needs to change. In Hawkins (2005) I, Peter, wrote: 'Leadership is not so much a role as an attitude: it begins when we start taking responsibility and stop blaming others.' Even within a framework of cascading conflicts, unclear goals, roles and processes, everyone must lead from where they are which means taking responsibility for their own reactions, behaviours and contributions.

As a leader, coach or consultant, it is essential to engage in self-reflection coaching or supervision, to recognize our own patterns and that of the leader, team and organization unconsciously showing up within us. We need to identify and process these patterns. It is precisely from this place of awareness that we can then effectively guide others towards constructive engagement and dialogue, ensuring that personal or team biases (shared mental models) are processed and do not exacerbate existing issues.

Furthermore, embracing a systemic mindset deepens both personal and collective responsibility within the team. Individual success is intrinsically linked to the success of the team. By attending to the well-being and effectiveness of the team, individuals acknowledge that their own success is intertwined with the collective's success. Team members must take ownership not only of their personal contributions but also of the collective outcomes, fostering a culture of collaboration, accountability, trust, openness and shared responsibility. When each member commits to the belief that 'we are all in this together', the team becomes more resilient, cohesive and capable of navigating challenges effectively. Teams of coaches must also embody this motto and model effective teaming.

Team coaches must attend to all systemic levels and the interconnections between them. However, as we have observed in training coaches, many tend to overemphasize personal and interpersonal dynamics of the team while underemphasizing the team's connections with the broader team of teams within the organization and its stakeholder ecosystem. This wider systemic focus is essential for teams to collaborate effectively. This raises their collective capacity to create value for all stakeholders, both internally and externally.

Systemic awareness is different from systems thinking, which focusses on the organization or team as a bounded system and the relationship between this bounded system and the parts within it. Systemic awareness recognizes that every whole is a part of the larger system it is nested within, which in turn is part of an even larger system; and that every part is in itself a whole, with parts within it. Systemic awareness also perceives how holographical every systemic level we are nested within, from families and teams to organizations and ecosystems, is also necessarily living within us. The whole lives through the parts.

A systemic approach requires coaches, consultants and leaders to view and sense everything within the ever-widening contexts of all the systemic levels they are nested within. To focus as much on the interconnections and flows, as on the parts; and not just the interconnections and flows between the parts, but also the flows and interconnections, up, down and between all systemic levels.

Perceiving multiple systemic levels and the flows and interconnections between them requires intention and practice. Knowing how to intervene once you can sense these flows and patterns is even more challenging. It's akin to climbing a mountain, where each step upward offers a broader and more comprehensive view, revealing the interconnectedness of the landscape below, as well as what lies beside, above and ahead.

The need for an integrative development profession

Every part of the world is calling out for radical new approaches to change and development. The world is not short of individual coaches, team facilitators, consultants, strategists, or those running leadership development programmes. But the world is desperately short of teams of development professionals who can enable and support systemic change and transformation, in and between the following levels: individual, team, team of teams, organization, networks across the wider ecosystems and between the human and the 'more-than-human' world.

In the last 80 years we have seen an exponential growth of many different development professions, from coaching, mentoring, counselling and psychotherapy at the individual level; management and leadership development to help people develop their skills for specific organizational roles; team development, team coaching and Systemic Team Coaching at the team level; organizational development, organizational transformation, culture change and organizational learning at the organizational level; and various approaches to developing communities and networks of organizations. But as the field has grown it has become more siloed, with competing approaches and professional associations, each with its own codes of practice, accreditations and approaches.

The Systemic Team of Teams Approach (STOTA) is not setting out to be yet another siloed profession, but rather an approach to integrate many of the existing approaches, and we will address this at greater length in Chapter 3.

From stakeholder to ecosystem partner

In the 'Welcome' chapter we discussed the problematic of the term 'stakeholder', with its roots in colonial forced occupation and 'staking ownership' of land previously occupied by indigenous communities. To date we have not found a term to fully replace the word for all individuals and groupings, including the ecology, that are intrinsically part of the team or organization's network. However, throughout this book we show the necessity of moving from a transactional relationship, seeing the stakeholders as either demands to be met, or resources to be exploited, to transformational, 'win-win-win' relationships, where we are working in partnership, nor just for mutual benefit, but also to create value and fulfil a wider purpose.

What is needed is not just a change in language, but in our consciousness, to seeing the need to move beyond seeing people, communities and 'more-than-human' world as 'other', to perceiving all life as interconnected and part of 'us'. We need to position ourselves not as owners of a stake, but as co-creators seeking to serve within an interconnected and dynamically changing world. This approach demands that we listen more deeply, think more broadly, and act more consciously. It requires us to continually adapt, innovate and work in ways that honour the complexity and interconnection of the ecosystems we inhabit.

To transition from stakeholding to ecosystem partnering isn't just a matter of words; it's a profound change in how organizations engage with everyone they touch – customers, suppliers, communities and even the natural environment. By forming deeper, more interconnected partnerships, organizations can generate value not just for themselves but for the entire ecosystem of which they are a part. This kind of integrated collaboration is essential in the complex, adaptive environments organizations face today.

In the Systemic Team of Teams Approach (STOTA) this evolution is critical. Teams that focus solely within their own boundaries miss the much larger opportunity to collaborate across the broader ecosystem. When organizations break down those boundaries and cultivate relationships that span the ecosystem, they unlock new paths to innovation, resilience and shared success. To thrive in the Anthropocene and navigate the complexity of our world, organizations must fully recognize their partners as co-creators in a shared ecosystem, working together to build a better future.

As Cooperrider and Godwin beautifully state (2022: 29), we 'are alive at just the right moment to help human systems at every level change everything. Ours is a once-in-a-civilization moment calling out for inspired transformation.' This is our moment for us all to respond in partnership and collaboration.

Conclusion

Coaching and team coaching have significantly contributed to developing more emotionally intelligent and resourceful individuals, as well as fostering more harmonious and effective teams. However, the larger challenges of the metacrisis that our species and planet now urgently face require us to extend empathy, compassion, partnership, collaboration and collective action far beyond individual teams and organizations. We must work across organizations, regions, countries and cultures to address these global issues.

This transformative work begins with ensuring that all individual coaching is systemic, meaning it is conducted as a partnership in service, not only of the client but also their team, the broader team of teams, their organization, and the wider stakeholders and ecosystem partners. Similarly, all team coaching must be systemic, functioning as a partnership that serves the organization and the broader world to which it is inextricably linked.

To ignite real change, coaching, consultancy and organizational transformation efforts must be directed not just towards the immediate part of the system they are working with but towards the larger team of teams. This broader perspective is crucial for driving meaningful and sustainable impact. The time is now ripe for extending the work of Systemic Team Coaching (Hawkins, 2021, 2022; Leary-Joyce and Lines, 2024) to develop Systemic Team of Teams Coaching (STOTC). In this book, we will uncover the strategies and practices needed to embrace this systemic approach, showcasing powerful examples from around the globe that illustrate its transformative potential in action.

02

What is a team of teams and a Systemic Team of Teams Approach?

Introduction

Having shown in Chapter 1 the urgent and large-scale need for a team of teams approach, in this chapter we will explore what is a Systemic Team of Teams Approach (STOTA) and the significant contributions it can make to developing organizational learning, strategy, culture change and organizational transformation. We will demonstrate how STOTA is essential in all forms of organizational development/transformation and is a key lens necessary for individual and Systemic Team Coaching.

Defining a team of teams

As soon as an organization becomes larger and more complex than can be managed by one team, the organization necessarily creates separate functions, each with its own team leading and managing it. Each team needs to have a clear commission from the central leadership team (or Board) so that there is clarity of expectations and delegation, knowing when it needs to obtain the agreement of the senior team, when and what it needs to report on, and when it can decide and act independently. This bounded autonomy is necessary for the team to function well and co-create beneficial value, with and for all its stakeholders, both internal and external (see Hawkins, 2021).

Once there is more than one team reporting into the top senior team, these teams need to engage and work together, rather than being a 'hub and spoke' organization, where everything goes up to the senior team and then down to another team. The senior leadership team need to avoid being the 'go-between' and communication channel between all the other teams. Instead, they need to provide the orchestration and culture that encourages teams to work together so that they accomplish shared goals and resolve any conflict or boundary issues directly.

The Team of Teams is made up of every team in the organization, working together. For the organization to truly flourish, not only must every team function as more than the sum of the parts, but the Team of Teams must also function as more than the sum of all the teams and co-create beneficial value with and for all the organizations stakeholders (Hawkins, 2021).

Defining a Systemic Team of Teams Approach

The Systemic Team of Teams Approach (which we also abbreviate throughout this book to STOTA), begins by looking at an organization as a living system, which is both nested within larger systemic levels, and has within it several semi-autonomous sub-systems (functions and teams).

The approach focusses on improving the inter-relationships, dynamics and partnering between teams, vertically, horizontally and transversally, to increase synergy, ensuring that the whole becomes more than the sum of its parts. This requires an approach that can perceive how the organizational culture plays out in the spaces and relationships between teams. By adopting this perspective, we can look at how this multi-level team of teams culture, both influences, and is influenced by, other systemic levels. This includes the two-way impact on team dynamics and individual employees, as well as the reciprocal effects on the wider stakeholder ecosystem, communities and the broader environment.

STOTA requires an appreciation of organizational design, culture, strategy and learning, as well as team and inter-team dynamics.

Defining a Systemic Team of Teams Coaching

Building on the concepts above:

Systemic Team of Teams Coaching is an organization and ecosystem-wide intervention, designed to foster effective collaboration and synergy among multiple teams, by focussing on partnering vertically, horizontally and transversally across the organization, as well as effectively teaming with stakeholders, beyond the organizational boundaries. It ensures that the team of teams function collectively and synergistically so that they are more effective than the sum of their parts through collaboration and partnering.

If we now take each of these aspects that are in the definition, we can see that STOTC is:

1 '... an organization and ecosystem-wide intervention'. Even when the coaching is just with a small number of specific teams, the approach must focus on how inter-team relationships can better serve the flourishing of the whole organization and their wider stakeholders.

2 '... designed to foster effective collaboration and synergy among multiple teams, by focussing on partnering vertically, horizontally and transversally across the organization'. The coaching is in service of more effective communication, engagement and synergistic partnering between teams and those above it, below it, upstream and downstream in the flow of work, as well as how it connects with teams diagonally across the organization.

3 '... able to effectively team with stakeholders beyond the organizational boundaries.' The coaching of the organization's internal teaming across teams, serves not only the organization's greater flourishing, but also its ability to team and partner with all essential stakeholders – its customers or clients, suppliers and allied organizations, funders or investors, the communities it operates within, and the 'more-than-human' world of the wider ecology.

4 'It ensures that the team of teams function collectively and synergistically and are more effective than the sum of their parts through collaboration and partnering.' In today's world all organizations are having to do more, at higher quality with less resource. To do this effectively, it is essential to maximize synergy and collaboration both within and between teams.

Team of Teams work addresses the complex challenges that require coordination across today's interconnected teams. It ensures that there is:

- **Cohesion and purpose:** Supports building trust, shared understanding and a common purpose among teams.
- **Collective alignment:** Focusses on aligning and integrating the work of different teams through a collective purpose to achieve collective goals.

- **Collective intelligence:** Facilitates the exchange of best practices, lessons learnt and knowledge-sharing among teams.
- **Capabilities:** Enhances strategic alignment, agility and adaptability in responding to dynamic environments and changing circumstances.
- **Capacities:** Evolves worldviews in navigating challenging experiences, integrating diverse perspectives and engaging in reflective learning.

An aspiration born of necessity

The Team of Teams coaching approach gained significant momentum with the work of General McChrystal (McChrystal et al, 2015) and his colleague Chris Fussell (2017) who highlighted the necessity of transforming traditional hierarchical structures into adaptable networks of interdependent teams. Their insights underscored the importance of shifting organizational culture and management practices to foster collaboration, agility and resilience in and between teams.

In 2005, US General McChrystal was given the unenviable task of coordinating the Allied forces in establishing a peaceful, democratic state in Iraq following the invasion and the overthrow of Saddam Hussein. As the leader of the Special Operations Task Force, he was charged with combating the rise of extremist terrorist cells. Despite leading one of the best-equipped and trained military forces in the world, McChrystal found that his forces were being out-thought and outmanoeuvred by an untrained, under-resourced network led by a Jordanian, Abu Musab al-Zarqawi.

This realization led General McChrystal and his senior officers to reevaluate their core assumptions and operating models. As McChrystal et al (2015: 20) put it, 'we had to unlearn a great deal of what we thought we knew about how war – and the world – worked'. They realized that they had 'developed tremendous competencies for dealing with a world that no longer exists' and that to be successful, they had to change. That change was less about tactics or new technology, than it was about the internal architecture and culture of their force. They needed an entirely new approach to management.

Al-Qaeda and Iran were outmanoeuvring the well-drilled, efficient command structures of the Allied forces with their superior adaptability, resilience and e-enabled networking capabilities. General McChrystal recognized that hierarchical command structures, whether in the military, healthcare institutions, or large corporations, were originally designed for 19th- and 20th-century challenges and were proving ineffective in the 21st century. In today's world, large corporate organizations are vulnerable to disruption by swarms of nimble, innovative startups operating out of garages. To remain competitive, McChrystal realized that large entities needed to emulate the innovation, adaptability and resilience of these smaller, agile competitors. This required a transformation in organizational culture, core assumptions, and fundamental principles of design. They needed a new model that was built on highly flexible, empowered and motivated teams. He spent sleepless nights grappling with the reasons behind this dilemma and pondering potential solutions. 'As the world grows faster and more interdependent, we need to figure out ways to scale the fluidity of teams across entire organizations: groups with thousands of members that span continents. But this is easier said than done' (McChrystal et al, 2015).

McChrystal's solution was to create a Team of Teams – an organization where the relationships between constituent teams mirrored those among individuals within a single team. His restructuring transformed traditional hierarchical structures into a dynamic network of teams, emphasizing fast knowledge-sharing, decentralized decision-making and a shared conscious-ness. The goal was to cultivate a cohesive environment where collaboration and agility could flourish, enabling teams to respond swiftly and effectively to evolving challenges.

Fussell (2017) adds depth to this model by emphasizing the critical role of shared purpose and trust among teams. Fussell's perspective highlights that for such a network to function effectively, each team must not only be aware of the broader organizational goals, but must also be fully integrated into the operational and strategic decision-making processes. This integra-tion fosters an environment where collaboration transcends organizational silos, enhancing overall agility and effectiveness.

Together, McChrystal and Fussell advocate for a dynamic and adaptable team of teams structure that leverages the collective capabilities and insights of all its teams.

We, like many others, have been greatly influenced by General McChrystal and Chris Fussell. However, their works draw heavily on a military and warfare perspective. Even the title of Chris Fussell's book, *One Mission*, evokes a combative, win-lose approach (see Hawkins, 2024: 52–53).

A key aspect of Systemic Team Coaching

Besides being influenced by the work of McCrystal and Fussell, STOTC has grown naturally out of Systemic Team Coaching (Hawkins, 2011a, 2011b (2nd edn, 2014), 2017, 2021, 2022b; Leary-Joyce and Lines, 2017, 2024). What sets Systemic Team Coaching apart from other team coaching methods is its emphsis on the broader, interconnected web of relationships that extend beyond the team itself. Instead of focussing solely on the dynamics within the team, this approach recognizes that the team's relationships with other teams – whether they are above, below or beside one another in the organizational hierarchy, are just critical, if not more so. These external connections are vital to the team's success and cannot be overlooked. Systemic Team Coaching is inherently stakeholder and future-oriented, prioritizing the question of who the team is creating value with and for. This perspective ensures that teams are not just functioning in isolation but are actively engaging with, and contributing to, the wider ecosystem of which they are a part, fostering a more holistic and sustainable approach to achieving their goals.

In our work on Systemic Team Coaching, we have delved into the intricacies of coaching, not just the team itself, but the vital connections between teams within an organization. We've crafted practices that go beyond the boundaries of individual teams, focussing on how these inter-team relationships can be nurtured and strengthened. By doing so, we help teams forge stronger bonds, creating a network of collaboration that enhances overall organizational effectiveness and adaptability. This approach ensures that teams are not working in silos but are actively contributing to a larger compelling and cohesive purpose. Chapter 10, is dedicated to the concept 'Every team is a Team of Teams', and further develops ways to systemically coach inter-team connections and partnerships as they show up within teams. Thus, we believe that all team coaches need to be able to adopt a STOTA, even if they are just coaching one team, or an individual team leader.

An essential bridging level in working across nested systems

Systemic approaches, unlike traditional systems thinking that tends to focus on bounded systems, emphasize the holographic and dynamic relationships between interconnected nested systemic levels (see Chapter 1). In the organizational world, the individual is nested within a team. This team is part of a team of teams, which is part of an organization, which belongs to a stakeholder ecosystem of suppliers, customers and investors and is held within the communities where the organization operates. This is all part of wider political, social, economic, technical and legal systems, which are themselves part of the broader more-than-human ecology (see Hawkins, 2015, 2025: Chapter 4).

I, Peter, have demonstrated elsewhere (Hawkins, 2025; Hawkins and Turner, 2020; Hawkins and Ryde, 2019) how every systemic level that we are nested within, is also nested within us. When an individual leader comes to coaching, their team dynamics, organizational culture, wider societal culture and the ecology all manifest within the coachee. These are often difficult for the coachee to articulate, as they have become integral to their way of perceiving, thinking, doing and being (see the section below, 'Culture as a key aspect of organizational transformation' and Chapter 12).

As we discussed in Chapter 1, the world does not lack individual coaches, facilitators, consultants or strategists, but there is a scarcity of individuals who can facilitate deep, integrated change and transformation, connecting individuals, teams, teams of teams, organizations, stakeholders, wider human partnerships and the broader ecology. There is an urgent need all round the world for such people, and a critical or pressing shortage.

To do this work effectively, we need individuals trained and experienced in working with individuals, teams, organizations and broader partnerships. Equally important are those trained and experienced in working at the intermediary team of teams level, including how teams collaborate internally to become more than the sum of their parts, as well as how they engage as partners and team externally.

Teamwork and teaming

In 2002 Patrick Lencioni wrote: 'Not finance. Not strategy. Not technology. It is teamwork that remains the ultimate competitive advantage, both because it is so powerful and so rare.' Teamwork remains essential for every successful organization, but since 2002, the speed of change and the interdependency of the world have grown exponentially. The organizations that hold the greatest competitive advantage now are those that:

- Have a well-developed teaming culture
- Operate as a team of teams that functions as greater than the sum of its parts

- Excel in teaming and partnering with all their stakeholders and ecosystem partners, including suppliers, partner organizations, customers, clients, investors, communities where they operate, and the broader more-than-human ecology.

Teaming is not just a buzzword; it's a critical capability that allows organizations to thrive in an increasingly complex and interconnected world. As the pace of change accelerates and global interdependencies deepen, the organizations that excel are those that can fluidly adapt, forming and reconfiguring teams as challenges arise. This ability to function as a Team of Teams, where each team is not just a silo but part of a larger, cohesive network, creates an additive synergy that propels the organization forward. In this environment, partnerships extend beyond traditional boundaries, engaging stakeholders/ecosystem partners at every level, from suppliers and customers to the communities in which the organization operates.

By embracing teaming as a verb, organizations unlock the potential for continuous innovation and resilience, ensuring they are not just surviving but thriving in a world where agility and collaboration are essential or imperative. As Edmondson (2012) notes, the real power of teaming lies in its ability to foster the kind of open communication and knowledge-sharing that turns individual efforts into collective success. This is the hallmark of organizations that are truly built for the future: flexible, connected and always ready to evolve.

Multi-team networks

Organizational contexts are now complex and interconnected. Even small businesses can be working with investors, suppliers, customers and employees from all over the world. They can be interfacing with legal and tax requirements from many different countries' governments, and impacted by global events, such as financial crashes, tsunamis or pandemics. The work of organizations can be viewed as multi-team systems that cross traditional boundaries (Carter O'Connor and O'Donovan, 2020; Edmondson, 2012; Zaccaro and DeChurch, 2012). Achieving success in these systems not only requires effective teamwork within individual teams; it demands strong inter-team collaboration. Shared mental models are a vital part of this process, as they help teams understand, not only their own objectives, but how their work fits into the broader system. This alignment fosters better communication, reduces friction and ensures that all teams are moving in the same direction. The networks exist not just through formal connections, but also connective tissue of informal meshworks, built on empathy, trust, influence and shared interests (Cross, 2003; Cross, Parise and Weiss, 2007; Ingold, 2011, 2015).

STOTC, working with leaders and teams, can help them cultivate these connections, fostering boundary-spanning behaviours that break down barriers between teams. In doing so, they create an environment where collaboration becomes the norm rather than the exception. STOTC can help leaders recognize and strengthen these networks and meshworks, creating an ecosystem in which teams aren't working in isolation but are collaborating seamlessly to achieve the organization's and wider partnerships' goals.

A key aspect of organizational learning

In the 1970s, I, Peter, worked as a leader in therapeutic communities. There I learnt that, if you were to help an individual flourish, you need first to focus on the health of the community and the wider organization. This work led to my doctoral research, 'Living the Learning' (Hawkins, 1986), in which I sought to discover how the approaches and practices found in therapeutic communities spiritual communities and intentional learning communities, could be applied to different work organizations, as all organizations, whatever work they did, also had to be learning organizations.

This research took me more fully into the world of organizational development and to participating in the early work to develop learning organizations (Garrat, 1987; Hawkins, 1991, 1994; Pedler, Burgoyne and Boydell, 1991; Senge, 1990). Much of this work focussed on how individuals and teams learnt more effectively within organizations, rather than how organizations learnt and evolved as a living organism. Thus, the work needed to bring together the learning organization with how organizational cultures learnt, developed and evolved, and how it was possible to work with culture change and transformation (Hawkins, 1997, 2019b).

At the heart of STOTA is how effectively an organization can learn, adapt and evolve; how quickly successes, failures and innovations can spread across every team in the organization. Price and Toye (2017) measured how quickly and successfully new innovations could spread and be adopted across an organization. In the UK's National Health Service, it took nine years for one life-saving new treatment for stroke patients to be adopted by half of the NHS organizations, whereas in the most successful company, a new innovation took 37 days to reach the 50 per cent adoption level. From their research they advocate four key organizational capabilities: ripple intelligence that joins the dots; fluidity of resources; liquid leadership that connects beyond the hierarchy; and dissolving paradoxes through reframing. All of these are key to developing a STOTA and are addressed in this book.

From strategic plans to strategizing

Strategy is not just a static plan; it's an ongoing process of strategizing; a living, breathing approach that evolves as the world changes. Planning is comfortable; it's about following a predictable path and maintaining control. But strategy is the opposite. It's about predicting what you think will happen in a world full of uncertainties and having a unique, creative response when things shift. It's less about comfort and more about embracing discomfort – the uncertainty, the unknown, the surprises. As Martin (2014) suggests, a great strategy is not just a set of instructions; it's a theory, one that guides how an organization will achieve its goals, but with the flexibility to adapt as needed by the changing context.

One key approach in moving from safe planning to bold strategizing is to continuously ask the hard questions:

- What is changing in our environment and stakeholder needs?
- How might these changes open new opportunities or challenges?
- How can we respond in ways that our competitors have not thought of yet?

This mindset of proactive inquiry, shifts an organization's focus from simply executing tasks to co-creating its own future.

Three horizons thinking (Sharpe, 2013) adds a crucial layer to this conversation by encouraging leaders to think in terms of the present, near future and long-term future simultaneously.

- The first horizon focusses on how to best operate current business.
- The second is about innovation, what we need to change about our products, services and processes to be future-fit.

- The third is about future foresight, what changes or disruptions are starting to appear that could challenge the status quo, and how stakeholders needs are likely to change over the next 3–5 years. These considerations show an organization what it needs to do to truly thrive in the long term.

Coaching leaders to think across all three horizons helps them balance managing today's reality with shaping tomorrow's potential. What must we protect, and what must we evolve? What does the 'third horizon' demand that we need to start building today? An effective example of this is Netflix, which started as a DVD rental service. It anticipated the shift towards online streaming and the leaders pivoted the business, investing heavily in streaming and content creation, before their much-larger competitors followed in their wake. This transformed them into a global entertainment leader. They did not just wait for the future; they created it.

Strategizing is also helped by scenario planning (de Geus, 1997; Kahane, 2012, 2019; Wack, 1985a, 1985b) which involves building multiple plausible futures and preparing responses to each. Instead of being blindsided by change, organizations are ready to respond to whatever scenario unfolds. Just like Netflix, companies must ask: if our environment shifts, what would we need to change today to stay ahead?

Real-time strategizing (Hamel and Prahalad, 1994; Jacobs, 1997) also plays a key role in this ongoing process, encouraging organizations to act as if their desired future state is already a reality. This is where strategy becomes truly dynamic, constantly adjusting and evolving as circumstances change, by exploring how the organization can start living their envisioned future, today. This helps organizations to begin aligning their actions with their long-term goals, constantly closing the gap between where they are and where they need to be.

Effective strategizing isn't just about planning for the future; it's about shaping the future, by embracing uncertainty, asking tough questions and adapting in real-time. Increasingly strategizing needs to be co-created by a team of teams across the organization, in partnership with all its stakeholders.

A key aspect of culture change

As organizations are increasingly required to adapt and transform with greater speed, flexibility and agility, one of the major barriers to this continuous change is people's deep attachment to the existing culture. Cultural norms and values, while essential for collective identity and stability, can hinder the flexibility needed for transformation. Another significant challenge is the strong identification individuals have with their local teams or silos, which can make it difficult to foster collaboration and cultural alignment across the organization during periods of rapid change.

Culture is not a tangible entity that can be measured; rather, it is a pervasive pattern that connects all aspects of an organization. Contrary to common belief, culture does not reside solely in the people and their behaviours. You can replace all the people in an organization, and if you don't change them all at once, the old culture can continue to dominate. Culture resides in the patterns of connection within the organization and in how it interacts with external stakeholder ecosystems. It is embedded in the organization's stories, rituals and oral history, as well as in the unwritten rules that are passed down through the 'unofficial induction programme' (Hawkins and Smith, 2013).

Recognizing one's own culture is challenging, as an old Chinese proverb suggests: 'The last one to know about the sea is the fish.' Our own culture is the medium through which we understand and make sense of the world. We don't perceive our own culture because it is the lens through which we view the world, ingrained in the language and grammar we use to shape our thoughts.

When we join a new organization, the culture is initially something we can observe as outsiders, but it soon becomes absorbed and part of how we perceive and make sense of the world. I, Peter, have previously defined culture as 'what you stop noticing and take for granted when you have worked somewhere for over three months' and explored how 'culture resides in the habituated patterns of relationships' (Hawkins, 1997). Business leaders, organizational behaviour academics and organizational development practitioners widely recognize culture as critical to both an organization's development and its success. Here are two examples from CEOs who faced significant challenges in transforming their organizations: Louis Gerstner, former CEO of IBM (2002), noted, 'I came to see in my time at IBM that culture isn't just one aspect of the game – it is the game. In the end, an organization is nothing more than the collective capacity of its people to create value.' More recently the CEO of a major international bank, when asked why his bank had flourished and their closest rival bank failed, replied with the one word 'Culture.'

The purpose of any culture, whether at the family, team, organizational or national level, is to create a collective shared identity. This identity is critical in enabling the collective to collaborate in service of a joint purpose, making it 'more than the sum of its parts' (Hawkins, 2021). A shared culture also establishes the boundaries of a community or a shared enterprise, defining who is part of 'us'. We often distinguish our culture by how it differs from others: they make sacrifices to multiple gods, we worship one transcendent God; we are black, they are white; we wear suits and blue shirts, they wear jeans and t-shirts.

I, Peter, developed, with colleagues, a model of organizational culture that builds on the earlier work of Ed Schein (1985 and 1992) and others (see Hawkins, 1997; Hawkins and Smith, 2013), which illustrates the levels of culture within all organizations (see Figure 2.1).

Artefacts. These are the tangible manifestations of how an organization presents itself to the world. These include: symbols of power and authority; dress codes; purpose and vision statements, and core annual reports, strategy documents; displayed objects such as photographs, certificates, artwork; and the layout of sites and offices.

Patterns of behaviour. These are the common patterns within the organization that illustrate how things are done. Key indicators include: how people engage with one another; how conflicts are handled; how resources are allocated; how mistakes are managed; and what behaviours are rewarded or given attention.

FIGURE 2.1 The Hawkins model of culture

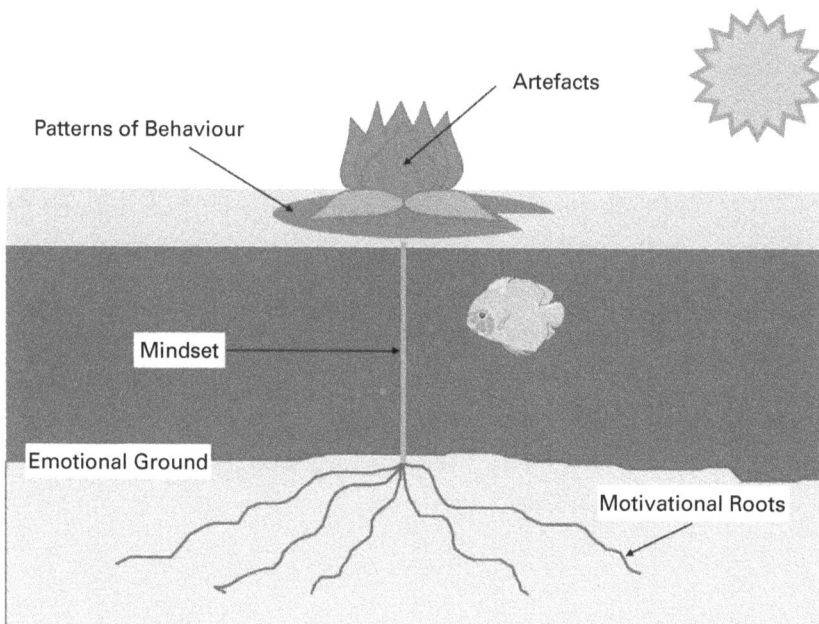

Mindsets. These are the underlying assumptions about what is good, bad, correct or efficient, as well as how problems are framed. These assumptions are usually implicit and need to be uncovered. These organizational worldviews generate: habitual ways of thinking, taken-for-granted assumptions and perceptions, and organizational values in use (see Chapter 12 on vertical development).

Emotional ground. This is shaped by significant events that have left an emotional impact on both staff and stakeholders. These are often emotional reactions that are not part of day-to-day awareness, such as: unprocessed reactions to major organizational changes and emotions imported from the organization's boundaries, such as those from work with clients, customers and other stakeholders.

The emotional ground also includes the emotional climate of the organization, and the characteristic patterns of emotional expression used within its culture.

Motivational roots. This deepest level of the organizational culture influences all the levels above. These roots grow from the purpose, values and motivations involved in both the founding and ongoing operation of the organization. They reflect the deeper reasons for caring about the organization beyond meeting individual needs. They include: the often-forgotten passions that inspired the organization's inception and later evolution; how people find meaning in their work; what connects the organization's purpose with the purpose and motivation of the individuals within it.

This model of culture acknowledges layers or levels of influence that exist like a rich tapestry, with each thread and pattern contributing to the whole with each layer contributing to the whole. As organizations evolve, these levels can easily become misaligned. Culture provides a shared way of perceiving, being, thinking and doing across an organization, and needs to evolve at the same speed of change as exists in the organization's ecosystem.

Culture as a key aspect of organizational transformation

In Chapter 1, we discussed how organizations today must transform not only their products and services but also their strategy, culture, leadership, partnerships, and reimagine their engagement with stakeholders as ecosystem partners. This is crucial because organizational changes in ownership, structure and focus are happening more frequently, and the life cycle of commercial organizations is often much quicker than that of individuals. Rapid growth, enormous expansion and success can be followed by sudden collapse (see Chapter 5).

In recent years, we have witnessed the phenomenon of unicorn companies - some privately owned startups that grow quickly to become valued at over \$1 billion, such as Airbnb, Uber and SpaceX - companies that have dramatically disrupted existing markets through technology. Fifty years ago, the life expectancy of a firm in the Fortune 500 was around 75 years; by 2011, it had dropped to less than 15 years and continues to decline (Denning, 2011). As of 2024, the average lifespan of a company on the Standard & Poor's 500 Index had dropped to under 15 years, compared to 32 years in 1965 (Investment Office, 2024).

Steve Jobs, the charismatic founder of Apple, attributed this decline to companies focussing too much on milking their 'cash cows' (their most successful products) and promoting their accompanying sales managers to top leadership positions, rather than continually developing new products to meet future customer needs and reinventing and transforming themselves (Isaacson, 2011).

Product leadership alone is no longer a safeguard against obsolescence, as the downfall of once-iconic companies like Kodak and Olivetti clearly illustrates. These former giants in film and typewriters failed to evolve, became habituated to their past success, and their demise serves as a cautionary tale for today's businesses. To be truly future-fit, organizations must develop the muscle and capacity to constantly transform not just their products, but also their strategy, culture, leadership and, most critically, the way they align and connect both internally and externally.

Without fostering internal synergy through an agile, adaptable and fast-learning Team of Teams approach, organizations will find it difficult to develop their culture at the pace required by the rapidly shifting political, social, technological and economic landscapes. Furthermore, without robust external partnerships and effective teaming, businesses risk being overwhelmed by the relentless demands of diverse stakeholders, and become ensnared in the complexities of a highly interconnected ecosystem. The key to thriving in such an environment is not just to lead in one area, but to evolve continuously, ensuring every part of the organization is aligned, thriving and responsive to the world around it.

Peel Regional Police: changing culture

In 2020, the Canadian Peel Regional Police felt the ricochet from a kaleidoscope of events including a pandemic, Black Lives Matter, the 'defund the police' movement and the tumultuous US election. The Peel Police Board hired a new progressive chief, Nishan (Nish) Duraiappah, and two new deputies. They believed that it was crucial to change the culture and the story about policing in the community and protect the rights and well-being of all, through service excellence and community engagement.

Chief Nish understood the gravity of change needed and commissioned his coach, Heather Clayton, along with internal leadership staff, to design a Systemic Team Coaching and leadership development programme based on Hawkins' Five Disciplines and his Creating a Coaching Culture model (Hawkins, 2021, 2012).

The early stages of this work are described in Hawkins (2022: 195–219). Now, almost five years into STOTC and transformational leadership work across the organization, the story continues, and is growing in energy, excitement and impact.

> I didn't realize how critical it was for the coaching environment to be one
> that was embodied by everyone in the organization. When we started... it
> was me, directly with my team. We weren't thinking about team coaching we
> were just thinking of individual work with top and aspiring leaders... but true
> effectiveness comes from your entire team embodying a team coaching culture-
> mindset and way of working (Nish Duraiappah)

An evolving strategy to 'saturate' the organization and create a team coaching culture has expanded to include the senior leadership team (which reports to the chief's executive team), middle managers programmes, partnering with external partners, a women-in-policing programme and the creation of an internal Leadership Development Office, supported by a constable who has trained as a coach.

Peel is recognized across Canada as an exemplary, forward-thinking policing organization, with other organizations visiting to learn from them. Chief Nish has also been invited to join the International Policing Commission.

Key principles of the culture that has developed at Peel Police can be summarized as:

- Encouraging leaders to ask questions, rather than tell, and be willing to challenge one another, including those in higher ranks.

- Modelling the behaviour expected from other leaders and police.

- Providing resources and support where needed.

- Aligning with the vision by focussing on strategic work that advances it most.

- In some ways it was simple – consistent, persistent messaging and modelling to shift practice and culture across all teams, as well as the teaming between Peel Police and their community partners. And it took an unwavering belief in their five-year vision.

Becoming a globally networked business

Effective alignment and synergy require strong teamwork across all internal teams, as well as effective teaming and partnering with key ecosystem partners.

GHD, a 95-year-old civil engineering business, was founded as a private practice in Melbourne, Australia, in 1928 by Alan Gordon Gutteridge, who focussed on water and sewerage consulting. The partnership of Haskins and Davey joined in 1939, establishing the formal partnership of Gutteridge Haskins & Davey. During the 1950s and 1960s, GHD grew to more than 400 employees while expanding into transportation, manufacturing plants, building and civil works, energy, mining and dams.

In the 1990s, GHD expanded its services into architecture, environmental and business consulting while growing its presence in South East Asia. During the 2000s, the company focussed even more on international expansion, growing rapidly through a series of mergers and acquisitions in the US, Canada, United Kingdom, Australia, New Zealand, the Middle East, China, Chile and Malaysia. By 2014, GHD had grown to over 8,500 employees, helped by the acquisition of the Canadian firm Conestoga-Rovers & Associates, making it one of the largest employee-owned engineering consultancies in the world. By 2020, GHD had over 12,000 employees and operated in more than 30 countries worldwide.

Under the visionary leadership of CEO Ashley Wright, GHD successfully embarked on a bold new strategy which aimed to forge deeper partnerships with their client customers across both the commercial and public sectors. This strategy wasn't just about expanding their service offerings – which were growing to include consultancy, digitalization services, architecture, and engineering – but about integrating these disciplines to tackle some of the most pressing global challenges. GHD's strategy started to focus on the 'future of water', 'future of energy' and 'future of communities', recognizing that these areas are at the forefront of issues facing societies worldwide. By focussing on them, they aimed to increase their contribution to facing the metacrisis of our time.

However, despite the ambitious vision of becoming a truly 'One GHD' organization, the reality was more complex. With many geographically spread acquisitions, the company faced the classic challenge of silos which stifled collaboration and innovation. Recognizing this, Jan Sipsma, the Head of People and Strategy, approached Renewal Associates for help in transforming GHD into a 'globally networked business'. The goal was to break down these silos and create a cohesive, interconnected organization, capable of leveraging its global expertise, knowledge and resources to address the both the challenges of tomorrow and their clients' needs wherever in the world they occur.

We will come back to this case study in later chapters when we explore the journey of a STOTA and team coaching journey. In Chapter 5 we will explore how GHD successfully transitioned from a national company with international outposts, to an internationally networked business, able to quickly move resources, expertise and learning to where they are needed most through being a 'team of teams'.

Conclusion

Every organization, in every sector, needs to discover how it can positively respond to the metacrisis of our times by becoming a future-fit and net-positive organization. To do this, we have shown in this chapter the essential aspects of successful organizational development and transformation, which include continual organizational learning, strategizing and evolving the organizational culture and leadership.

To enable such a journey, organizations need help from every part of the development professions, including coaching, counselling, team development, strategy consulting, culture change, organizational development and organizational transformation. However, these professions are often siloed and tend to compete with each other. In the next chapter, we will highlight the urgent need for them to integrate and how a Systemic Team of Teams Approach can play a significant role in this endeavour.

03

The role of a Systemic Team of Teams Approach in creating an integrated development profession

Introduction

Over the last 80 years we have seen an exponential growth in many different professions that are focussed on development of either individuals, teams or organizations. These include:

1 Counselling, psychotherapy, coaching, and mentoring for developing individuals.

2 Management and leadership development for developing individuals for specific roles.

3 Team development, group coaching, relevant team training team coaching and Systemic Team Coaching for developing teams.

4 Organizational development, organizational transformation, culture change, change management, and the learning organization for developing whole organizations.

5 Many different strategy approaches for developing the relationship of organizations to their stakeholder ecosystem and their potential futures.

Each of these has become an international industry, with its own trainings, research and competing professional associations. While working with organizations to overcome silos, the development profession that works with developing individuals, teams, leaders and organizations, has itself become siloed.

In this chapter we will first look at the need for integration across the development professions, and then briefly explore the evolution of several key separate professional approaches and finally show how a Systemic Team of Teams Approach can play a role in bringing together the best of many different development approaches.

The need for a new integrated profession

The world does not need lots more independent coaches, consultants, strategists, facilitators or experts. What the metacrisis urgently requires is people, internally and externally, who can enable change and transformation at depth, and who work relationally to enable development in the connections between individuals, teams, functions, organizations, stakeholders, communities and between the human and 'more-than-human' world of the wider ecology.

Over the years, we have dedicated ourselves to training coaches, team coaches, counsellors, psychotherapists, supervisors, HR and OD consultants and leaders. Yet, we have observed that even these training programmes can become overly siloed. Professional associations often exacerbate this fragmentation by imposing rigid pathways, such as requiring one to be accredited as a coach before becoming a team coach, or requiring specific accreditations, thereby excluding equally qualified professionals from other bodies. This growing specialization has led to a fragmentation of knowledge, where disciplines and professional communities become increasingly isolated from others.

I, Peter, highlighted this issue in my last book (Hawkins, 2025), referencing the great physicist Erwin Schrödinger, who expressed concern about over-specialization as early as 1951. In his lectures at Cambridge University, Schrödinger (1951) said, 'the isolated knowledge obtained by a group of specialists in a narrow field has in itself no value whatsoever, but only in its synthesis with all the rest of knowledge and only inasmuch as it really contributes in this synthesis toward answering the demand, "Who are we?"'

Another profound thinker, Arnold Toynbee, also warned against the dangers of growing specialization, 'Specialization… leaves critical questions not only unanswered but unasked. And they will remain unasked if the microscopic approach is not supplemented by a panoramic one. Without a combination of the two, there can be no stereoscopic vision' (Toynbee, 1961: 633–34).

There is a telling joke that the definition of a top specialist is someone who knows more and more about less and less, until they know everything about nothing.

In the research that I, Peter, led for Henley Business School on 'Tomorrow's Leadership and the necessary revolution in today's leadership development' (Hawkins, 2017), there is an insightful quote from a CEO, who said:

> I have lots of coaches who coach my people and lots of consultants that consult to different parts of my organization, but that is not where our challenges lie. All our significant challenges reside in the connections – not only between individuals but between teams, divisions, countries, and between us and our stakeholders. Where are the coaches and consultants skilled in coaching these connections?

What is needed is a new, integrated profession comprising individuals who can partner with organizations, communities and alliances to enable, support and orchestrate transformational change in, and between, all key systemic levels. This includes the individuals, the team, the team of teams, the organization, its mergers, acquisitions, and partnerships, its stakeholder ecosystem, communities, and between the human and the wider, 'more-than-human' ecology.

The team of teams is a critical systemic level that serves as a vital bridge, linking the development and transformation of the organization with the ongoing work of developing individuals and teams through coaching. It represents the key intersection between the best practices in systemic individual and team coaching, and the most effective systemic approaches to organizational development, strategy and transformation.

Creating the 'future-fit function'

Ten years ago, I, Peter, delivered a keynote address at a major HR conference in South Africa, where I argued for a radical transformation in Human Resources. I pointed out that HR was often too disconnected from broader business issues, focussing solely on employees while neglecting other key stakeholders such as customers, suppliers, investors, the communities in which the organization operated and the wider ecological environment. Internally, many large HR departments were also siloed, with specialized sub-functions like recruitment, compensation, international mobility, communications, coaching, learning and development, and organizational development operating in isolation.

I proposed that these HR functions, along with the strategy function, should be unified into a single, cohesive entity, called the 'Future-Fit Function'. The overarching purpose of this integrated function would be to ensure that the organization, its teams, employees and the entire stakeholder ecosystem is developing to be future-fit and equipped to thrive into the future, enabling long-term success and sustainability.

Since then, we have helped numerous organizational reviews of their internal functions to create much greater alignment, integration and synergy between all these future-fit functions, greatly increasing the return on investment in these activities.

Coaching

I, Peter, have written extensively about how, in the 45 years I have been involved in coaching, mentoring, counselling, psychotherapy and supervision, I have seen an enormous growth and development in each of these fields (Hawkins, 2021, 2025; Hawkins and Ryde, 2019; Hawkins and Smith, 2013; Hawkins and Turner, 2020). However, the urgency of the metacrisis of our times means that we no longer have the time to try and change human perceiving, thinking, doing and being, one person at a time. We need to move from individual and human-centric coaching, to systemic and eco-centric coaching, where we no longer have a coach as the supplier of coaching, with the coachee as the client, but rather a coaching partnership, together focussed on exploring how the coachee can develop themselves in a way that co-creates value, with and for their team, team of teams, organization, its stakeholder ecosystem and the wider ecology.

In Hawkins (2025: 57–61) I outline seven tenets of the new systemic coaching paradigm:

1 seeing the coachee as your coaching partner and the coaching as co-created
2 seeing the client as all the stakeholders that the coachee's life and work serves
3 bringing the stakeholder's voice into the coaching room
4 attending to the wider ecology from the very first meeting
5 jointly working at the learning edge, rather than believing that either the coach or the coachee has the answer
6 coaching connections, not problems
7 moving beyond insight and action plans to focussing on embodied change in the room

Leadership development

The leadership development industry has become massive, with the website futuremarketinsights.com reporting that economically, in 2022, the industry's revenue was $67,311 million and was growing at over 10 per cent a year; and they estimate that by 2032 it would be $179,916 million. Yet in 2012, Professor Barbara Kellerman from Harvard University wrote:

> Leaders of every sort are in disrepute; we don't have much better an idea of how to grow good leaders, or of how to stop or at least slow bad leaders, than we did a hundred or even a thousand years ago... the leadership industry has not in any major, meaningful, measurable way improved the human condition. (Kellerman, 2012: xiv)

We believe that this is still the case 13 years later despite positive changes in how leaders are taught and developed, with a decrease in the studying of past case studies of great heroic leaders, and more time focussed on personal and individual development.

In Hawkins (2025: 49) I wrote: 'The dominant paradigm is still human-centric individualistic leader development, rather than leadership development that develops collective leadership that can partner with their followers, stakeholders and communities to address the urgent challenges of our times.'

I went on to say (2025: 49–50):

> If we look at the purpose of leadership at any depth, we discover that its role is first to sense and make sense of the changing world and the context in which the organization they lead exists, and then to continually realign the organization, including its focus, priorities, connections, teams and people, to best respond to the changing needs of the coming times.

And that this requires:

> collective leadership, where leadership teams function at more than the sum of their parts... The role of the leader is not only to ensure that this happens in their own team, but also to develop the right culture, processes and support for this to happen across the organization, so the organization matures into a 'Team of Teams' that is more than the sum of its parts.

Many so-called Leadership Development programmes are actually 'Leader Development' programmes, but leadership is co-created between a leader, followers, and most importantly a shared endeavour or collective purpose.

Thus, all true leadership is contextual, relational, collective and purpose generated. It needs to be in service of all the systemic levels that it is operating within, and hence we have the development of ecosystemic leadership (Hawkins, 2025). Ecosystemic Leadership has much in common with other approaches as 'Regenerative Leadership' (Hutchins and Storm, 2019) 'Eco-leadership' (Western, 2013) and leaders as visionary, architect, catalyst, coach and human (McKinsey, 2023).

To develop the collective and collaborative leadership needed for the future, it is often far more effective to bring development and learning into the real-time work of leadership teams, and their orchestration of an organization-wide team of teams, rather than sending individuals away to expensive leadership development programmes.

Organizational development

Organizational Development (OD) emerged in the late 1940s and continued to evolve through the 1950s and 1960s, primarily applying social psychology and group dynamics to address challenges such as poor communication, unhealthy conflict and resistance to change. Early pioneers like Kurt Lewin, Richard Beckhard and Ed Schein significantly influenced the field and our work. Initially, OD was characterized by a more traditional, expert-driven consultancy model. However, by the 1960s, it became clear that a more collaborative, action-oriented approach was necessary – one that involved partnership and dialogue with key stakeholders within teams and the organization. Schein (1969) defined organizational development as encompassing 'all the activities undertaken by managers, employees, and consultants aimed at building and maintaining the health of the organization as a complete system'.

This was a positive shift, although organizational change was still viewed as episodic, driven by shifts in the market or broader context that necessitated a corresponding adjustment within the organization. Effective change management was commonly understood through Kurt Lewin's three-step model: 'Unfreeze, Change, Refreeze' (Lewin, 1947; Lewin and Lewin, 1948).

Since then, we have increasingly recognized that change is a fundamental and constant aspect of the present; nothing remains static – everything is in a state of movement and transformation. As Henry Miller (1957) aptly stated, 'all is change, all is flux, all is metamorphosis'.

Early-stage organizational development typically began with a specific presenting problem that needed immediate attention, focussing on diagnosing and resolving issues within the existing framework.

- What specific problem or challenge is the organization currently facing?
- What is the root of the issue (diagnosis)?
- How can they address communication breakdowns or conflicts that are impacting their performance?
- What internal processes need to be improved to resolve the issue?

Later-stage organizational development work, exemplified by the contributions of Schein (1985, 1988, 1999, 2003, 2010), delved into uncovering deeper issues such as underlying patterns, cultural themes, and structural challenges within organizations.

Schein's approach helped organizational development shift from a problem-centric approach, where experts focussed on solutions, to one that moved beyond the presenting problem towards a 'humble inquiry' into the underlying patterns of the organization and its culture. In the last chapter we showed how organizational culture becomes part of the way you begin to see the world, how you think, behave, relate and prioritize. Despite popular conceptions, it does not just reside in the people. We have worked with organizations where we have seen all the key leaders replaced, but the organizational culture remains relatively unchanged. The organizational culture resides in the 'habitual patterns of relating', which are like a riverbed, formed originally by the flow of the water, but which, in time, plays a major role in directing where the water will travel.

In exploring culture in organizations, we focus on the following:

1 key challenges facing the organization's leadership
2 changing stakeholder needs
3 underlying assumptions and values
4 how decisions are made and by whom
5 patterns and flows of communication
6 roles and responsibilities of the key players
7 how conflict and change are managed
8 organization's history and how has it evolved
9 espoused values versus the enacted behaviour
10 reward and recognition processes

We also incorporate an 'appreciative inquiry' approach (Cooperrider and Srivastva, 1987) moving further away from a problem-centric approach, by beginning with a focus on what teams and organizations already do well. Appreciative inquiry seeks out the very best of 'what is' to help ignite the imagination of 'what might be' (Cooperrider and Srivastva, 1987). In (Hawkins, 2021: 401–03), I describe the four stages or 'Ds' of appreciative inquiry:

1   Discovery: the discovery of the best of what is already happening.

2   Dreaming: dreaming what the team or organization could become.

3   Designing: collaboratively designing what is necessary to make this happen.

4   Delivery: of the design into new behaviour, practices, processes and structures.

At the same time there were many approaches being developed on ways of engaging people from across an organization, to collectively explore, vision and create new ways forward for their organization. In our work from the 1980s onwards, we have drawn on many approaches for working with large groups (Brown and Isaacs, 2005; Jacobs, 1997; Owen, 2008; Weisbord and Janoff, 2010). In Chapter 14 we have a whole section on how to enable large leadership gatherings using STOTA to vision, design and implement organizational transformation.

As the world has become more digitalized and virtual these approaches have also been adapted for effective implementation online. The most well-known approach which we have used are 'Hackathons' and 'Jams' (Hawkins, 2021: 236–37). Hackathons typically have a core group working closely together, while engaging a much larger disparate group online, testing ideas and gathering inputs. 'A jam is a focussed transformational intervention through a high-profile online event, with a clear context and strategic question' (Hawkins, 2021: 357). It may run over several days, or one or two weeks, but is always time limited so it has a similar focussed energy to an agile sprint. It can engage the participation of thousands of people from across the organization and even involve wider stakeholders or others within the same sector. As with Agile sprints, there will be several iterations of what is designed and created, allowing for continued feedback and input.

Both types of large group engagements are designed to achieve large-scale participation of key people who, because they have shared the strategic challenge, and been part of co-creating the response and way forward, take much greater ownership for ensuring the outcomes are implemented throughout the organization.

Alongside innovation in structuring large engagement events, there has been the growing emphasis on relational approaches to understanding change and transformation. Many build on the social constructivist theories of Gergen (1999; Gergen, McNamee and Barrett, 2001) and the concepts of inter-subjectivity (Stolorow and Atwood, 1992) to create dialogic approaches to organizational development (Bushe, 2013; Bushe and Marshak, 2015; Isaacs, 1999). This approach focusses on enabling generative dialogue, not just between the OD consultant and those they are working with, but also across the organization, both vertically and horizontally, as well as between the organization and its ecosystem partners. STOTA builds on this work to enable generative dialogue between teams, horizontally, vertically and with stakeholders.

The organization as complex co-evolving organisms

Organizations, as we indicated above, are always in flux and continually changing and evolving. Thus, the term 'change management' has been an unhelpful one, implying that change only happens in managed and structured ways, and can be controlled from the top-down. Increasingly we have had to recognize that change is emergent, happening in multiple dimensions. The internal dimensions include:

- within individuals
- between individuals
- in collective teams and workgroups
- between teams
- horizontally across organizations
- vertically up and down the organizational hierarchy
- influenced by history
- shaped by the perceptions of possible futures

The organizations, like all living and social organisms, are also open adaptive systems (Bushe and Marshak, 2015; Kauffman, 1993, 1995; Stacey, 2001, 2010), which are constantly adapting to their ecological niche and context. Daily interactions with the changing needs of all their stakeholders bring new information and challenges, that require some small and some substantial adapting within the organization. However, we would contend that the emphasis on adaptation is reductive, as the organization is also influencing and impacting all its stakeholders. The process is one of continual co-evolution and co-creation.

This therefore requires any change or transformation process to not only work across the organizational system but with the co-evolution and co-creation happening between the organization and its wider ecosystem.

There has been a gradual increase in focussing on creating value for all stakeholders, and moving away from the very reductive Milton Friedman (1970) doctrine that organizations are only there to maximize returns to their shareholders. Porter and Kramer (2011) argued that we need to move from creating share value, to created 'shared value' for all stakeholders, and Polman and Winston (2021) showed how 'net-positive' organizations 'can thrive by giving more than they take'. I, Peter, have long argued that we need to move beyond the focus on 'High performing teams' to 'High-value creating teams, that co-create value, with and for, all their stakeholders' (Hawkins, 2021). In this book we go further and argue that to thrive we need to transform our relationships with 'stakeholders' into genuine collaborations with ecosystem partners.

Organizational development involving the wider community and network

Addressing the new paradigm of organizations as complex, co-evolving organisms that is responsive to wider challenges (discussed in Chapter 1), requires an organizational development approach that develops organizations to evolve in partnership with their wider systems, creating a 'systemic organization of organizations', working on shared challenges.

Some writers such as Cooperrider and Godwin (2022) distinguish between micro- and macro-organizational development. Micro OD focusses on the internal aspects of an organization, such as enhancing individual and team performance, improving communication, fostering positive organizational culture and enhancing leadership capabilities. It involves day-to-day operations and relationships within the organization and engaging and aligning the workforce with the organization's goals. Macro OD, on the other hand, addresses the larger, systemic factors that influence an organization, such as strategic direction, external stakeholder engagement, responses to market changes, and anticipating and adaptation to global trends. Successful organizational development requires a balanced approach that integrates both micro and macro perspectives – ensuring that internal improvements support and are supported by the organization's broader strategic goals and external challenges.

Several key theorists and practitioners have made major contributions to Macro OD (Boulton, 2024; Bushe and Marshak, 2015; Waddock, Ansari and Haider, 2022; Stacey, 2010), combining relational and complexity based ways of understanding adaptive systems. The approach sees OD as in service of supporting organizations to become 'net positive' (Polman and Winston, 2021) and ones that continually co-create value with and for all their ecosystem partners (Hawkins, 2021, 2022b). These approaches challenge leaders by asking: is the world better off because your organization is in it? And what can your organization uniquely do that the world of tomorrow needs? David Cooperrider leads strengths-based Appreciative Inquiry summits with multi-stakeholder engagements, where they utilize the 4-D cycle that we mentioned earlier. Summits commonly involve anywhere between 300 to 2,000 stakeholders and are designed for prototyping innovative solutions. An example is that of a sand mining company that held a design summit to 'do all the good you can possibly do' (Cooperrider and Godwin, 2022: 34) where sand loader operators developed a low-cost scalable sand water filter for providing clean drinking water. This initiative is now used in over 44 countries and led to the company being named the number one corporate citizen in America by the US Chamber of Commerce.

The third way beyond individual coaching and consultancy

The Systemic Team of Teams Approach (STOTA) goes beyond simply facilitating one of these systemic levels; it embodies an entirely new way of perceiving, thinking, being and doing at all levels.

For several years, we have critiqued both conventional coaching and traditional organizational consultancy. We often caricature the former as being overly reliant on asking questions, under the assumption that 'the client has the answer', and the latter as being addicted to providing solutions, convinced that 'they have the answer!'. What we believe is necessary is a third way – one that transcends this polarity by integrating the strengths of both approaches while moving beyond their limitations.

This third way has several key features that are central to STOTA.

1   It recognizes that transformation happens at the 'learning edge' where neither partner has the answer, but both recognize that the world around them is requiring them to find a totally new response.

2   Finding a new response requires skilled, collaborative and orchestrated inquiry, with generative dialogue that can produce new perception, thinking, being and doing, and which no one could have arrived at by themselves.

3   It is rooted in an ecosystemic way of perceiving and engaging with the world around us.

4   It focusses on the connections and disconnections, rather than the parts, and on the flows, rather than the structures.

5   It understands teams and organizations as complex organisms, co-evolving in relationship to their wider context.

Organizational Transformation and Systemic Team of Teams Coaching

Both Organizational Transformation and Systemic Team of Teams Coaching draw on OD, Systemic Team Coaching and transformational change. It begins with a forward-looking approach, starting from the future and working backward ('future-back') and from the external environment inward ('outside-in'). Questions start with:

Who and what does the organization serve?

and

Who and what does the organization create value with, and for?

Only then can the organization begin to explore what those stakeholders appreciate and value about the organization and what they need different in the changing world of the future.

Systemic organizational transformation is not trying to return an organization to some notion of organizational health, but working with the organization to discover what is needed for that organization to be 'future-fit' and able to be a 'net-positive organization' (Polman and Winston, 2021) which co-creates greater beneficial value with, and for, all its stakeholders.

Our research as well as our work with partnering organizations in developing their leadership culture, their teams, team of teams, and with their organizational transformation, has led us to propose that there are five keys that are essential for organizations to be future-fit and successful in the mid-21st century.

1. Purpose led

After many years of helping organizations craft their 'mission statements', I, Peter, came to realize that this terminology was misguided and ultimately inadequate. The term 'mission' has its roots in warfare and was later adopted in the contexts of colonization and evangelism. It conveys a sense of individual and collective ambition – focussed on what we want to achieve, how we can be the most successful, and dominate our sector or the broader ecosystem. Even Jim Collins, who developed the Collins-Porras Vision Framework that moved from 'core values' to 'purpose' and then to 'mission' (Collins, 2001), eventually shifted away from the concept of 'mission' towards the idea of a compelling goal designed to motivate a company over a 10- to 25-year period (Collins and Lazier, 2020).

Purpose is very different than mission. At the personal level it comes from discovering what we can uniquely do that the world of tomorrow needs? As Braks (2024) writes: 'When we are taking action in the world in accordance with our life purpose, it feels fulfilling.' Our work is in service of a greater whole, it makes a positive difference and feels meaningful.

For an organization, 'Purpose is the fundamental reason for your company's existence, its ultimate reason for being' (Collins and Lazier, 2020). Having a meaningful purpose is essential for any organization to thrive. The purpose provides the sense of direction that can align the separate activities of different functions and teams. It provides the meaning that attracts customers, suppliers, investors and employees, and motivates them not just to stay in a relationship with the organization, but to want to partner with it. As individuals, teams or organizations we do not create our purpose-we discover it, through our co-creative relationship with the world around us. Purpose arises neither solely from within nor entirely from without, but from a moebius flow and dance between the two.

2. Stakeholder centric

Since Porter and Kramer published their influential paper in 2011 on the need to shift from an overemphasis on shareholder value to the concept of 'shared value', there has been growing recognition that organizations can only thrive by creating value *with* and *for* all their stakeholders. Even Jack Welch, the former CEO of General Electric and an icon for many of successful leadership, famously stated that 'strictly speaking, shareholder value is one of the dumbest ideas in the world' (as quoted in Erdal, 2011: 373).

For an organization to be sustainable and successful, it must continually create value with and for a diverse range of stakeholders, including its customers; suppliers and partner organizations; employees and contractors; investors, funders and taxpayers; the broader communities in which it operates; and the more-than-human world of the wider ecology.

It is important to recognize that customers don't buy products and services, but rather what those products can do to enhance and sustain their lives, and the lives of those they care about.

3. Partnering

Often organizations become overwhelmed by the competing needs of the wide variety of stakeholders listed above and revert to siloed functions each focusing on separate stakeholders needs: sales looking after the customer; supply chain managing the suppliers; finance or investor relations serving the investors; HR responsible for the employees, and so on.

Organizations must explore ways to create a 'win-win-win' scenario for all their stakeholders, fostering a virtuous cycle throughout the entire stakeholder ecosystem rather than addressing each group's needs in isolation. Additionally, organizations need to recognize that stakeholders are not merely demands to be met but potential resources and partners. This shift involves evolving their relationships with stakeholders from simply asking, 'How do we meet your needs?' to working alongside them and considering the broader context such as the customer's customer, the investor's investor, the employee's future career and family, and the sustainability of the environment. The key partnering question then becomes, 'What can we achieve together that neither of us could achieve alone?'

4. Learning as fast or faster than the world is changing around it

Many years ago, Reg Revans (1982), the founder of Action Learning, argued that organizations would only survive if they could learn at the same rate, or faster, than the environment around them was changing (L ≥ E.C.). Since that time, much has been written about the importance of the 'Learning Organization' (see Chapter 2).

During this period, the pace of change and the rapidly growing interdependence of the world have both increased exponentially, leaving organizational learning and evolution struggling to keep up. In this book, we explore why developing a fast-learning organization is impossible without fostering a strong teaming culture and adopting an approach, that serves as the fifth and final key to success.

5. Creating a team of teams that is more than the sum of the parts

Faced with the need to 'do more with less' while maintaining high quality, many organizations respond by driving harder, working faster and relentlessly pursuing greater productivity and efficiency. While this approach may yield short-term gains, it often leads to diminishing returns over time and burn-out. To truly work smarter, every team within the organization must operate as more than the sum of its parts by fostering collaboration and synergy. Similarly, the team of teams must function as more than the sum of its individual teams, leveraging collective work, learning and innovation. Effective collaboration involves eliminating redundant efforts, resolving conflicts and problems horizontally rather than escalating them, and ensuring that lessons learnt, whether from successes or failures, are quickly shared and applied across all teams.

Conclusion: transforming development with a Systemic Team of Teams Approach

This chapter emphasized the critical need for a Systemic Team of Teams Approach (STOTA) to address the growing complexity of organizational challenges and the interconnected nature of modern systems. As we've explored, the development professions, ranging from coaching and leadership development to organizational transformation, have often become siloed, creating barriers to holistic growth. The metacrisis of our time demands more than isolated interventions; it calls for a collaborative, integrated approach that operates across all systemic levels.

STOTA bridges these divides by aligning individual, team, organizational and ecosystem development. This approach shifts the focus from isolated performance improvement to creating networks of collaboration, where teams of teams collectively co-create value with and for all ecosystem partners. It's no longer just about achieving high performance; it's about building systems that are future-fit, resilient and capable of adapting to the rapidly evolving demands of the 21st century.

The journey towards integration is not without its challenges, but as we've seen, it also presents immense opportunities. By embedding coaching principles into systemic frameworks, organizations can cultivate cultures of trust, shared accountability and collective learning. Leaders are no longer solitary figures but part of a relational network that prioritizes purpose, aligns diverse stakeholders into ecosystem partners and fosters innovation at scale.

In this chapter, we've outlined how STOTA is uniquely positioned to navigate this complexity, combining the strengths of coaching, organizational development and transformational change. This integration enables organizations not only to thrive in their current environments but also to contribute meaningfully to the broader ecosystems in which they operate.

As we move forward, the vision is clear: to evolve the development profession into a dynamic, interconnected practice that reflects the very principles we advocate. In doing so, we can co-create a future where organizations, communities and ecosystems flourish together, addressing the urgent challenges of our time with courage, creativity and collaboration.

PART TWO

The 'how' of a Systemic Team of Teams Approach to Organizational Development

04

The Systemic Team of Teams Coaching journey

Introduction

In Chapter 1, we emphasized the urgent need for all organizations to adopt a Systemic Team of Teams Approach (STOTA). In Chapters 2 and 3, we delved into the details of what this approach involves, defining the concept and illustrating how it integrates with other key fields, such as organizational development, organizational transformation, systemic coaching, Systemic Team Coaching and organizational learning. We also discussed how this approach ties into integrated strategy, culture and leadership development, as well as the pressing need for ecological change and bridging the gap between the human and the 'more-than-human' worlds.

In this chapter, after examining the 'Why' and the 'What' of the Systemic Team of Teams Approach STOTA, we now turn our focus to the 'How'. Drawing from research involving over 70 organizations globally and our consulting experience with more than 150 different organizations, we will outline what we've identified as the most effective journey. We will highlight the various stages of this journey and explore the different pathways organizations can take, depending on their unique context and circumstances. Our aim is to provide:

- a wheel of best practice based on what organizations report makes the greatest difference
- a range of options for each stage of the journey
- a flexible playbook for organizations to chart their own course of development

From our research, we identified two distinct types of journeys organizations undertake:

1 **The Incremental Journey** involves taking a step-by-step approach, learning and adapting as the process unfolds, with each new step informed by the outcomes of the previous ones.

2 **The Planned Transformational Journey,** in contrast, occurs when leadership recognizes the need for a significant overhaul of the business either because the strategies that once drove their success are no longer aligned with the needs of is the world around them. Or because the organization is entering a major transition stage in its growth and development. This could include becoming an international company, undergoing a merger or acquisition, or being publicly listed for the first time, all of which demand fundamental organizational transformation (see Chapter 5). Organizational transformation cannot be achieved through selective leadership coaching, team development initiatives, hiring decisions, strategic planning or structural changes alone. Instead, a more fundamental and holistic transformation is necessary; one that must be undertaken in partnership with the entire organization.

Both approaches have their benefits and limitations, and at the end of Chapter 6, we will explore how organizations can develop a third approach that combines the potential benefits of both. In this chapter we will explore the first approach and various pathways within it.

The incremental approach

At the core of this approach is the principle of starting small and learning as you progress, taking the journey step by step, evaluating and learning from each stage and then refining your focus for the next phase based on those insights.

In our review of many organizational 'team of teams' journeys, we observed various strategies. However, a clear pattern emerged in what organizations found most effective and, conversely, what they wished they had done differently (see Chapter 8).

Organizations overwhelmingly reported that the most successful journeys began by engaging the top executive team and quickly expanded to include the broader leadership of the organization – not just those with

FIGURE 4.1 The team of teams wheel of best-of-the-best practice

senior titles, but also a diverse range of people across the organization, including those poised to be the leaders of tomorrow.

The research also underscored the importance of avoiding the trap of cascading the change process down through the existing siloed structures. Instead, it is crucial to work with the necessary connections, vertically, horizontally and transversally, throughout the organization.

Many organizations emphasized the importance of the change process itself modelling the culture and the outcome they were striving to achieve. This sentiment is captured in the famous quotes from Marshall McLuhan (1964), 'The medium is the message', and as attributed to Mahatma Gandhi, 'Be the change you want to see.'

None of the organizations followed the exact journey plan outlined below; some began at later stages and then revisited earlier ones, while others overlooked critical steps. However, by synthesizing the most success-ful elements from a variety of these journeys, and focussing on those that produced the best outcomes, we have arrived at the following 'best of the best' journey plan.

1. Systemic Team Coaching of the leadership team

Nearly every organization we reviewed either started the process by coach-ing the top executive team or regretted that they did not start by doing so. The latter group commented on how the lack of prioritizing the process, support and role modelling from the top made it much harder to sustain the work throughout the organization over time. None of the many organiza-tions that did start with Systemic Team Coaching of the top team regretted having this as their starting point.

To have an aligned organization, you need to have an aligned top team. I, Peter, have written extensively (Hawkins, 2021, 2022b) on how, in today's world, the level of complexity and the speed of change make it impossible for an organization to be successful, if the only point of integration is the CEO. What's essential is a collaborative 'Leadership Team' at the top, rather than a collection of individual leaders managing their respective regions and functions. A true leadership team takes collective responsibility for the entire organization, with each member not only accountable for their own perfor-mance, learning, development and well-being, but also for that of their colleagues.

The journey from being a group of leaders to a leadership team is neither straightforward nor easy. We have outlined elsewhere (Hawkins, 2021) the Five Disciplines that every leadership team needs to develop, along with the Systemic Team Coaching journey necessary to establish and master them. In brief, the leadership team must focus on these core practices:

- **Commission:** Clearly define not only the purpose of the organization and the value it creates for those it serves, but also the unique purpose of the leadership team and how it contributes distinctively to the enterprise's success.

- **Clarify:** Establish the organization's and team's core purpose, values, strategy, objectives, roles and processes, along with collective Key Perfor-mance Indicators (KPIs). Additionally, outline a comprehensive roadmap for the transformation journey.

- **Co-create:** Discover how team members can work together to become more than the sum of their parts through effective collaboration and synergy.
- **Connect:** Identify the current key stakeholders and ecosystem partners and those that will be critical in the future, and determine how the team can connect, collaborate and partner with these major groups.
- **Core Learning:** Evolve beyond being a healthy and effective team to one that is constantly growing its capacity to be future-fit and ready to meet the increasing challenges of tomorrow.

This first step must be integrated throughout the entire journey as the leadership team needs to be the key architects, role models, evaluators and re-designers of the whole journey as it unfolds. In many cases that we studied, the top team was coached by an external systemic team coach, but in the most successful cases, the journey and this crucial step continued beyond the tenure of the coach. The leadership team had both learnt and been empowered to become a self-coaching team, consistently reflecting, learning and refining both their actions and their approach with different team members taking on coaching and facilitation roles to support the team's ongoing development.

2. Developing the executive-board partnership

Almost all organizations, except for a few early-stage ones, have a governance structure that sits above the top executive team. In the private commercial sector, this is typically a board of directors; in the public sector, it might be politicians; and in the charity or not-for-profit sector, it could be trustees. Regardless of the sector, the relationship between the board and the executive team is crucial to the organization's success.

In our research, we identified two common but opposing pitfalls in companies that struggled with their change process. The first was waiting for the board to take the lead in defining the future strategy and direction of the organization. The second was delaying the involvement of the board until it was too late, missing the opportunity to engage them as full partners in the transformation process.

Many boards and executive teams often find themselves in debates over who is responsible for strategy, transformation, leadership appointments and financial performance, treating these issues as an 'either-or' decision (see Hawkins, 2021: Chapter 9; Hawkins and Hogan, 2022).

However, we argue that both the board and the executive team have crucial roles to play in all four areas. In this stage of the journey, it's vital for both parties to first focus on what the organization and its stakeholders will need most from their collaborative partnership in the future. Only after this shared vision is established should they clarify how each will contribute to these responsibilities, in distinct yet complementary ways.

3. Coaching the key teams across the company

Our research clearly shows that leadership teams alone cannot achieve successful and sustainable organizational transformation or culture change. To succeed, they must engage key teams across the organization, involving them in shaping their best contributions to the transformation. For these teams to fully commit, it is crucial that the leadership team engages with them; directly, clearly and consistently, communicating about why the change is necessary, the direction and roadmap, and the specific support needed from each team. However, it's equally important that the top team avoids being overly prescriptive. They should be clear about the 'Why' and the 'What' of the change, while allowing each team the autonomy to determine their unique 'How', in contributing to the overall effort.

In Hawkins (2025), I, Peter, talk about one of the rarest and yet most powerful leadership abilities: the ability for leaders to ask for help from their hearts in a way that invites others to step up and come alongside them. One of the most critical responsibilities of leaders is to encourage and nurture leadership at all levels in the organization.

Through our practice and research, we've identified various strategies for effectively managing this crucial step in the Team of Teams journey. We will now explore a diverse range of these approaches, highlighting the strengths and weaknesses we've observed in each.

3a. *Coaching the next tier of teams with a team of external systemic team coaches*

In this approach, the top team collaborates with the teams they directly oversee, to bring in a systemic team coach or a pair of co-coaches, to work with each team. This strategy necessitates a coaching team with a shared philosophy, fully apprised and aligned with the overarching goals and values of the organization's transformation journey. It's crucial that these coaches possess a deep understanding of Systemic Team Coaching principles and are adept at applying them, across the diverse teams within the organization.

If you just employ a panel of independent team coaches, they can inadvertently increase the separation and disconnection between teams, with different models and language, and supporting the team they coach in its own local success. The systemic team coaches need to see the support of the organizational journey as their number one priority, and the development of the team as in service of the wider team of teams. To help this process we have developed a series of 'Team of Teams nudges', which we adapt for every organization we work with, that all team coaches can use to help teams balance their internal focus, with focussing on how they better connect with the whole network of teams, above and below them, upstream and downstream of them, and externally with the stakeholders. We have included this in the Chapter 14.

This approach offers several key advantages:

- **Consistency:** By leveraging a unified team of coaches who share a common philosophy, the organization ensures that systemic principles are consistently applied across all teams, maintaining coherence throughout the entire organization.
- **Scalability:** With multiple coaches working in tandem, the organization can scale its coaching efforts, reaching numerous teams simultaneously and accelerating the overall transformation process.
- **Diversity of perspectives:** Different coaches bring unique insights and styles, enriching the coaching process by offering teams a broader range of tools and approaches.

However, it also has potential pitfalls:

- **Coordination challenges:** Involving multiple team coaches introduces the risk of misalignment or inconsistent messaging if the coaching team is not well-coordinated.
- **Dependence on external coaches:** While external coaches offer valuable outside broader perspectives and experience, there is a risk that the organization may become overly reliant on them. It's crucial that the coaching process gradually builds the internal capacity of teams to coach themselves and one another, as well as training a cohort of internal systemic team coaches.

3b. Coaching the teams with a pair of internal and external team coaches

Another option is to select and develop and train a team of internal team coaches or organizational change agents from various levels and functions across the organization. These internal systemic team coaches then can be partnered with external systemic team coaches, ensuring they work with teams outside their immediate business areas.

This approach offers several advantages. It fosters greater internal ownership and credibility in the change and coaching process, enhances cross-organizational awareness and learning, and provides significant development opportunities for those selected. For example, in one organization we worked with, the team of eight external systemic team coaches partnered with one of the 13 carefully selected and trained internal team coaches/change agents, to develop each of the 54 teams. Each one of these 13 was promoted within 15 months. When asked about this, the senior leadership team noted that these individuals distinguished themselves by focussing on the organization's overall goals and future, rather than solely on their team's short-term performance. They also developed a better understanding of the different parts of the organization, and key interdependencies by coaching teams from elsewhere in the organization.

However, there are potential challenges in this approach. Many organizations struggle to release senior people for these roles, or they may lack individuals with the necessary personality, skills and credibility to succeed. Therefore, selecting the right people is crucial, as is matching the appropriate internal and external team coaches, both with each other and with the right teams.

3c. Selecting key teams, rather than all second-tier teams

Some organizations choose to focus on a select few critical teams at different levels within the organization, rather than working consistently across all teams that report into the top team. They may determine that short-term business pressures, or the need to demonstrate the effectiveness of this approach to their board or to themselves, necessitate starting with a few key teams. This allows them to showcase how the approach can drive beneficial change in areas that are business-critical, before expanding to other less-critical areas of work.

The challenges with this approach include the need for leaders and team coaches to clearly communicate the rationale for prioritizing certain teams over others and to outline when other teams will have the opportunity to participate.

However, the advantages are that it can deliver short-term gains and build visibility and creditability of the approach, which, if leveraged effectively, can generate enthusiasm among initially reluctant teams to become part of the process.

3d. Leaders coaching their own teams

A few of the organizations we researched chose to follow up in-depth work with the top team by requiring each team member to take responsibility for coaching and developing their own teams. The potential risk in this approach is that individuals' capabilities, capacities and motivations for this responsibility may vary significantly. Leaders can also return to the pressures of their workload, after team coaching sessions and lose momentum in the busyness of the day-to-day work that has piled up while they were away. However, the advantage is that it embeds a cultural expectation that a core aspect of every leader's role is to develop and coach their team (see Hawkins, 2021: Chapters 12 and 13).

To mitigate the potential downsides of this approach, I, Peter, implemented a strategy with a major leading UK company, where each team member was provided with a template for them to use to devise a team development plan for their respective teams. After completing the plan, they presented it to their colleagues in the top team, who then critiqued and helped refine it, ensuring that it included clear objectives and outcomes, aligned with and supportive of the overall transformational journey. The team leader was then responsible for carrying out this agreed-upon development plan with their team and reported back to the top team every three to six months on progress. During these updates, the leader, in collaboration with their colleagues and myself as the external team of teams coach, discussed how to enhance the next phase of team development based on the experiences and outcomes to date.

For other organizations, we have facilitated a process where each team undergoes a Team 360 assessment, completed by all team members as well as key stakeholders. The insights from this assessment are then integrated into the team leaders' presentations of their team development plans to the senior team.

3e. *Training leaders and members of selected teams to coach their whole team*

Some organizations have chosen to engage this stage with another approach of training leaders and members of selected teams to coach their whole teams. In Hawkins (2022: 316–18), I included a case study of the work I, Peter, and colleagues, have done over the last nine years with Deloitte UK. This approach has been successfully implemented, enabling senior partners who lead multi-million-dollar businesses to take their leadership, their team and their business to the next stage of its development. Here is a another case example of this approach:

For the past three years, Christophe, one of our research partners, partnered with Guerbet, a global pharmaceutical company, in developing the company culture through a team-based approach. In the early phases of the programme, they worked with the top team and 180+ representatives from across the company to co-create the desired culture, which was crystallized through five behavioural principles: customer-centricity, focus, audacity, accountability, cooperation.

In the next phase, they chose team development as a key driver for cultural change for several reasons. First, they saw teams as the organizational 'units' of culture, the collective context in which company culture comes to life. Secondly, they believed that the five behavioural principles are present within each team and can be developed in the life of the team. Finally, building on the five-disciplines model of high-value creating teams (Hawkins, 2021), they felt that team Systemic Team Coaching ample opportunities to connect the behavioural and business dimensions, and to facilitate Systemic Team Coaching as key driver of value creation and stakeholder impact.

In this spirit, they codesigned a programme to coach seven teams in parallel, working through the team leader and two to three team members from each of the six teams. The team leader and the two to three members participated in the team coaching programme and then shared and applied their learning in the day-day work of the team between the team coaching modules. A major part of the learning came from the sharing that took place across the seven teams.

The intention in involving both the team leader as well as two to three team members was to coach directly across the hierarchical boundary and to ensure that both levels would be represented and actively engaged in the programme. This was a way of enabling a 'team-driven' dynamic from the set-up of the programme, rather than reinforcing a 'leader-driven' dynamic.

In this way, the relationship between the two hierarchical levels was brought directly 'into focus' and actively worked on in the sessions.

The seven teams were selected jointly with the Transformation Office and the sponsors, with the aim of representing different functions of the company, ensuring motivation to engage in a learning journey, considering the business impact of each team and securing the support of a senior executive member.

The team coaching programme was a year-long journey which included:

- Tailored team 360° feedback was provided at the beginning of the programme, based on the five behavioural principles applied to team effectiveness.

- Ten half day modules delivered over the course of one year, addressing the five disciplines of high-value creating teams (Hawkins, 2021) and the company's five behavioural principles.

- A tailored team 360° progress review was conducted at the end of the programme, focussing on two to three key team development goals.

- Action learning sequences were used to support the development of the team and its members.

- Co-coaching between an internal coach, from HR or the transformation team and an external coach,

- Particpant learning application through coaching the whole team between modules.

They collected progress feedback from more than 170 stakeholders to evaluate each of the seven teams on its two to three main development goals, as well as to collect further feedforward suggestions for continued improvement. This feedback indicated solid to strong progress on all team development goals across the seven teams. It further fuelled the learning process of each team while also providing a clear measure of progress.

They interviewed participating team members from each team regarding the impact of the team coaching journey. They recognized the significant impact of the programme, and reported the following areas of impact:

- 'Our interactions within the team have changed: we are aligned, people are closer, informal spaces have been created. We think about working together in a more efficient way, both on what we do and how we act together.'

- 'We have learnt from our stakeholders: we understand how our stakeholders think and work, what they need, what their challenges are. We plan with them, and we listen to them. We have increased our capability to work together with them.'

- 'Through the exchanges with people from other departments, we have benefited from different views and creating connections between us and across functions.'
- 'We have developed greater empathy and ability to mediate tense situations within and outside the team.'
- 'We have reinforced the clarity of our roles and responsibilities.'
- 'We are conducting regular feedback sessions.'
- 'We have organized visits of customer sites and made improvements to the customer journey.'

Both sources of feedback pointed to significant impact of the programme both for the teams and their key stakeholder relationships.

The strengths of the approach included:

- The participation of team leader with two to three team members opened up the hierarchical boundary of the team and created a context that fostered a team-driven learning dynamic.
- The combined training programme for leaders and members of seven teams created high-value creating connections across multiple parts of the organization.
- The use of stakeholder feedback at the start and at the end of the programme had a significant impact on the quality of partnership between each team and its key stakeholders.

The potential difficulties with this approach:

- The joint participation of the team leader with team members can be countercultural in very hierarchical cultures.
- The involvement of a sub-set of the team can create an internal boundary in the team (the participants in the team coaching programme vs the others), as well as a high dependency on the ability of the participating members to share their learning and coach the rest of the team. We found that this could be partly addressed by coaching the team members on this aspect as part of the programme.
- When the teams are not the direct reports of ExCom members, it proved important to involve the sponsoring Exco member directly and regularly, e.g. through alignment/review sessions at the start, the middle and the end of the programme with the team leader and the two to three team members.

4. Coaching the horizontal connections

Leaders often manage up and down their organization but often forget to partner across the organization.

As a standard practice, we conduct one-on-one or group network mapping sessions with leaders and teams, helping them to identify crucial stakeholders and ecosystem partners and develop strategies for deliberately engaging and activating their networks (see Chapter 14).

5. Embedding teaming into the organization's core processes

Teaming is a verb. It refers to the dynamic process of real-time working together collaboratively, often across organizational boundaries, to solve problems, innovate and achieve collective goals. Teaming involves fluid and flexible groups that come together as needed, often with members from different departments, disciplines or even organizations.

In the work with Guerbet mentioned above, they managed this stage by embedding a team feedback culture as part of the HR processes used in management teams. As mentioned earlier, we had helped our client define their desired culture through five behavioural principles and committed to a team-based approach to supporting cultural change.

To further embed this approach into the day-to-day operations of the organization, the top team committed to establishing a team-based feedback culture across all the management teams to make the yearly setting of behavioural goals a real source of meaningful growth and learning.

The systemic team of teams coaches worked with the organization to develop a simple structured grid of desired behaviours for each of the five behavioural principles. They then coached the ExCom to practise peer feedback based on those five principles. The team committed to do so at least three times a year. Then the ExCom members role-modelled openness to learning by asking for 180° feedback from their own team members as well as from other functions. Finally, they trained HR directors and HR business partners to facilitate team peer feedback sessions, which they did with all management teams. They collected feedback from the HR directors and business partners on the level of engagement by management teams in this process, which was reported as very high, and seen as a key enabler for embedding a feedback culture within each team.

6. Training leaders, managers, HR and internal coaches in Systemic Team Coaching and development

To ensure a strong teaming culture is sustainable, it is essential to build team leadership and Systemic Team Coaching skills into a range of regular internal training programmes. We have worked with many organizations to develop internal training and development programmes particularly focussed on the following four key groups:

- **Internal coaches:** Many organizations have developed their own internal community of internal coaches (see Hawkins, 2012).

  o We have long advocated that every individual coach should receive foundational training in both systemic coaching, (Hawkins and Turner, 2020) and team development and Systemic Team Coaching (Hawkins, 2021, 2022b). Some of the most common issues brought to individual coaching include: how can I develop my team? How do I deal with difficult team members or team conflict? How do I have more effective team meetings? We have thought about how to equip them to conduct individual coaching within a broader systemic context. To facilitate this, we have partnered with Coaching.com to develop an online programme called 'Team Development Essentials'. The programme consists of six modules, each featuring short videos, accompanied by handouts and tools. After completing the modules, participants join practicum groups where they apply the models and tools in a collaborative learning environment.

  o This programme is offered as a global open course, and customized versions are also available for in-house training. Some companies choose to involve their managers, HR and internal training and development professionals in this training, further integrating team development principles throughout the organization.

- **HR business partners:** Often the HR business partner plays a key role in supporting the development not only of team members but also the whole team.

We have worked with many HR business leaders of international companies as well as governments, to develop their internal systemic team coach practitioners.

One training model we have used runs as follows:

- o virtual half day introductory webinar and pre-reading, followed by a
- o three-day intensive workshop in which participants engage in a comprehensive, hands-on workshop where they learn to coach across the Five Disciplines of high-value team creation and navigate the team coaching journey. Participants practice coaching in real-time, with live supervision, as they guide teams through an enacted business simulation. This immersive experience ensures that participants not only understand the concepts but also apply them effectively in realistic scenarios.
- o Supervision groups: These internal systemic team coaches join supervision groups that meet over the next six months as they apply their learning to coaching teams.

- Managers: Several organizations choose to involve managers alongside internal coaches and HR business partners, in either the 'Team Development Essentials' training or in becoming an internal team coach. These companies have found that involving managers in coaching teams elsewhere in the company has enormous benefits in how they not only subsequently lead their own team, but also in how they understand and work with the complexity of team of teams right across the business.
- Leaders: Structured programmes for senior leaders helps them not only acquire skills, but also implement them to develop and coach their own teams.

7. Teaming in partnership with all the key ecosystem partners

In Chapter 3 we talked about the five keys for organization success in the 21st century. One of these was the ability to partner with all the organizations stakeholders and ecosystem partners, and shift these relationships, from transactional to transformational.

While working with one of the largest professional services firms in the world, I, Peter, assisted them in conducting research to understand what the senior leaders of their key client organizations valued most, and found most difficult about working with them and their competitors. The research revealed that having the best thought leadership, processes and tools was becoming less of a competitive advantage, as these could be easily replicated by competitors. However, the ability to create joint teaming between the client organization and the professional services firm emerged as a highly valued differentiator. Senior leaders of client organizations have made comments such as:

- 'Don't do the work for us, but with us.'
- 'We need you to leave our people more skilled than before, through working with your expertise.'
- 'We need you to coach our people to do what you do for us.'
- 'We need you to not just work with the core internal team but to help create connections across the business.'

Building on these insights, we coached several key client account teams within the firm, helping them add value far beyond the technical services they were originally contracted to provide (see Hawkins, 2021: 162–67). We also facilitated live workshops where both the professional services team and their client team collaborated, exploring how they could achieve outcomes together that were greater than the sum of their parts.

The CEO of one client organization involved in this partnering process told us, 'It would be very hard to switch to another professional services firm, as it would take years to train a new partner to understand our organization, our culture and collaborate with us the way this firm does.'

Organizations must learn to partner with all their stakeholders, not just their clients and customers, so they become ecosystem partners. Each of these relationships-involving a shift from viewing stakeholders as mere demands or resources to seeing them as true ecosystem partners-involves several key elements:

a. moving from 'win-win' to 'win-win-win' relationships

b. focussing on the stakeholder's stakeholder to focussing on the ecosystem partner's partner

c. exploring what we can uniquely do together than we cannot do apart (see the section on mergers and acquisitions in Chapter 5).

8. Evaluating and evolving

Throughout each stage of the change process, the organization must continuously review, evaluate and evolve its approach. This involves building on and amplifying successful strategies, adjusting what isn't working and ensuring that each subsequent stage is even more effective.

A thorough review should also consider the broader context, including new challenges coming over the horizon and those already impacting the organization. The external environment doesn't pause while an organization focusses on internal change. Shifts in financial revenue or funding, whether positive or negative, can have significant implications for the resources available to support these change initiatives. Additionally, new leadership may enter the organization, and it will be essential for them to become fully engaged in understanding the 'why', 'what' and 'how' of the change process, and to have the opportunity to influence its direction and form.

Moreover, if the organization has expanded into new product divisions, entered new regional markets or restructured some of its functional units, these developments must be integrated into the ongoing redesign of the change journey. By staying agile and responsive to both internal changes and emerging challenges on the horizon, the organization can ensure that its transformation efforts remain relevant, effective and aligned with its evolving goals.

Effective ongoing evaluation and evolution requires putting in place the right metrics, that can evaluate both short-term 'lead' indicators and longer-term 'lag' indicators. It is important not to introduce an additional layer of costly bureaucratic measurement, but rather to look at how existing evaluation processes and metrics can incorporate data collection, that supports evaluating the change process.

In Chapter 7, we return to the evaluation of Systemic Team of Teams Coaching, focusing on how to establish and measure the outcomes and value created through team of teams development.

A case example of the Systemic Team of Teams journey

The Systemic Team of Teams Approach was highly impactful at a multinational food company over an eight-year period between 2013 to 2021. The internal coaching lead reflected on the key ingredients.

> First, we had strong support from the CEO and CHRO at the time. Secondly, we had a business context in which team coaching could make a difference. The company had to issue a profit warning almost for the first time ever, which was a trauma for the organization. A restructuring was in progress: 1,000 positions of key leaders were being eliminated, with a clear risk to damage the high level

of engagement. We felt the need to support the teams that were building the organization of the future. By 2018, two major divisions were merging, creating new leadership teams which needed to be able to lead the integrated organization, both at the level of Executive Teams and Regional Boards. Fortunately, I was a recognized internal team coaching leader, and garnered support to build a team of seven internal team coaches over the following 4 years.

Building on these favourable starting conditions, the internal coaching lead established four pillars that ensured the success of the team coaching initiative. The first pillar was our **co-coaching model** that paired an internal and external team coach. We found in our experience that the combination of an internal and external coach was extremely effective and impactful. The internal coach brought the immediate connection to the organization context, and the external coach brought an external perspective and way of coaching. Each of the coaches in the co-coaching duo has a specific role. One coach is focussed on the team leader and having individual coaching sessions with the team leader. The other coach is focussed on the team members.

The Second pillar was the creation of our **own team model**. We found that the fundamental needs of executive teams in the group were often similar, while the ways of addressing them needed to be tailored to each team. Our approach aimed to enable new leadership teams to achieve a step change in collective leadership behaviours, lead transformation, and drive sustainable growth. This was delivered through a six-day team coaching programme over 9–12 months, structured in three phases:

- Preparation of the team coaching seminar: each team member participated in a one-on-one conversation with the team coach to engage them in the coaching dynamic. A synthesis of verbatim feedback, grouped by themes, was also created.

- Team kick-off seminar: two day workshop focussed on sharing perceptions of team dynamics, building personal connections, developing trust, co-creating a shared vision, and identifying priority team development goals.

- Three seminars of 1–1.5 days each: continued development of the priority team goals: trust, ability to give feedback, decision-making process, clarity of roadmap. Each seminar also included a review of progress: what did we achieve, how did we get there, what do we learn about our success factors and areas for improvement as a team…

The third pillar was the **continued professionalization** of our team coaching approach. We built a 3.5 days' Train-the-Trainer programme for both internal and external coaches. This enabled us to establish a robust common language and approach across our team of internal and external coaches, while also building a growing network of trained external team coaches. Every four months we bring together the internal and external coaches, for a supervision session facilitated by an external supervisor involved in the team coaching design.

The fourth pillar was the development of our team of **internal team coaching capability.** We expanded from two internal team coaches to twelve, with four full-time and eight part-time. As a network, we met regularly (45 minutes each month and two hours every quarter) to share best practices and learning. In addition, the internal coaches also had group supervision (three hours every two months). The development of our team enabled us to become a real and recognized developmental force within the organization.

The internal coaching lead identified three main levels of impact after listening to the participating teams, sponsors and key stakeholders.

1 Performance acceleration through greater effectiveness and collective engagement.

2 The facilitation of organizational change through team coaching, including restructuring during 2013–2014, and the merging of divisions in 2018–2019.

3 The team coaching helped to mitigate/offset the challenging human impact of the organizational restructuring. It reduced the risk of turnover, departures, and demotivation, and disengagement that could have happened if there had been no team coaching. For teams impacted, it created the feeling that the dual purpose of the company (economic and social) was not only words but a tangible reality! Corporate was bringing in real (human) support to help them navigate through the crisis.

* * * * *

Conclusion

This chapter reveals the transformative potential of a Systemic Team of Teams Approach (STOTA), offering a powerful framework for organizations navigating today's complex, interconnected challenges. By diving into the 'how' of STOTA, we've outlined a path that organizations can follow to move beyond isolated successes and into sustainable, enterprise-wide development.

What makes this approach truly effective is its flexibility – it's not about a one-size-fits-all solution, but about creating a living, breathing process that evolves with the organization's needs. The journey begins with small, deliberate steps: coaching one to a small number of teams, then connecting across those teams and down through the organization. The coach supports the leaders and sponsors to build towards a network of aligned, high-value creating teams. Each step serves as a building block for something much larger – an ecosystem of collaboration where teams don't just work in silos but in synergy.

A key insight from our research (see Chapter 8), and the cases in this chapter, is that leadership teams must lead this change from the front. These teams are the linchpins of systemic transformation, not only modelling collaboration and accountability but also setting the tone for the organization's culture. By shifting from individual accountability to collective ownership, leadership teams inspire the kind of trust and cohesion that ripple outward, empowering teams across the organization to embrace the same mindset.

What sets the Systemic Team of Teams Approach apart is its focus on the 'spaces in between' – the often-overlooked horizontal connections that are vital to organizational success. These connections represent the glue that holds a network of teams together, enabling seamless collaboration across boundaries and silos. Organizations that intentionally cultivate these connections can unlock latent potential, foster innovation and co-create greater value with their stakeholders.

This chapter also shines a spotlight on the importance of partnerships in this journey. The most successful organizations understand that real transformation requires a blend of internal insight and external expertise. Collaborations between internal leadership and external systemic team coaches create a powerful dynamic: internal players bring cultural depth, while external partners offer fresh perspectives and systemic thinking. Together, they create a partnership that drives lasting change and builds the organization's capacity to sustain its ongoing development.

Perhaps the most compelling aspect of this journey is the cultural shift it inspires. As teams embrace systemic thinking, they move away from static hierarchies and into a more dynamic, team-centred and collective way of working. This shift fosters agility and resilience, enabling organizations to navigate disruption and seize opportunities faster, more effectively and in a way that builds team energy and health rather than depletes it.

Yet, what makes the iterative journey of STOTA so engaging is its adaptability. There's no rigid roadmap or singular prescription. Instead, this approach thrives on iteration, learning and continuous reflection. Each team, each connection, each insight builds on the last, creating a momentum that fuels ongoing growth and innovation.

As organizations embark on this journey, they discover that Systemic Team Coaching is not just about improving teams but about unlocking the collective power of the whole. It's about creating networks and a meshwork of collaboration, shared purpose and lasting impact. And as we look ahead, this chapter serves as both a guide and an invitation, to rethink how we develop our organizations, inspire our teams and shape a future that's not just ready for change but capable of thriving in it.

05

Transitions and transformations in the organizational life cycle

Introduction

Neither the life of individuals nor organizations flow at an even pace or in predictable directions. Both individuals and organizations go through a series of life transitions where looking back, or viewing from the outside, one can discern the end of one phase transitioning into the beginning of another.

For individuals, these phases often include birth, going to school for the first time, puberty, leaving home, starting employed work, marriage, having children, mid-life with children possibly leaving home and a change in the focus of one's life, retirement, beginning to feel the effects of growing old, and finally dying. Then there are the interruptive transitions such as: divorce, sudden illness, death of a child, spouse, friend or sibling, being let go from a job, changing one's life direction, or mental illness.

Every transition, whether predictable and part of the natural course of events, or arriving as an unexpected loss, interruption or trauma, takes the individual into a liminal state, an open space between two worlds. Van Gennep (1909) wrote the classic book on 'rites of passage', for as an anthropologist he was interested in how different cultures used ritual and ceremony to assist the passage of individuals through these life transitions. He described three stages that most rites include:

- the dying to, and letting go of, the old phase
- the liminal state between one stage and another
- the re-entry back into life, in a new phase and role

We need to let go of our attachment to the previous stage, before we can fully enter the next stage. In the global research on 'tomorrow's leadership' (Hawkins, 2017), I, Peter, interviewed a CEO of a large international insurance business, who talked about the transitions he had been through between each stage of his leadership career. He stunned me by saying: 'At each stage of being promoted, I had to learn to eat my children.' I had no idea what he meant and found the image shocking. He explained, 'I had to consume, digest and destroy what made me successful at the previous level, in order to discover how I needed to be at this next level of leadership.' What is necessary in one role and one stage of our lives must often be unlearnt, in order that we can learn what is required from the next phase or role.

In modern leadership and coaching, however, we often want to pretend we can transition to the new state, without a death and letting go and unlearning of the previous phase. The three-stage model, used to describe organizational change, 'Unfreeze, Change, and Refreeze' (Lewin, 1947), is mechanistic and removes the deep emotional and psychological work that all major transitions require. Systemic coaches and consultants are in the business of helping leaders manage transitions and rites of passage, and one of their roles is as the modern secular celebrant, shaman or priest.

Every transition can be a moment of crisis, a time when the individual, team or organization break down, and indeed the onset of many mental health problems happen at the juncture of a life transition. Likewise, many team and organizational crises and failures happen at times of transition, where the organization is unable to navigate the transformation to the next stage of its development.

Transitions in teams

The systemic team coach is frequently in the role of supporting teams through transitions. Such transitions may include: a team leader leaving and a new leader being appointed; several team members leaving at the same time; the teams being downsized and having to readjust and reallocate its work; two teams being merged; the team being relocated to a new function and new reporting line in an organizational restructuring; or new technology requiring a very different process in how it operates. Each of these transitions can be opportunities for the team to grow and develop its collective maturity, or they may lead to stress and collectively feel victimized by events.

We recommend that in all periods of transition, the team take a pause amid the busy extra demands and rework the 'five disciplines of high-value creating teams' (Hawkins, 2021, 2022b).

a. **Commissioning:** Discover its changing purpose in the light of its new context.

b. **Clarifying:** Reclarify its team charter – its collective team objectives and key performance indicators, its roles and processes.

c. **Co-creating:** Consider how it can use this transition to change its team dynamic and culture and the ways it holds meetings and communicates.

d. **Connecting:** Remap and re-prioritize its key stakeholder groups and plan how it is going to inform, communicate, engage and partner with its stakeholders through this period of change.

e. **Core learning:** Harvest the learning from both the successes and the failures of the previous stage of the team and consider how this can inform the next stage. It is also important to attend to how the team can collectively learn through this period, about effective transitioning and transforming.

Recently I (Peter) was helping the global executive team in GHD manage both a change in their team leader, with the CEO retiring and a new CEO being appointed, as well as a subsequent appointment of new team leader to head up one of their largest regions.

The short-list for the new CEOs had come down to two members of the team, who currently were heads of the two largest regions: the Americas and Asia Pacific. Having previously seen the enormous cost in other companies not handling the process and dynamics of such internal competition for the CEO role well, I offered to help them with this process.

This top team all knew the contenders for the role and the timetable for the process. I met with the team and took them through a process of each person sharing their way of completing the following seed sentences:

a. What I think I, and we as a team, can best do to ensure that the current CEO leaves well is…

b. What I think I, and we as a team, can best do to support both the successful and unsuccessful candidate for the future CEO role is…

c. What I think I, and we as a team, can best do to manage a successful transition is…

The current CEO and the two candidates participated as equal members in this collective sharing. Once we had heard from all team members, I facilitated a process for agreeing on key protocols and steps for the transition. Then they individually and collectively committed to how they would be actioned.

Two months later after the appointment had been decided and made public, but the current CEO had not yet left, I again met with the team for an off-site workshop.

I invited the team to form a standing circle based on a clock of how long they had been in the team, with longest serving team member being at 12 o'clock, then second at 1 o'clock, right round to the just appointed new member being at 11 o'clock (for an outline of this technique see Hawkins and Presswell, 2022). The CEO, who was longest serving member of the team, then told the other team members, and particularly the new arrival, what the team was like when they joined and how it had developed up to the time the next member arrived. The second longest serving member then took up the story, until they passed on to the third. Finally, the new member, having heard the collective narrative of the team's development, told the story he would like to be able to tell the next future member of the team.

This process proved to be a very effective rite of passage, demonstrating how the whole team is responsible for its collective journey and maturation, how each member honours the legacy they have inherited, and how they pass on the baton of leadership to the next stage in a better and more developed condition than when they received it.

Organizational life-cycle transitions

The organizational development coach is likewise often supporting an organization through a 'rite of passage' from one stage of development to the next. In this chapter we explore the major transitions that organizations commonly encounter and how these can best be supported to ensure they become opportunities for transformation. As part of our team of teams research, we looked at the variety of transitions that different organizations were undertaking. Based on this and our research of the best models and theories of organizational life stages, including Greiner (1972, 1998) and Adizes (1990), we developed our own model (Figure 5.1).

We will now explore the different aspects of this model and show the different pathways and challenges in each stage.

FIGURE 5.1 A simple five-stage model of organizational life cycle

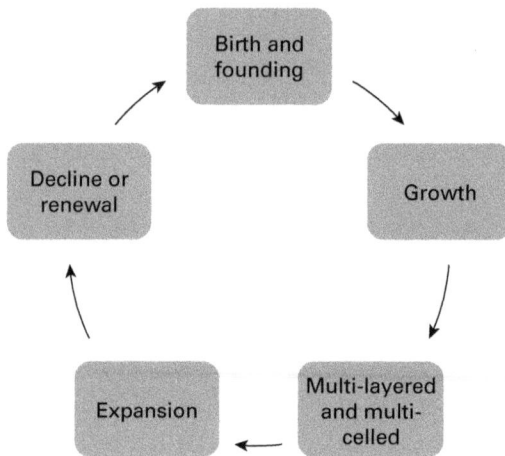

Birth and founding of the organization

Many organizations are started by entrepreneurial individuals, who driven by a mix of personal passion and recognition of a need in the world, set out to start something new. It is also increasingly common for organizations to be started by a small group or team of friends or colleagues, who bring different skills, personalities and experience to the birth of the organization.

I, Peter, have started five different organizations, some by myself and some with colleagues. Each approach has its different benefits and dangers. Organizations that are started by one charismatic founder can quickly reflect both the strengths and the hidden weaknesses of the founder. Such founders may also attract dependent followers who are less likely to challenge them, or surround themselves with people who are similar to them, leading to an imbalance imbalance in the requisite diversity of the team.

Entrepreneurial founders are often driven by confidence and optimism and less likely to see the dangers and pitfalls in the path they are driving. They can be greatly helped by a good mentor or coach, who often at this stage will fulfil the role of a quasi-non-executive director, without the formal role or shareholding. This coach or mentor needs to help them:

- see their shadow-side and how they will manage this
- realize the potential risks and dangers on the way ahead, without denting their essential confidence
- think long term as well as short term, and anticipate further stages in the organization's development and how they prepare in advance for them

- find, recruit and develop the core team that will be essential for the organization to grow and flourish.

It is therefore important that such mentor or coaches are team literate and understand the requisite diversity needed for a good team, and help the leader create a leadership team, rather than a group of followers.

The growth transition

We have also worked with many organizations at the point of transition from being a one-team business, to requiring separate but connected teams. For most organizations this marks the beginning of becoming a team of teams.

This transition poses many challenges. The founders may have become attached to knowing everything that is happening in their business, and feel their fledgling business is like a child they need to protect. Their own sense of identity may be caught up with the identity of the business, and losing a sense of being in control can feel personally very threatening.

The members of an early-stage pioneering business may fear losing their sense of being part of the core and at the heart of everything that is happening. The central team may feel like a family, with a strong sense of belonging and camaraderie – a feeling of 'we are all in this together'. However, as the business grows, involving everyone in every aspect of the work becomes inefficient. Too much time can be spent on internal meetings, when there is often a growing need to be externally focussed, actively engaging with the growing number of stakeholders.

Many organizations we have coached at this stage have an over-stretched leadership group, that are trying to simultaneously combine the roles of: ownership and governance, strategic leadership, and operational management.

At this transition, the coaching needed for the core leaders, who often but not always will also be the founders, is from someone skilled in organizational design and 'team of teams architecture'. The design needs to focus on both the vertical and horizontal clarity of functions and interconnections.

Vertical clarifying

Even when core leaders need to be owners, strategic leaders and operational managers and 'doers', it is important that they are aware of which role they are in, and that others know which hat they are wearing when listening to them.

I, Peter, worked with one fast-growing and successful consultancy and training business that had expanded internationally. The company was still a partnership, even though the original partners had left. Before starting to work with them I was invited to attend one of their monthly meetings. This went on all day, and it quickly became clear that their meetings constantly shifted between short-term operational detail, longer-term strategy and policy and governance issues that should belong to a board. Conflict arose as it was not clear, at any one time, whether partners were speaking as an owner, a collective leader of the company or as an employee. This led to frequent misunderstandings and an ensuing dance of complaint and defence.

At the beginning of the afternoon, I called a 'time-out', and said: 'Being with you over lunch and in the coffee break, it is clear you all like each other and get on well informally, but as soon as you get into the meetings it seems you all become frustrated very quickly. Please can you each write down a score on a scale of 1 low to 10 high, a) how much you enjoy the meetings, b) how effective and productive are your partner meetings?'

The scores for a) ranged from 1 to 7 and for b) no one scored the effectiveness and productiveness of the meeting more than 5. 'So, what needs to change?' I asked. The responses included, 'we need clearer agendas', 'better chairing', 'greater discipline'. I noticed a pattern that they were locating the problem in the process, or in the managing partner, but decided to refrain from commenting, as this would have the danger of being heard as blaming them for blaming others!

Later, the managing partner shared with me how she felt that she was in a catch-22. The partners had elected her as managing partner, but as fellow owners of the business, resisted being managed by her, and all wanted the freedom to work and lead in their own way. This was a pattern I had previously seen in other organizations, particularly partnerships, even when working as a consultant to two of the largest global professional services firms.

Gradually I worked with them to separate out the distinct purposes they needed their meetings to fulfil. Together we designed quarterly **board meetings**, where they were clearly there in the role of owners and shareholders, and the managing partner would present a business update and the finance manager the performance against budget and the forward projections. The partners agreed very clear protocols for how they would all operate in this meeting, including leaving personal employee agendas outside of the room.

Their monthly partner gatherings were redesigned to have three different forms of meeting:

a. **An operational planning meeting** – including updates on all key current client work and key programmes, and allocation of new work, led by a new role of one of the partners being elected COO (Chief Operating Officer).

b. **A strategy meeting** that looked at how the business needed to develop: including new areas of research, new work streams, marketing focus and organizational culture. This was led by the managing partner.

c. **A peer learning/supervision meeting** where one or two members would present a current piece of work and the whole group would explore how this work could be taken to the next level and where else in the business the learning from this could be applied. For several months I acted as an external group supervisor, until the processes were well established, and they could operate on a peer supervision basis, with different team members rotating the role of group facilitator.

Horizontal clarifying

At the same time as we were working on designing vertical clarity in the structure of the consultancy business above, we were also helping them get clarity and empowerment in their horizontal organizational design. We worked with them to map out a matrix of regional, client and project leadership. Each leader in the business was freed up to be totally responsible for how they led their geographical region, key client accounts and or training programme. From Netflix, they adopted the phrase, 'Every leader has to be captain of their own ship' (Hastings and Meyer, 2020), but we added: 'We need to sail as an integrated flotilla'. This was a phrase we used again when working with the much larger GHD (see Chapter 2).

Becoming multi-layered and multi-celled:
the emergence of separate tribes

The solution, which is the way out of one problem, can often be the cause of the next problem (Senge,1990), and each organizational transformation brings new challenges in its wake.

Having helped growing organizations to develop differentiated meetings vertically and different teams horizontally, very quickly this can lead to the development of separate tribes and competing teams. In many finance, investment, and law firms we've worked with, regional teams viewed each other as competitors, each trying to outperform the rest. This requires the senior leadership to change their dominant focus from managing the separate regions and functions, to orchestrating the connections between the team of teams, to create an aligned and synergistic performance. Like all great orchestral performances, this requires not only a shared score, translated into separate parts for different sections of the orchestra, and good conducting, but also every section being able to listen and attune to everybody in their section, and all other sections, as well as respond to the acoustics of the setting and the response of the audience.

The emergence of a multi-layered structure

In the late 1980s, British Aerospace had difficulties with its Airbus division, which was part of the international partnership between France, Germany, Spain and the UK to build the Airbus passenger jets. The British contribution was the design and building of the wings and engines, and as the business grew, they had to build and assemble four wings a week and have them flown out to Toulouse in France for the next stage of assembly.

When I, Peter, was brought in, I found that the business was struggling to deliver to the increasing demands for more production. Senior leaders were coming in over the weekend to 'chase parts' that had gone missing and were holding up the assembly. They were also working extremely long hours and constantly fire-fighting emerging problems and crises.

Some of the workers I met told me how they had been trained for 20 years to leave their brains outside the factory gates and do what they were told. Another said: 'They at the top call it "cascade change", we call it being p***** on from on high!'

Having spent two days touring the hangars, and more time interviewing all the team members and some key stakeholders, I told them they had the most expensive postal service I had ever seen. They were shocked. I said, correct me if I am wrong, but it seems you have five levels of management whose main task is to take problems from the front-line workers, up through the levels of management to the leadership team, and then take the solutions back through these five levels. We explored how they could change this and move to a new culture where the role of the leadership team was to frame the challenges and engage the managers and workers in solutions coming up through the company.

As soon as you have a multi-layered organization, employees can become over-focussed on the vertical dimension and feel they are working for their boss to meet the boss's targets, rather than for the whole organization and even more importantly the stakeholders it serves.

Also, the separation into 'us and them' with blaming the people above you or beneath you for your difficulties can develop, and at the same time a growing dependency on the people above you to make all the decisions. This can lead to what we term 'delegating upwards' rather than resolving issues directly at your own level.

In a hospital where I, Peter, carried out team of teams coaching. The top team set themselves a key performance indicator, to reduce by 80 per cent the number of issues that were delegated up to the top team or one of its members, that could have been resolved at a lower level either by an individual leader or by partnering horizontally across the organization. This quickly transformed the culture.

Expansion and its challenges

There are many ways an organization can grow and expand:

- taking their product and approach into new regions and countries
- developing new products and brands
- occupying more of the value chain, by doing more of the production previously done by their suppliers, or owning their own retail outlets
- moving beyond selling products to also providing ongoing servicing and being a service company
- acquiring competitors or linked businesses that given them new products, brands, regions or entry into new markets

Each of these bring several challenges in its wake. These include, how to:

1 maintain and develop a clear collective identity both internally and externally

2 avoid diluting the brand identity of the business and being seen as trying to be 'all things to all people'

3 avoid the fragmentation into separate sub-businesses and the centre just being an expensive overhead that tries to oversee and control the different parts

Many organizations have come to us, unsure of whether to organize their business based on geographic region, product, key customers or key customer sectors. The exploration always involves exploring the pros and cons of each one of these being the vertical pillar of the company's organizational design, while recognizing the need to build strong horizontal connecting processes for the other dimensions. This inevitably creates some form of matrix organization, which brings its own challenges and dangers. Managers can complain about having to report to different bosses along different reporting lines and receiving conflicting demands and messages. The leaders of the different reporting lines can start competing for people's time and for resources.

What is needed is for the vertical and horizontal leaders to come together to co-create and clarify protocols and processes that enable a 'win-win-win' – for all dimensions, and most importantly for the whole delivery of products and services to the customers and clients.

There needs to be requisite complexity, no more or no less complexity than is required to meet the needs of customers, clients and key stakeholders and provide the speed and agility of responding to changing contexts and circumstances.

Becoming a globally networked business

In Chapter 1 we argued that every business, however small, has to think globally, for even a single corner store may be selling goods that have come from many different countries, and their customers, although living locally, may have cultural origins from many distant places, and their bank loan may be from a bank that works internationally. However, there is a specific transitional challenge when an organization develops from being a nationally headquartered business, with international outposts to being a fully globally networked business.

I, Peter, worked extensively with one of the big four professional services firms through a global merger. It became clear that this was not just a merger between two professional services firms, but an organizational transformation challenge to get over 50 separate country partnerships to become globally networked and able to deliver seamless service to global clients. The research, they and we had carried out with global clients, yielded quotes such as:

- We need you to be more integrated than we are.
- We want you to help us join up our business by linking all the different work you are doing for us.
- We don't want to waste time having to tell your people where else you are working with us around the world.
- When you meet with our senior leaders – don't just report on all the different projects you are doing, but help us see the bigger picture and patterns, and how we can do projects better in the future.

The challenge for companies becoming a globally networked business, is that staff are mostly appointed locally, remunerated on what they achieve in their region of function, and their sense of belonging and identity is local. Supporting client work or projects in other regions is something that depends on goodwill and is done outside of the 'day job'.

We helped the organization develop global sector teams that pooled knowledge and know-how on current and future trends in that sector, so that they could deliver best-of-the-best global thought leadership and processes to companies in that sector right around the world.

We also worked providing Systemic Team Coaching to their global account teams for their global clients. There is a write-up of this account team coaching in Hawkins (2021: 162–63).

In GHD, the engineering firm which we described in Chapter 2, we have been partnering with them over the last three years to evolve into being a globally networked business. Three transformations have been critical to their success:

1   **The transformation of the Executive Committee (ExCo) into an Enterprise Leadership Team (ELT).** The ExCo was originally located in Australia, the country where the business first started. The current ELT now has no 'headquarters' and holds its face-to-face meetings in different regions around the world, always engaging with staff groups and client organizations that are in that area. The ELT also needed coaching to move their mindset and agendas from over-focussing on the operational management of the business to focussing 'outside-in' and 'future-back';

how they could develop the company to meet what their stakeholders needed and the future would be requiring. They also transformed to being collectively responsible for orchestrating the connections across the company not just managing their part.

2 **Transforming their leadership and partner forums** from presentations from the senior leaders on stage, to large numbers of leaders from across the world working together to co-create ways of responding to the current and future challenges facing their business and their client's worlds (See Chapter 14 to discover how we helped them supercharge leadership forums).

3 **Developing team leaders to focus horizontally as much as they focus vertically.** Team meetings at all levels were dominated by 'how do we manage our clients, our people, our numbers, to achieve the targets that our bosses have set us?' This vertical looking up and down, built and reinforced silo thinking and operations. To balance this, we trained team leaders in using 'Networking Nudges' in every meeting to prompt team members to look sideways in order to:

a. acquire and share learning and best practice

b. to access expertise not available locally

c. to partner on winning and carrying out major projects (see Chapter 14)

Going public and being listed, or being bought

For many companies a change in ownership and governance is a major transition. In the early 1990s, I, Peter, along with colleagues, worked with 3i, the largest venture capital/private equity company in the UK and western Europe at that time. It had been stablished in the late 1940s as 'Investors in Industry' to bridge what was known as the 'MacMillan Gap', which was to support companies, when their growth and capital needs had outgrown bank financing, but they were not yet ready to be listed.

3i had been owned by a number of the major UK banks, but the board had decided that now was the time for it to 'go public' and be listed. The capital size of the business meant that once it was listed it would immediately be one of the UK's largest companies and part of the FTSE 100 rankings.

Being catapulted onto the public stage, with much greater investor and media scrutiny, they recognized that this would require a major culture change for the company. The company would need to be far more 'stakeholder centric' – building partnerships with its investors, the media, the companies it invested in and the future purchasers of these growing companies. They wisely decided to start this culture change journey prior to going public.

We started by working with the executive committee, mapping the key stakeholder groups and the gap between how they were currently seen by these stakeholders and how they needed and wished to be seen. We used our own method of 'Descriptor Analysis' (see Hawkins, 2021: 355–57). Externally the top descriptors used by their stakeholders included 'institutional, bureaucratic and slow to respond'. They were wanting to be seen as 'leading edge', 'innovative' and 'European'. We built descriptor analysis into their employee surveys. Internal descriptors of the current culture from their employees included 'siloed, hierarchic and unaligned'; while the descriptors they would like to see included 'strategic, visionary and focussed'.

This gave both the organization and team a sense of the cultural journey that needed to be undertaken. Along with the executive team we appointed a change team of 13 people made up of a diagonal slice across the business, with representatives from different levels, regions and functions. The criteria for the selection to the team was, people who were innovative, creative and had high influence and peer credibility. Working closely in partnership with this team we designed a 'Team of teams' intervention, which involved taking all 54 teams across the business through a team coaching process. Each team was co-coached by one of our team coaches working in partnership with one of the 13 internal change teams. Several of the methods used with the Systemic Team Coaching of every team can be read in Hawkins (2021).

This was one of first whole organizational transformation projects I, Peter, carried out. Three key ways in which it developed STOTA were:

1   Having every team identify which teams vertically and horizontally it needed to receive feedback from, and then looking at how it turned these internal stakeholders into what we now term ecosystem partners.

2   A carefully coached generative dialogue between every team and two members of the ExCo, in which we coached the connection (see Chapter 9).

3   Transforming their leadership forums of their top 120 leaders, into real-time strategizing sessions held in cross-level and cross-team groups (see Chapter 14).

Mergers and acquisitions

Mergers or acquisitions are nearly always a great challenge and an opportunity for transformation, and fraught with many pitfalls. Acquisitions and mergers are a very popular approach for many companies whose speed of annual growth is beginning to plateau and slow down. It is easier to grow a business with double digit growth when your annual revenue is $1 million to $5 million dollars, than when you are $50–$100 million annual revenue. However, it is variously estimated that anywhere between 60 and 80 per cent of mergers fail to meet their predicted financial targets (Bragg, 2009; McKinsey & Company, 2021). It is easy for a due-diligence report to show how the acquisition could create greater economies of scale, remove duplication of functions or provide a new product or client base, and from these estimates extrapolate target figures for the possible return on the investment. Realizing that benefit and managing the post-acquisition integration is much, much harder. Various research studies, and our own experience, indicate that the main reasons for failure include:

- Having too long a period of uncertainty, between first discussions and full integration; for in this period key staff can leave and both parties can be distracted from focussing on their key markets and core tasks.

- Not finding a way to bring the two very different cultures together to create something totally new. At the time we were involved in the merger of Glaxo and SmithKline, to create GSK, the people in SmithKline were still talking about people as 'Beecham's people' or 'SmithKline people', indicating the unfinished merger integration from the previous merger.

- People issues, including the inability to create a harmonious new board and top leadership team, who can put past competition behind them and all be aligned on their future purpose and strategy.

All these major challenges can be addressed by focussing on the transformational opportunity, supported by a strong 'Team of teams' approach, rather than just focussing on the transactional, structural and financial terms or project implementation.

Too often partnerships start in a contractual way with each partner saying what they want from the partnership. This creates a negotiated transaction between the parties. Paul Polman, the ex-CEO of Unilever, who oversaw many successful acquisitions, wrote:

> Too many people think in terms of trade-offs that if you do something which is good for you, then it must be bad for someone else. That's not right and it

comes from old thinking about the way the world works... We have to snap out of that old thinking and move to a new model (Polman and Winstone, 2021).

For a partnership to be transformational, the partners need to develop their 'future-back' and 'outside-in' strategy – addressing questions such as:

- Who and what does our partnership serve?
- What can we achieve together that we cannot achieve apart?
- What massive transformational purpose can we pursue together?
- How will we know the partnership is successful?
- What criteria will we use to evaluate our collective success?

Only when a new partnership has clarified the potent future can it clarify the strategy and road map to get there. Then and only then can it formulate the strategic objectives with action plans and measurable targets, and clear roles and responsibilities, its merger charter.

In another example, two large financial investment companies had decided to merge, and as usual they had set out targets for realizing the synergies and economies of scale by pooling resources and removing duplicated activities. They asked me (Peter), to help them with the merger of their two cultures. I innocently and naively asked them what they were trying to achieve. Their immediate answer was: 'the best of both'. I must have unintentionally grimaced, as they asked: 'What is the problem with that?'

I replied: 'please don't set that as your goal, because from my experience it will lead to two or more years of internal competition, competing over who has the best investment products, best investment managers, best HR processes, best marketing etc.' 'So, what should we focus on?' they inquired. After some more exploration with them I said: '*What about focussing on the question: What together can we uniquely give birth to, that the financial world of tomorrow needs?*'

Hitting the buffers and renewing or dying

From the data available in 2024, only about 60 of the Fortune list of the world's largest 500 companies from 1980 are still on that list today. Unlike the life expectancy of individuals, which has grown steadily over this period, the life expectancy of organizations is getting shorter. Even very successful companies can quite quickly go into administration, be bought up or cease to exist. Peters and Waterman's book *In Search of Excellence* (1982) focussed on 43 successful companies that they believed were exemplars. Over the decades, many of these companies faced considerable challenges and changes, leading to varying degrees of success. Some companies like Xerox and Digital Equipment Corporation, faced significant declines, or were acquired, while others, such as Polaroid, have gone bankrupt and others have lost their former prominence.

We can also look at other companies that have dominated their sector, such as Kodak in film and photography and Olivetti in typewriters, whose successes made them blind to the major disruptive trends in their wider ecosystems. Being number one and leader in your sector is a dangerous place to be, as not only will all the others be trying to leap-frog you, but more crucially you are the last to feel the impact of any disruptive storm in technology or social trends.

Other 'excellent companies' in Peters and Waterman's study have continued to thrive or adapt successfully, such as IBM, AT&T and PepsiCo. But each of these has gone through fundamental renewal and organizational transformation.

Sometimes sudden decline comes from global events that the organization had not anticipated. Recent examples that have impacted organizations in our research have included the war in Ukraine and the Covid-19 pandemic. One of the case studies and interviews was with Casa Amica, an amazing Italian charity that provides 'homes of love' for individuals and families when they or family members are attending hospitals far from their homes. The organization was still in its transition from being centrally led by its amazing charismatic founder when the Covid-19 pandemic swept through Italy. The team of eight systemic team coaches worked with all teams in the organization using a Systemic Team of Teams Approach. The goal was to help them move from separately battling with these and many other challenges (e.g. increased migration, greater funding needs etc.) separately, to working across the organization both vertically and horizontally, to collectively renew and regenerate the organization (we hope to publish a fuller account of this and many of the case studies in a future book).

Reinventing oneself as an organization is never easy. The time to reinvent yourself as a company is best done before the peak of your current success, rather than waiting until you are already in decline, when both morale and resources are declining. Handy's (1994) double S or Sigmoid Curve model, gave shape to this important realization. It shows the rise and fall of organizational stages and products:

1 **Introduction phase:** This is the initial stage where growth is slow as new ideas or products are introduced.

2 **Growth phase:** Here, growth accelerates rapidly as the idea or product gains acceptance and momentum.

3 **Maturity phase:** Growth starts to slow down as the idea or product reaches its peak potential.

4 **Decline phase:** Without innovation or change, growth eventually declines.

By starting a new curve before the old one declines, organizations and individuals can renew and regenerate themselves and avoid stagnation and decline.

Conclusion

In this chapter we have seen that organizations, like individuals, go through significant life stages and transitions. Each transition can be an opportunity for renewal and regeneration, or a time of decline and dying as a separate entity. Systemic Team of Teams Coaching is particularly needed at these critical life junctures. We have provided several examples where it has made a significant difference.

FIGURE 5.2 The adaptative change cycle (building on Holling and Gunderson, 2002)

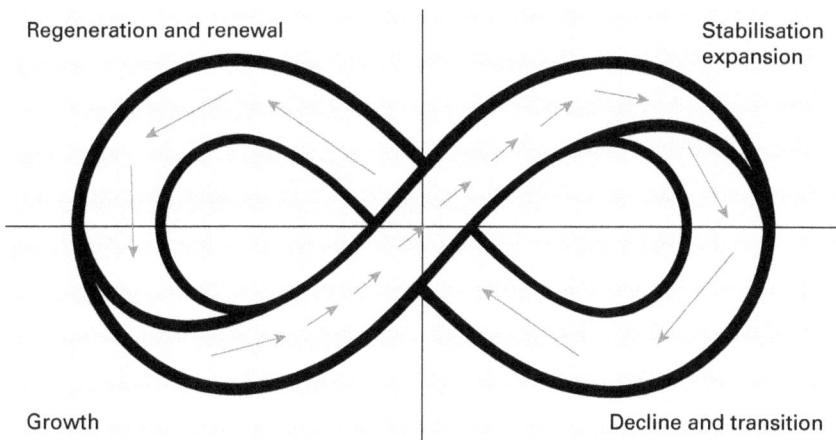

Regeneration and renewal

Stabilisation expansion

Growth

Decline and transition

Organizations are complex ecosystems, and we have built on the work of many scientists (see Holling and Gunderson, 2002) to evolve our original life-cycle model into a continual moebius double-loop adaptive change cycle (see Figure 5.2). The organization can move through this cycle many times, and so can different parts within the organization. Successful long-living organizations often have different regions and product divisions simultaneously in different phases of the model (de Geus, 1997).

In the next chapter we will focus on how Systemic Team of Teams Approaches (STOTA) can help organizations turn the challenges of a life-cycle transition into an opportunity for an integrated organizational transformation.

06

Organizational transformation and the Systemic Team of Teams Approach

Introduction

In Chapter 4 we showed how a STOTA can be adopted in two very different ways. The first that was explored and illustrated is an exploratory and emergent journey to gradually develop a stronger teaming culture and an organization that is more networked and connected, both vertically and horizontally. The second, which we address in this chapter, arises when an organization is either facing an important life transition which requires, or is an opportunity for, major organizational transformation, or when a major external disruption compels the organization to fundamentally rethink its business, strategy, structure, culture and how it partners with the external world.

In the previous chapter we introduced our model of the organizational life cycle and explored the various stages organizations can go through, each accompanied by different challenges. In this chapter we will outline some of the history, key principles and stages in organizational transformation. We will then lay out the Systemic Team of Teams Approach to organizational transformation, with illustrations both from our research and our practice.

We start from the belief that change is always happening and cannot be managed, for as the ancient Greek sage Democritus said: 'The cosmos is change, life is discourse' (Democritus fragment 115 quoted in Rovelli, 2022: 155). Henry Miller more recently and memorably put it, 'It is almost banal to say so yet it needs to be stressed continually: all is creation, all is change, all is flux, all is metamorphosis' (Miller, 1957). However, change is not uniform. Jean Bouton, a complexity scientist, writes: 'There are times of relative statis, and there are times of incremental drift, when not much happens. There are other times, when there is a shift into something radically, and irreversibly new' (Boulton, 2024: 81). Some scientists talk about change and evolution as being punctiform, sometimes slow and unfolding, but then punctuated by a sudden, often unexpected fast transformative change.

In organizations, as in all life forms, we can see periods of relative stability, with slow change, and other times rapid change encompassing every aspect of the system. Organizational transformations are larger, more fundamental change processes, that affect every part of an organization. These often occur at times of organizational transition (see Chapter 5). Just like being a human being where you are constantly changing, there are periods of life transitions, which are much more transformative.

Systemic Team Coaching and Systemic Team of Teams Coaching are not extensions of coaching into larger systems. They are distinctive approaches born out of the coming together of:

- the best of organizational development and transformation theory and practice
- the best of coaching principles, processes and practice
- key aspects of systemic theory including complex adaptive systems, two-way nested systems, and Batesonian approaches to the ecology of mind

What is organizational transformation?

With the gradual dissolving of the mechanistic and atomistic materialism of 18th-century science, through quantum theory, holism, systemic thinking and awareness, relational and process philosophy and inter-subjectivity, organizations began to be seen as dynamic, living organisms, rather than as structured mechanistic and economic apparatus for manufacturing products or delivering services.

Organizational transformation refers to a significant and fundamental change in the way a company or organization operates, which often involves shifts in its strategy, culture, structure and processes. The concept has evolved over time and been influenced by several theories and models, each offering unique insights into how organizations adapt and change.

The concept of organizational transformation is rooted in an epistemology that views organizations as dynamic living, and ever-changing, social organisms (de Geus, 1997). Its development parallels other systemic approaches that view families (Minuchin, 1974), communities (Capra, 1996), the whole earth's biosphere (Lovelock, 1979; Margulis, 1998), or indeed the whole universe (Whitehead, 1929) as living evolving systems, rather than the sum of their parts.

At the same time science is increasingly viewing living systems, from microbes to humans, as interdependent networks, rather than separate beings. Whether we study an individual human, who is composed of 10^{13} billion human cells, but 10 times as many bacterial cells of many different species or consider that, as Pross (2012: 187) states, 'each human is more a super-organism – a giant network, than an organism' or we study a whole species within its ecological niche, or an ecological niche within its changing lithosphere, hydrosphere and atmosphere, all life can be seen as networks, nested within larger networks.

Pross (2012: 144) wrote that 'evolution is a process that populations undergo not individuals'. He later goes on to outline a theory of nested network systems, very similar to my own (Peter's) where 'The functioning of the network at any level is dependent on the functioning of the network both below and above' (Pross, 2012: 188). Thus, we would contend that it is not individual populations that evolve, but networks, that are entangled with other networks, both horizontally (of the same level of complexity) and vertically (the networks nested within itself and in which it is nested). So ultimately it is the dynamic meshwork web of life that evolves, not individual organisms or the population of a species. 'Biology is the study, not of being, but of becoming' wrote Woese and Goldenfield (2009: 14–21).

Organizational transformation also views organizations as growing out of a necessary purpose that they fulfil. Thus, they can be described as teleonomic, being purpose-led. When the core purpose of an organization no longer exists, then the organization either has to repurpose itself, or it dies. When the purpose of large mainframe computers was no longer needed as computers became portable, Microsoft was born and IBM only survived by repurposing itself: 'We decided that we would build the company around a services strategy, not a products strategy… It was the idea that this company, at its roots, could be a solutions company' (Gerstner, 2002). Those that did not adapt fast enough, such as digital engineering, were swallowed up into other organizations that were more future-fit.

Some of the modern drivers of organizational transformation which are more and more crucial are:

- **Global metacrisis** (see Chapter 1).
- **Global challenges:** All being interconnected.

- **Ecological crisis:** All the crises are symptoms of human consciousness and without a radical transformation of human consciousness our very species and much of the ecology will not survive.
- **Technological disruption:** Innovations such as artificial intelligence, automation and big data require organizations to fundamentally rethink their strategies and operations.
- **Globalization:** Increasing interconnectedness and competition globally push organizations to become more agile and adaptable.
- **Sustainability and social responsibility:** Growing demand for organizations to adopt more environmentally sustainable and socially responsible practices.
- **Diversity, equity and inclusion:** Companies are increasingly recognizing the importance of creating inclusive cultures as part of transformation efforts.
- **Pandemics** and their social and ecological consequences.

The roots and history of organizational transformation

Organizational transformation has grown and developed out of the field of organizational behaviour and organizational development.

In the 1980s, the consulting firm McKinsey (2008) produced their **7-S Model,** for delineating the different facets of an organization all of which need to be addressed in a change or transformation process. These are:

- **Strategy:** The plan to achieve competitive advantage.
- **Structure:** The way the organization is arranged (e.g. hierarchies, teams). '
- **Systems:** The procedures and processes that support day-to-day operations.
- **Shared values:** The core values that guide behaviour.
- **Styles:** The leadership style and organizational culture.
- **Staff:** The people within the organization.
- **Skills:** The skills and competencies of the organization's employees.

The weakness of this model is it can lead to believing that you can focus on these facets independently. This has led to many organizations having multiple siloed change processes, with the strategy department changing the strategy, the IT department the systems and the HR department working on leadership style, culture and staff. This we have described as 'death by a thousand initiatives'. In our consulting work, we have always emphasized that the challenges lie in the connections between these different aspects, and helped a number of organizations and leadership teams integrate their many change initiatives into one overarching transformation process, with a number of closely integrated parts.

Other approaches focussed on the necessary steps in a successful change process, of which the most well used is Stephen Kotter's (1995) 'Eight-step model for change'. This proposes the following advice:

1 **Create a sense of urgency:** Convince employees and stakeholders that change is necessary.

2 **Form a guiding coalition:** Build a team of influential leaders to drive the change.

3 **Develop a vision and strategy:** Outline a clear vision and strategy for the future.

4 **Communicate the change vision:** Ensure everyone understands and buys into the change.

5 **Empower employees for broad-based action:** Remove obstacles and empower people to act on the vision.

6 **Generate short-term wins:** Create small victories to build momentum.

7 **Consolidate gains and produce more change:** Use early successes to further drive change.

8 **Anchor new approaches in the culture:** Make the change stick by embedding it into the organizational culture.

This was later somewhat simplified by the ADKAR Model (Hiatt, 2006; Hiatt and Creasey, 2012):

- **Awareness:** Ensuring people are aware of the need for change.
- **Desire:** Building the desire to participate in and support the change.
- **Knowledge:** Providing the information needed for employees to change.
- **Ability:** Developing the skills and behaviours necessary to implement the change.
- **Reinforcement:** Ensuring the change is sustained and embedded into the culture.

Other approaches to understanding change have emphasized the emotional stages humans need to go through, drawing on Kübler-Ross's model of understanding the grief process (Kübler-Ross and Kessler, 2005), or William Bridges' (1991) model of the change house, which highlights how human emotional reactions can derail change processes. Scharmer (2009) and Scharmer and Kaufer (2013) developed 'Theory U' which combines the emotional descent and re-emergence process inherent in Kübler-Ross with the need for collective inquiry and dialogue. This process begins with letting go of attachment to currents ways of thinking and existing answers, to arriving at the learning edge where past experiences and individual solutions are no longer fit for purpose. Through presencing – being fully present with 'open mind, open heart and open will' – and by attuning to the wider contexts of both the present and future, new possibilities can emerge.

Other developments that have focussed on the strategic management of change include Michael Porter's (1980, 1985) work on competitive strategy and the need to transform in response to industry dynamics, technological advancements, social and economic changes and market competition. Porter later moved to a more stakeholder centric approach with his seminal work (Porter and Kramer, 2011) on the need for organizations to create 'shared value' for all its stakeholders, not just its shareholders. Hamel and Prahalad (1994) focussed more on leveraging the organization's strengths and unique capabilities to respond to the emergent challenges and find the fastest route to meeting tomorrow's needs. I, Peter, built on these two different perspectives, in my core strategy question: 'What can you uniquely do, that the world of tomorrow needs?'

Other methodologies have emerged in the last 30 years that have helped organizational transformation move beyond seeing an organization as an entity and as a bounded system. As far back as the 1950s, the work of the Tavistock Institute and in particular Emery and Trist (1965, 1972) started to look at organizations as open systems. In this view, inputs such as raw materials, finance and labour, flow in, are processed and changed, and emerge as outputs of products and services delivered to customers and service users. Thus, they started looking at organizations not as structured hierarchies, but as horizontal value chains. The organization's success was linked to its ability to create added value to the inputs, before they became outputs.

Business process engineering (Hammer and Champy, 1993) built on this process by looking at every step in the process of the value chain, and how to remove unnecessary steps, address blockages in the flow and create greater efficiency.

Since then, this way of thinking has been applied to whole industries and market sectors, and organizations have sprung up and been very successful by disintermediating a whole business sector, by connecting customers more quickly and directly with a resource they need. Well-known examples include Airbnb, bypassing hotels by connecting visitors directly with rentable unutilized rooms, or Uber providing transport in a way that cuts out the intermediate taxi company.

Agile methodology (see Hawkins 2012: 155–58) builds on the Rapid Application Design (RAD) processes that were developed in the technology sector in the late 20th century for creating fast and iterative innovation of bespoke computer software systems. Agile has developed a number of linked methodologies such as: Scrum, prototyping and Kanban, that enable incremental change, self-organizing teams, collaboration with current and future customers, and fast responsiveness to changes in the wider context.

We worked with Data Sciences, a British IT services company in the early 1990s up to the time it was bought by IBM in 1996. They presented to us a great challenge, by telling us that it took them nearly 18 months to design and implement a bespoke new software system for an organizational customer, and by the time it was implemented, the problem it was there to solve was gone and there were new and different challenges. We asked how long it took other similar companies, and the reply was, about the same, 18 months. I then asked how long the technological design and prototyping took. They proudly told me that with icon libraries and suppliers around the world, they could achieve this in just three weeks. 'So, what takes the other 17 months?' I naively asked. 'The liveware issues', they replied. 'We know how to redesign the hardware and software, but not the liveware.' Puzzled, I asked what was the liveware. 'The people and the politics', came their reply. We worked with them and several of their key clients, ensuring the organizational transformation was happening in sync with the technology design. In several instances this approach reduced the change process down to three months from the previous 18.

Appreciative inquiry

The key feature of appreciative inquiry (AI) is its focus on what currently works well, using this as a starting point for improvement and change. We described this approach in Chapter 4. The assumption is that, there have been times when the organization has worked well which participants can identify and build on, to en vision how they want to work together well in the future.

For a more detailed account of appreciative inquiry in Systemic Team Coaching, read Hawkins (2021: 401–03).

More recently David Cooperrider and colleagues have developed concepts and methods for what they first termed 'Macro OD' (Cooperrider and Dutton, 1999). This approach focuses on large-scale change and transformation, not only within an entire organizations, but also between organizations and wider networks.

In spring 2022, *The OD Review* published a special edition titled 'One giant leap: How organization development and change can help organizations, industries, and world-changing megacommunities lead the net-positive earthshot'. It includes several articles focussed on the potential of organization development in fostering sustainable and positive global changes, including Cooperrider and Godwin's excellent article 'Our earthshot moment: Net positive OD for the creation of a world of full spectrum flourishing'. In this article they build on the pioneering work of Polman and Winston (2021) to explore how to create a 'net-positive organization', defined as 'an organization that improves well-being for everyone it impacts and at all scales: every product, every operation, every region and country, and for every stakeholder, including employees, suppliers, communities, customers and even future generations and the planet itself'.

Their rallying cry for the whole field of OD and organizational transformation is:

> OD's Earthshot moment means ending the climate crisis in a generation and creating a regenerative economy in the service of life – a future of full-spectrum flourishing. And because of the unthinkable high stakes of failure, this emerging world macro-project will call all of us in the field to dare in scholarship, to stand up, step up, and scale up in practice, and to reach far beyond our competence.

Another key recent development in organizational development has been Dialogical OD (Bushe and Marshak, 2015), which contrasts 'dialogic OD' with 'diagnostic OD' and focusses on the role of generative conversations and emergent change. Their work builds on appreciative inquiry (Bushe, 2013), process consultancy (Schein, 1988, 1999), social constructionism (Gergen, 2009), transformative dialogue (Bohm and Nichol, 1998; Gergen et al, 2001; Issacs, 1999) and other postmodern perspectives (Marshak and Bushe, 2009).

In conclusion, organizational transformation is a complex and multi-faceted process, influenced by a range of historical, economic, social and technological factors. Theories and models like Lewin's Change Model, Kotter's 8-Step Model, the McKinsey 7-S Framework, and Agile methodologies offer structured approaches for managing and guiding these changes. Successful transformation requires alignment across strategy, culture, systems and leadership, with an emphasis on adaptability, human engagement and continuous learning.

The Systemic Team of Teams Approach to organizational transformation

As we have explored earlier in this chapter and in Chapter 4 our approach starts from the following key principles and perspectives.

1 Seeing all life as existing through networks, rather than in separate entities.

2 All networks are open systems, constantly exchanging with their wider context.

3 Every network is constantly evolving and becoming, rather than changing from one fixed state to another.

4 All networks are made up of smaller networks nested within them.

5 All networks are nested within larger networks.

6 Every network that a system is nested within, is also nested and living in and through its parts.

7 All organizations are teleonomic- that is they exist through having a collective purpose. However, this collective purpose can evolve and change.

8 Networks are living evolving organisms, that are born, develop, transform through a number of life transitions, and eventually die (although their parts may just scatter into other forms and networks).

9 Networks are interconnected both vertically within nested systems and horizontally with other networks at the same systemic level.

10 Boundaries between networks are conceptually created, rather than having a material fixed reality.

11 The web of life is better described as an evolving meshwork of becoming, rather than a network of networks made up of beings and systems.

12 Adaptation is relational and co-creative.

13 In a fast-changing context, organizations need to not just focus on and develop what is already happening, but what is coming into being-in order to be future-fit.

The five disciplines of organizational transformation

Based on the above principles and informed by both the research and our own combined 70-plus years of working with organizational transformation, we have created a model of the key five disciplines of organizational transformation. This model builds on the model that I, Peter, created between 2000 and 2011, for the five disciplines of high-value creating teams which became the foundation for Systemic Team Coaching (Hawkins, 2011b, 2021, 2022b) and which is now used successfully right around the world.

Like the earlier Five Disciplines model, this approach starts by seeing organizational transformation as having an internal and external aspect (placed on the left and on the right respectively). It also highlights the need to focus on both *what* it does including its products or services, and *how* it engages (placed above the line and below the line respectively). This creates the four quadrants which, rather than representing four steps or four different areas they are a constantly turning wheel. At the heart of the wheel is

FIGURE 6.1 Five disciplines of systemic organizational transformation

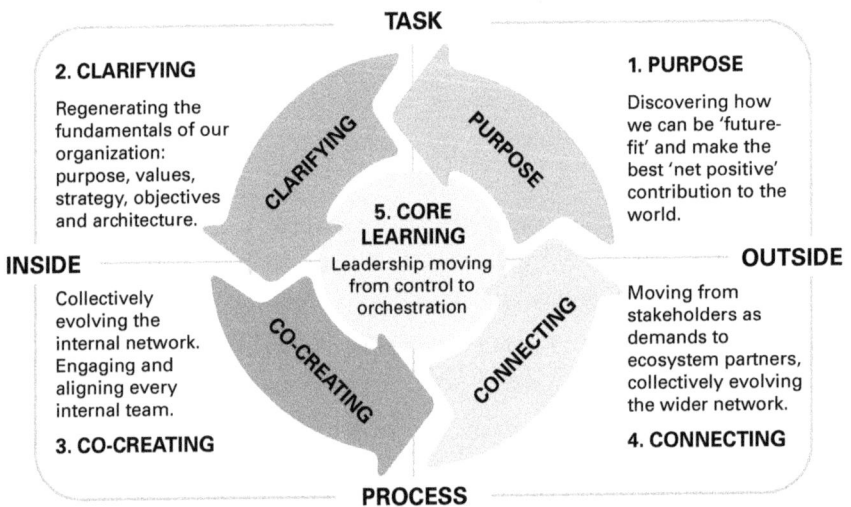

TASK

2. CLARIFYING

Regenerating the fundamentals of our organization: purpose, values, strategy, objectives and architecture.

CLARIFYING

PURPOSE

5. CORE LEARNING

1. PURPOSE

Discovering how we can be 'future-fit' and make the best 'net positive' contribution to the world.

INSIDE

Collectively evolving the internal network. Engaging and aligning every internal team.

Leadership moving from control to orchestration

CO-CREATING

CONNECTING

OUTSIDE

Moving from stakeholders as demands to ecosystem partners, collectively evolving the wider network.

3. CO-CREATING

4. CONNECTING

PROCESS

core learning as this is where the organization is not only continually learning and evolving in and between all four domains, but is also learning and
evolving how it best learns and evolves – a form of Level II or double-loop
learning (Argyris and Schön, 1974, 1978; Bateson, 1972; Hawkins, 1991,
1994, 2004).

We can now look at each of the five disciplines in turn but always remembering that they are all interconnected and much of the work lies in the
dance between two or more disciplines.

Purposing and repurposing

The primary discipline is in purposing and repurposing, for it is the purpose
that gives rise to the organization. When communities needed tools to hunt,
organization-making tools emerge when medieval travellers require a form
of exchangeable currency, mints and banks came into being.

An organization does not create its purpose, neither can it repurpose by
itself. Purpose is always co-created between an organism and its changing
context between an organization and the dynamics in its wider ecosystem. It
is thus an evolutionary process of two-way co-evolution, the organization
transforming in relation to the changing needs of its stakeholders and wider
context, and by so doing changing its context.

Failure to adapt in relation to the changes in the wider context, will
always lead to death of the organism/organization and to extinction.

For the purpose to be meaningful, it must be much more than a brand
slogan. It must include who the organization serves and creates value with
and for; what is the unique value it creates; how it does this; and the principles by which it operates. This is why we always come back to the core
question for every system and every organization – 'What can you uniquely
do that your world of tomorrow needs?'

For the purpose to be compelling, it must also become a vision - a
narrative story of what the organization would be doing, being and
becoming, if it was truly fulfilling its purpose.

Clarifying

*A vision without a task is but a dream. A task without a vision is but
drudgery. But a vision with a task can change the world.*

(BRAHMA KUMARIS, 2023)

The purpose has to be translated into not only a compelling vision, but also a plan. The collective needs to bring key players together from across the organization to work out how to turn this purpose into:

1 a strategic direction

2 with clear organizational choices and priorities

3 with measurable KPIs (Key Performance Indicators) or OKRs (Organizational Key Results)

4 ways of adapting its internal network to deliver the above, and a

5 new commission for internal teams and role descriptions for individuals

This is the organizational equivalent of the team charter (see Hawkins, 2021: 114–16).

Co-creating

But the organizational strategy and charter is just a blueprint design, and as Peter Drucker famously said, 'Culture will always eat your strategy for breakfast' (see Wartzman, 2011). Culture cannot be defined or planned for, as in yogurt, it is a living process, with a life of its own. The charter is equivalent to an orchestral score, but the culture is experienced in the style of the music that emerges live from this specific orchestra, at this particular time.

Culture can evolve and transform, albeit often at a much slower rate than organizational strategies and plans. Cultures live in the thousands of daily interconnections up and down, side-to-side, and transversally within an organization, and is also reflected in the thousands of interconnections that the organization has with its wide variety of external stakeholders, what we have elsewhere referred to as the 'lived-brand' (Hawkins, 2019; Hawkins and Smith, 2013).

Culture change cannot be mandated or imposed top down. Senior leadership can set the challenge by defining what is required by the changing context and the direction of travel, but the 'how' needs to be co-created. This co-creation cannot just be an intellectual discussion group, it must be a living embodied process, where the new culture is being experimented with through enactment.

Connecting

Whereas co-creation focusses on evolving the internal cultural network of the organization, the connecting discipline is doing the same process with the lived culture in the many interconnections that the organization has with its wider systemic context, within which the organization is inextricably nested.

Here again, evolving the external network or meshwork cannot be done through espoused brand statements or preaching how the organization will be different. The new culture of relational interconnection needs to be evolved through co-creation with all the key stakeholders as ecosystem partners.

Core learning and leading

Core learning and leading is at the heart of the wheel as this is where the organization is not only continually learning and evolving in and between all four domains, but is also learning and evolving how it best learns and evolves - a form of Level II or double-loop learning (Argyris and Schön, 1974, 1978; Bateson, 1972; Hawkins, 1991, 1994, 2004).

In today's fast-changing world, which is becoming ever more interconnected, every organization we have encountered are having to do more, at higher quality with less resource (Hawkins, 2021). This leaves two main choices, one is to drive harder and faster through effort, the other is to learn and adapt more effectively, collaboratively and with greater agility (Hawkins, 2019).

Collective organizational leadership also has to be continually learning and transforming. This involves a constant unlearning, letting go of what was successful in the world of yesterday, and discovering the difference that is needed for the world of tomorrow. You cannot have a future-fit organization without collective future-fit leadership. This leadership transformation includes moving from the old competencies of deciding, directing, controlling, implementing; to new roles and capacities such as: sensing, presencing, orchestrating, co-creating and partnering, internally and externally. There are different questions in each of the five disciplines that can be used by either organizational leaders or by organizational transformation consultants and in Figure 6.2 we have included just a few examples for each of the disciplines.

FIGURE 6.2 Five disciplines of systemic organizational transformation – key questions

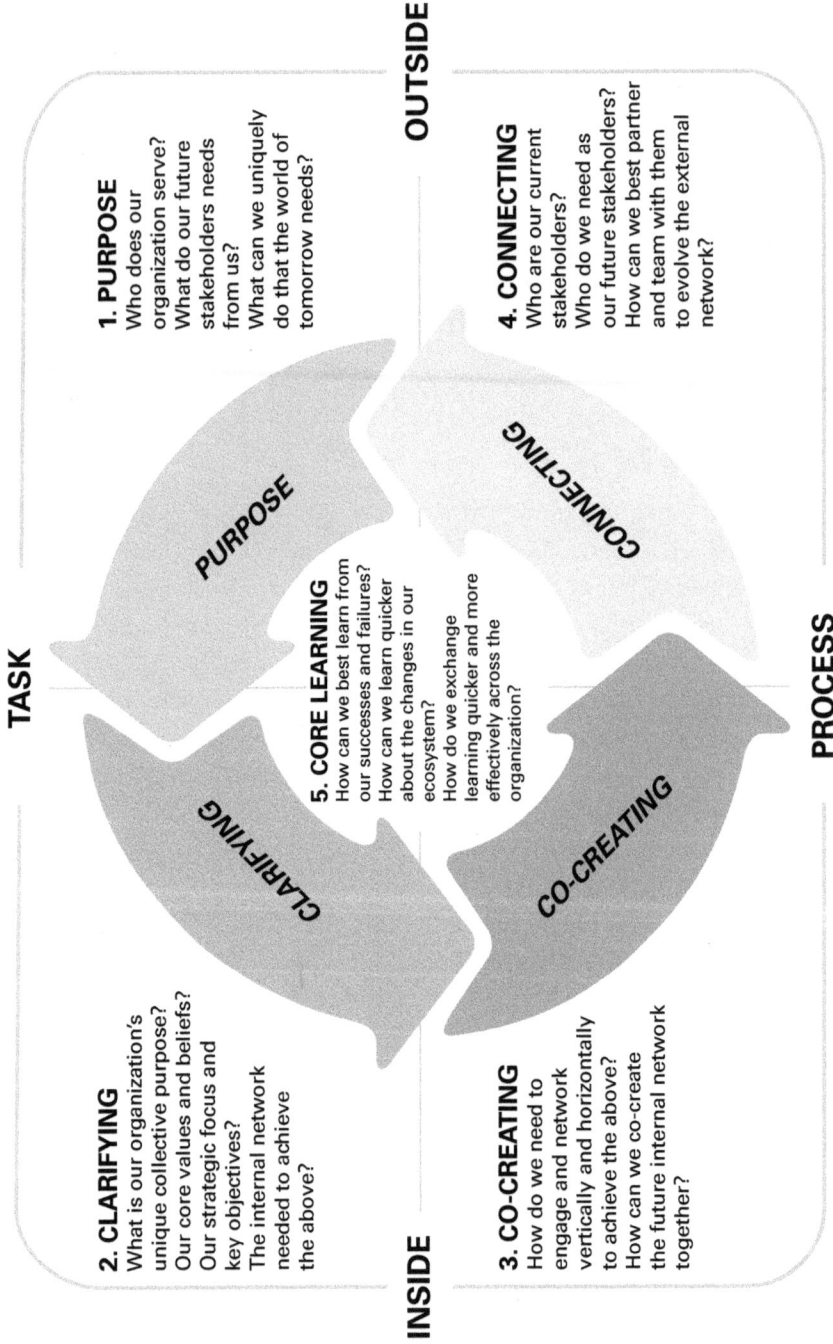

1. PURPOSE
Who does our organization serve?
What do our future stakeholders needs from us?
What can we uniquely do that the world of tomorrow needs?

4. CONNECTING
Who are our current stakeholders?
Who do we need as our future stakeholders?
How can we best partner and team with them to evolve the external network?

2. CLARIFYING
What is our organization's unique collective purpose?
Our core values and beliefs?
Our strategic focus and key objectives?
The internal network needed to achieve the above?

3. CO-CREATING
How do we need to engage and network vertically and horizontally to achieve the above?
How can we co-create the future internal network together?

5. CORE LEARNING
How can we best learn from our successes and failures?
How can we learn quicker about the changes in our ecosystem?
How do we exchange learning quicker and more effectively across the organization?

PURPOSE

CONNECTING

CLARIFYING

CO-CREATING

TASK

PROCESS

OUTSIDE

INSIDE

The five disciplines function like a living ecosystem, continuously evolving and interdependent, with learning and leadership at the core, sustaining the whole system.

The key stages in organizational transformation

From our practice and our research with organizations on how they have used both systemic teams coaching and an organizational Systemic Team of Teams Approach, we have assembled a model of the current stages that successful organizational transformations seem to progress through. No organization we have encountered or worked with is currently using all aspects of this model, and every organization has a somewhat different context and challenges. However, we believe all these stages are important elements for transformation.

1 **Awakening** to and amplifying the signals from the wider context that a transition is needed

2 **Presencing**

3 **Re-purposing** as discussed above

4 **Re-clarifying** as discussed above

5 **Working with the teams and the interconnections between teams,** both vertically and horizontally simultaneously. This requires joined-up systemic coaching of the individual teams and network events that bring teams together, or team leaders together, to co-create how the interconnections need to evolve

6 **Co-creating and prototyping the future organization.** This needs to include how we evolve the internal network

7 **Transforming leadership to focus on orchestration**

8 **Aligning the flows** of information, communication, people, rewards to support the new network system

9 **Structure. Process and Technology aligned** to support the newly evolved network system

10 **Moving from stakeholders as demands to ecosystem partnering,** where working jointly with partners we evolve the external network of the wider ecosystem

11 **Evaluation and evolution.** As in Chapter 4 this needs to be a continuous process

The following is an example of a team of teams approach to organizational transformation.

Hitachi Energy, HVDC: Successful growth through teaming and sustainability

Hitachi Energy, HVDC is a world leader in High Voltage Direct Current (HVDC), a technology that enables the transmission of large amounts of electricity over long distances. With a strong focus on integrating renewable energy into power systems, the company is a key player in the transition to sustainable energy. The company has experienced strong growth. In Sweden, the number of employees has quadrupled in recent years, and the company continues to expand its facilities to meet market demand. Hitachi Energy in Sweden is currently hiring 1,000 new employees per year. This rapid expansion has been necessary to meet the increasing demand for renewable energy for large industrial projects.

Here is the background as described by the consultant Jenny Sima:

In the year 2023, Hitachi Energy, HVDC was faced with the challenge of managing this rapid growth at the same time as winning one of the largest industrial deals in the world, valued at approximately $13 billion. The dilemma they faced was how to ensure the sustainability of employees and managers, while increasing efficiency to ensure the ability to deliver without compromising quality. They quickly realized that simply increasing the number of employees would not be a viable solution. Instead, they needed to double their efficiency and productivity without doubling their workforce. In order to achieve this, the company recognized that it was critical to strengthen the sustainability and resilience of its managers and their ability to lead in a rapidly changing environment and to create collaborative synergy in and between teams. Initially, the company considered offering individual coaching to all managers but realized that a more sustainable approach would be to strengthen the collaboration and partnership skills of its teams, building a teaming culture with dynamic teams.

Coaching the team of teams

This is a recent case of using STOTA, with a Swedish renewable energy company provided by the consulting company Gällöfsta Perlan Ledarskap (GPL), with an account of the process as seen by Dr Magnus Callavik, SVP and Global Head of HVDC Engineering at Hitachi Energy, HVDC.

In a dialogue between Hitachi Energy, HVDC and GPL, it was decided to offer Systemic Team Coaching within a Systemic Team of Teams Approach (STOTA) to all management teams in order to strengthen the teams' cooperation and partnership skills. The aim was to support the transformation by building a teaming culture. The first department to start was engineering with its 12 management teams. The Systemic Team Coaching was broken down into a process that took place over a period of 18 months, with each team coming together for four off-site team sessions. The initiative started with the management team, and gradually the subgroups were included in the process. This allowed each manager to attend as a member of their management team and subsequently lead a parallel process with his or her own team. Through this iterative process, the initiative became more widespread and has contributed to a successful transformation across the department. I think this exercise came at the right time for us; just as we were accelerating. We [Hitachi] really hit the ground running.

We secured the major contract and gained the trust from upper management to expand, hire and do everything in our power to capture this market. This led us to truly reflect on how to build our own team. It was crucial to develop an understanding between the different teams, that we're all connected.

We were very fortunate with the timing. First of all, we had the transformation journey. We were a fairly new team. We had just reorganized the whole company and my team felt that there was a need to better understand where we were going. Further, we were open to a team coaching process at my engineering department. That way, we could also pave the way for the rest of HVDC by showing that it actually works. It was important to dare to expose ourselves a little, otherwise we wouldn't succeed.

The goal was to strengthen the managers' abilities to support each other and create synergies through collaboration and partnership, which in turn improved both individual and organizational sustainability.

We did a lot of thinking about the purpose of our management team meetings and the purpose of the project team meetings. Why do we exist as a team?

In our management groups, we've restructured the meetings as part of the team coaching. What is the purpose of this meeting? How often do we need to hold it? What should happen and how long should it be? The team has become quite independent in solving issues. If there is an open question, someone will pick it up and come forward with a proposal. As a result, many things fall naturally into place.

In other groups where we haven't had the opportunity to work with Systemic Team Coaching, we find it more challenging to achieve this level of spontaneity in meetings.

Stakeholders, teaming and partnering

Another focus has been on the identification and interaction with stakeholders, both internal and external, in order to build stronger relationships and ensure long-term partnerships.

We thought about who our stakeholders are, those we depend on and those dependent on us. The simple fact that we asked them for feedback meant they were taken by surprise, for they wondered how we had the time to think about that. They were really pleasantly surprised, of course, but in this rat race nobody has the time for that. You only relate upwards in the organization and to those who you are directly dependent on, but you do not look around more broadly.

By enhancing their teaming and partnership skills, they improved their collaboration both internally and externally. Teams learnt to work more flexibly and solve problems together instead of getting stuck in hierarchical structures, which led to improved efficiency.

We have broken down the hierarchical structures and created better networks between teams. This allows us to address and solve problems directly at the level where they arise.

Long-term partnering

Hitachi Energy, HVDC have changed the way they collaborate with customers. Rather than treating each project as an isolated event, we now actively work to build long-term partnerships with our customers, thereby reducing friction and increasing productivity and improving quality in delivery.

In the past, it was common for us to have a bidding process where everyone worked intensively for years and then we competed for a single project. Now we work in a much more partnership-oriented way. When we do several projects together with the same customer, it makes it easier to prevent and resolve conflicts earlier and avoid getting stuck in unnecessary problems. There's no point arguing when you know you'll be working together on the next project. It calms the situation and makes the cooperation more constructive. It's important to find solutions instead of passing blame.

You create long-term relationships with different people and groups. As an individual, you build friendships rather than just being business partners.

While professionalism still is key, it transforms into a different, long-lasting relationship.

The fact that HVDC has so many parallel teams, all of which are built much in the same way, also enables a learning process in how they work in their projects. There is a lot of knowledge within the organization for a new employee to absorb. In addition, the projects are large and last for several years and it is important to continuously include new employees and keep the effort alive. We have to remind ourselves that we are constantly onboarding new people. They must be included on this journey, otherwise the results will be diluted.

Reflections on the process

We had to become much more efficient. Hiring more people isn't a viable solution. If our workload doubles, we can't simply double our team's size. This realization was incredibly important, and so we had to enhance our efficiency as a management team. We had to start with ourselves. And I would say, today we have become more informal within our team.

When we started this journey my team showed some concern with the strategy, whether we could truly manage this. Now, two years later, I would say the vast majority of my team has fully embraced this change and feel confident about the journey ahead.

They feel they get the support they need from the group as well as a speaking partner they can talk to. And then parallel to this they also got help from the team development process in their own teams to make them more effective. On this journey, many new people, and a large number of new projects and tasks are coming in all the time. But the number of ongoing challenges and projects are actually pretty constant. And we have managed to keep the output and the results.

Also, I believe it was strategic to include the sub-management teams in the team coaching initiative. This was done simultaneously, and my managers could step in to it with confidence since they had already experienced it with me in the management team. I didn't have that benefit, but the others got that help.

Our project teams were also important in this since we have a project-oriented organization. Parallel to this we needed to strengthen the line in order to be more productive. The team coaching effort really contributed to that.

Lessons learnt

When we started this, we made a plan that extended over 18 months, which initially felt a bit excessive. It's a rush but you get results all the time, so it's important to allow this journey the necessary time from start to finish. Additionally, in larger structures, it's vital to work top down. This approach gives lower-level managers much more confidence to engage in the process. Nobody felt challenged in their leadership role. They received support from their coaches, of course, but it can still be challenging. Overall, it has been very successful with all the teams.

One of the lessons we learnt was that we had a very strong driving force. One motivator was that we were a new team. The other was that we were on a significant growth journey. In contrast, if you're a part of a team in a state administration facing zero growth year after year you need to find the incentive for change. We got that from the outside and realized we had to act now. You're either on the journey or you're not.

There are three key findings. First, it's been so well received that we're now repeating it in all other groups, and we can be an inspiration to them. Second, while my managers remain under pressure, their stress levels have significantly decreased compared to two years ago. They have increased confidence and resilience in their management teams, and they have grown in their roles with the support of this. It is fantastic that we have been on this journey.

Third, is that we have been successful in achieving an all-time high performance last year.

When you're expanding as much as we are it is crucial to maintain the quality of your delivery and not to lose your margins. A couple of years ago we occasionally made huge mistakes which was incredibly costly due to people not talking to each other and not being transparent.

I really don't know what would have happened if we hadn't done this. We had these trends around teaming and partnership in the organization. But without the Systemic Team Coaching initiative it would have been extremely challenging for us to succeed.

In conclusion, Hitachi Energy, HVDC's commitment to building a teaming culture by providing its management teams Systemic Team Coaching has been a key factor in managing the rapid growth while maintaining high levels of quality in the deliveries. By strengthening collaboration and transparency between managers and teams, and building long-term partnerships both internally and externally, the company has been able to increase its efficiency and resilience. The process has also helped create a more sustainable organization where all employees have a clearer understanding of their purpose and role in the bigger system.

REFLECTIONS ON THE CASE

In reflecting on this case, we can see all five disciplines being addressed.

Purpose: The organization was alert to the growing need for large renewable energy supply to industrial projects and the need to repurpose itself to respond to this challenge. This brought the challenge of how to scale up quickly, but in ways that provided alignment and synergy across the organization.

Clarifying: Several strategic objectives emerged:

- Focus on customers who could become long-term partners, where they did multiple projects.
- Grow the size of the business faster than you grow the headcount of employees.
- Achieve alignment and efficiencies through effective teaming in both management teams and project teams.
- Increase collaboration and learning across teams.

Co-creating: The senior team were involved in co-creating the strategic direction, and having first participated in Systemic Team Coaching in the senior team, they then became active leaders in developing each of their own teams.

Connecting: At the same time as reshaping the internal network they developed new ways of teaming with their customers, so they became long-term partners, solving emerging challenges and conflicts together.

Core learning and leadership: As part of the teaming culture, they fostered fast learning across all the project teams and the leadership were learning how to become team orchestrators and team coaches (see Hawkins, 2021: Chapter 13) while also increasing their partnering skills and collaborative capacity.

Conclusion

Change is continuous, and many scientists and philosophers would now argue that life is always 'becoming', and that life can be seen as flowing through events and processes as opposed to being built out of things (Hawkins, 2025; Prigogine, 1980, 1984; Rovelli, 2022; Whitehead, 1929). However, continuous change is punctuated by large and more fundamental processes of transformation. This is true for all living organisms and collective living systems such as organizations. These often happen as a result of a life transition, or a major change in the wider context.

Organizational transformation is also a professional discipline that has developed from previous forms of organizational development to deal with the greater internal and external complexity that organizations now face.

Our research and practice have shown that a Systemic Team of Teams Approach (STOTA) can be an important process in enabling a successful whole organizational transformation. Through out our work we have developed a model of the key five disciplines that are essential aspects of organizational transformation as well as some of the key stages organizational transformation needs to undertake.

We ended with a case illustrating a recent use of STOTA in helping a large renewable energy company undertake an organizational transformation.

In the next chapter we will explore how to embed learning and evolution into every change and transformation journey and how to evaluate the beneficial impact that the work is creating.

07

Evaluation and evolution

Introduction

In this chapter we explore what a Systemic Team of Teams Coaching (STOTA) requires for evaluating success, not just at the end of the development programme, but continually through the process. By integrating continuous evaluation and outcome measurement, we can more effectively determine what needs to be adjusted as the journey progresses. This ongoing assessment is crucial not only for refining the current programme but also for ensuring that the organization and Systemic Team of Teams Coaching (STOTC) can capture valuable insights from each iteration. These insights, in turn, can be used to improve future processes, increasing their effectiveness and the value they create.

For many years we have been training, supporting and challenging team coaches to incorporate measures that demonstrate the effectiveness of their coaching and strengthen their team coaching approach (Carr and Peters, 2012; Hawkins, 2012, 2021, 2022a, 2022b; Peters and Carr, 2013a, 2013b). Specifically, we encourage team coaches to capture the value their work brings not only to the team but also to the wider organization and the stakeholders and ecosystem partners they serve. This chapter continues that call to action, urging team coaches to go beyond traditional metrics that often evaluate only inputs and outputs, to include and measure the outcome impacts and value creation of their work.

It was great!

Have you ever faced this situation? Your team coaching work is gaining traction, and then the enthusiastic team leader who initially brought you on board leaves or shifts roles? Suddenly, you find yourself in an advocacy vacuum with no one left to champion the ongoing team coaching. You and the team are left wondering whether you continue this coaching journey.

This change can create a ripple of uncertainty, disrupting the continuity, momentum, and even the perceived value of the coaching process. It raises a critical question for the organization concerning whether to continue investing in external coaching without the person who sponsored it.

For you as the leader or team coach, this scenario highlights a number of challenges:

- What could you have done earlier to prevent this dependency on a single advocate?
- Did you paint a clear picture of why coaching is not just a nice-to-have, but essential for making the organization to be future-fit, aligned with key strategic drivers, and focussed on achieving critical business outcomes?
- Could you have built broader sponsorship across the leadership team, created more shared ownership of the coaching outcomes, and developed internal coaching champions?
- Had you jointly agreed upon and established clear measures to demonstrate the value of team coaching? Did you do this early on to document the changes created in the period of the team coaching?
- Did you use data as you went along to get a pulse check, to course correct, and to strengthen what was working?

Imagine you had helped the team develop a clear understanding of what being future-fit meant for them, supported them in aligning around their values and purpose, and co-created a vision of success. From there, you used existing measures and co-created additional tools to track progress. You considered establishing or linking to key team performance indicators (KPIs), implementing regular short feedback loops, and conducting pre- and post-assessments, with both the team and the wider organization.

Now, as the leader steps away, the team coaching impact speaks for itself through clear, quantifiable data. People recognize its value and see improvements in team cohesion, leadership effectiveness and critical business outcomes. In this scenario, the tangible proof of the coaching's success was shared with the new leader and broader organization. As a result, they requested a proposal to expand the team coaching programme, so that other teams could experience similar progress, and the wider team of teams could learn from each other more effectively.

This proactive, measurement-based approach ensures that the value of team coaching is not tied to one individual but is embedded within the organization. Even in the face of leadership transitions, the team coaching initiative can continue to thrive because its impact is clear, and its benefits are woven into the fabric of what matters in the organization.

Understanding evaluation and evolution

In Chapter 4 we provided a best-of-the-best model of the STOT journey, which had evaluation and evolution as a continuous ring flowing around every stage. Evaluation should not be limited to a retrospective process after team or team of teams coaching is completed. It must occur continuously throughout, supporting the ongoing evolution of the development journey as it unfolds.

Evaluation needs to be a key part of the start of every development process from organizational transformation to leadership development, to team development, right down to each team member's individual development plan. Crucially, starting with the end in mind enables evaluation to go beyond simply monitoring satisfaction or other short-term outputs. Instead, evaluation should aim to answer: What is the impact that the development of the individual, team, organization or partnership, is there to create? We need to assess how the development will contribute to the organization's purpose and the increased net-positive value that the individual, team, team of teams and organization will co-create with and for all their stakeholders and ecosystem partners.

Our five-stage model of evaluation

I, Peter, have previously developed a model of the four types of evaluation for evaluating individual coaching (Hawkins and Turner, 2020: 182–99); for team coaching (Hawkins, 2022b: Chapter 14) and for developing a coaching culture (Hawkins, 2012: Chapter 13). This has been informed by important work by others including Kirkpatrick's (1977) and Kirkpatrick and Kirkpatrick's (1994) model of evaluating training and development, and Philips and Philips' (2007, 2016) and Philips, Philips and Edward's (2012) work on assessment.

Building on this earlier work we can now propose a model that distinguishes between five levels of evaluation, each level inclusive of and dependent on the previous levels:

1 **Inputs** (resources, information, and actions): The quality of the team coaching interventions, relationships built between the coaches and team, and the quality of the team coaching models, processes, resources and tools that are used.

2 **Outputs:** The new insights gained, learning achieved, decisions made, and new plans, policies, workflows or initiatives launched.

3 **Outcomes:** how these changes translated into sustainable shifts in behaviours, team processes, team performance and the quality of stakeholder engagements.

4 **Value creation:** The measurable value created for all stakeholders, including team members, the team as a whole, their wider organization, customers/clients, supplier and partner organizations, employees, investors or funders, communities where they operate and the wider ecology.

5 **Return on Investment (ROI) and Return on Effort (ROE):** These can only be evaluated once we have assessed the value creation at level 4. At that point we can calculate the ratio of the value created to the cost of the development, which includes not only financial, but also the effort and time invested.

Each level of evaluation in this model builds on the previous one. Effective design begins 'future-back' and 'outside-in', focussing on the **value creation** by the organization, teams and individuals, for stakeholders and ecosystem partners. This clarity guides the desired **outcomes** – such as changed processes, relationships and partnerships – and determines the measurable **outputs** required at each stage.

We have built upon a model in Hawkins and Turner (2019: Figure 12.5) that looked at methods for each of these evaluation stages for individual systemic coaching and created a model for evaluating Systemic Team Coaching in Table 7.1.

We believe it is essential to have both qualitative and quantitative assessment methods at all five stages and then develop mechanisms for assessing the connections between them. Building further on this we can now show a model for Systemic Team of Teams Coaching in Table 7.2.

TABLE 7.1 Ways of evaluating along the value chain

	Inputs	Outputs	Outcomes	Value Creation
WHAT	Dialogue with the coaches	Team Purpose Team Charter More effective meetings	Measuring the difference created by the team as a result of the team coaching	Measuring the value created as a result of the outcomes
HOW (Internal)	'What have you most appreciated and valued and what could have made the team coaching more effective?'	Reflection on what the team has achieved 'Reflecting on what you have co-created through this team coaching – what are you proud of and what would you do different next time?'	Re-running the Team Connect 360 Re-run Descriptor Analysis. Individual 360 feedback or upward appraisal	Staff retention and ease of attraction Customer retention and attraction and share of spend
HOW (External)		Our observations of differences in the team	The above plus: Changes in Employee or pulse surveys Changes in Customer/client net-promoter scores	Profitability Sustainability targets
How (External to organizations)			Most Admired Company Survey Best Company to work for Other awards	Investor ratings/analysts reports Share Price changes

TABLE 7.2 Ways of evaluating STOTA along the value chain

	Inputs	Outputs	Outcomes	Value Creation
WHAT	Dialogue with the team of coaches	Team Purpose Team Charter More effective meetings	Measuring the difference created by the team of teams as a result of the team of coaching	Measuring the value created as a result of the outcomes
HOW (Internal)	'What have you most appreciated and valued and what could have made the team of teams coaching more effective?'	Reflection on what the team has achieved 'Reflecting on what you have co-created through this team coaching – what are you proud of and what would you do different next time?'	Re-running the Team Connect 360s for all teams Re-run Organization Descriptor Analysis	Customer retention and attraction and share of spend Staff retention and ease of attraction
HOW (External)	Reviewing the process against the 'best of the best practice	Our observations of differences in the team	The above plus: Changes in Employee or pulse surveys Changes in Customer/client net-promoter scores	Profitability ESG targets
How (External to organizations)			Most Admired Company Survey Best Company to work for Other awards	Investor ratings/analysts reports Share Price changes International benchmarking Contribution to Sustainable Development Goals (UN)

Inputs

Most organizations we have worked with or included in the research have instituted formal processes for collecting standardized feedback from both coach and coachee, as well as from team coaches and teams on all coaching processes. These processes gather feedback on what aspects were most helpful or unhelpful. This feedback supports learning in how team coaches are allocated to teams, the different needs of each team and in the collective learning for all those involved in developing the organization and particularly its teaming culture.

Outputs

Some of the feedback processes have also included a section on **outputs**, asking both team members and team coaches to comment on new learning they acquired, and how it has been applied at work. 'It is important to distinguish between insight learning about what needs to be different, and applied embodied learning, that has created new behaviours and ways of engaging back at work' (Hawkins and Turner, 2019: 192).

Sophisticated evaluation processes would then include a question on what it was in the team coaching process that facilitated these significant actions, a link back to inputs.

One of the most important outputs that needs to be tracked is how the individual learning in coaching impacts on team and organizational learning. It is rare that coaches focus on the spread and amplification of the individual learning to others in the organization and ask: 'How could you help others benefit from what you have learnt and developed here?' This kind of knowledge transfer is typically poorly measured and understood, yet is critical to organizational learning.

This approach has been used with a number of organizations and is called 'Harvesting the Learning' (Hawkins, 2012: 99–101). It has five stages:

1 Regularly convening the community of internal and external team coaches to hear the challenges the organization is facing. This provides a forum for asking questions about the organization's strategy, as well as its plans for the development of its business, organizational growth, culture, leadership and people.

2 Working with all the team coaches in supervision trios (coach, supervisor and observer) to discuss key team coaching relationships with managed

confidentiality. The observer is given a pro-forma to capture some of the emerging themes in such areas as:

    a. Clarity and alignment concerning the direction of the organization and what this direction requires from leaders and managers.

    b. The organizational culture, including the five levels: artefacts, patterns of behaviour, mind sets, emotions and motivational roots (see Hawkins and Smith, 2013).

    c. Connections and disconnections across the organization.

    d. Connections and disconnections with stakeholders.

    e. How team coaching is perceived and suggestions for improvements.

The trio has 20 minutes in each role, with additional time allocated for feedback to the supervisor on their supervision – thus providing additional developmental learning.

3 The trios are then asked to look for patterns emerging across the themes collected from the three supervision sessions. We sometimes provide a short explanation and handout on systemic pattern identification.

4 These patterns arising from all the trios are written on Post-it notes and placed on different themed flip-chart boards. The whole group is then divided into small groups by each themed board. They work on clustering the emerging themes, identifying the patterns that connect them, and then presenting these back into the whole group. They are asked to identify the key patterns that either enable or block the organization in meeting its strategic and developmental objectives.

5 These enabling and blocking patterns are then brought together and a dialogue is facilitated between senior executives and the team coaches on these emerging key themes. This can take place either at the same event or at a later meeting between the senior leadership team and a representative group of internal and external team coaches. Having explored the emerging themes, the dialogue can then shift to how team coaching can contribute more effectively to the next stages of the organization's development.

This process requires facilitation from a consultant who is not only an experienced team coach and skilled Systemic Team Coaching supervisor, but also one who understands organizational strategy, culture change, systemic dynamics and organizational development and transformation. Most importantly, this facilitator needs to translate between the language of senior leadership and the language of systemic team coaches.

This full process for harvesting the learning may sound rather daunting for many organizations, but simpler forms of the process can be adopted as part of the annual review of team coaching and other development activities in the organization. In Hawkins (2012: 101–03) there is a case study of such a process with the Electricity Supply Board (ESB), Ireland's premier electricity utility company.

Outcomes

Few evaluation processes assess the outcome of these new behaviours and ways of engaging. Some organizations include 360° feedback using either the High Value-creating Team Questionnaire or the TeamConnect 360 (see Chapter 4) to evaluate the team before and after the team coaching. These tools assess how the team's stakeholders are experiencing the changes resulting from the team coaching. It's important not only to conduct feedback immediately after the team coaching but also to follow up six months or more later. Many benefits of team coaching take time to fully manifest, as new processes and behaviours often take time to embed and produce noticeable changes in external relationships and performance.

One can also use the Team Contribution Grid (Hawkins, 2021: 376–77). In this process, the team leader and every team member self assesses and then receives feedback from the other team members on their current value contribution both to and from the team and along with suggestions on how this could be developed. After the team coaching is completed, they receive feedback on how their contributions have changed, and suggestions for further development.

Value creation

Much has been written about the elements for inputs, outputs and outcomes and ways of effectively assessing them (see for instance Philips and Philips, 2007, 2016; Philips, Philips and Edwards, 2012). Much less has been written about the measurements of value creation.

Organizations spent over $60 billion on leadership development in 2023, yet many still struggle to assess whether these programmes delivered the desired shifts and outcomes (Yemiscigil, Born and Ling, 2023). Without robust qualitative and quantitative data, it's often unclear if this significant investment is driving meaningful change. Too often, organizations remain uncertain about the true impact of development programmes on leadership behaviours, team performance or culture. They need leaders and leadership to think, feel different and act differently, not just for a few days after a leadership development programme or team workshop.

Value creation is defined in Hawkins (2021) as: 'co-creating beneficial value with and for all your stakeholders'. Internal stakeholders include:

a. the more senior teams, or board, the team reports to

b. the teams and individuals that report into the team

c. the teams and individuals the team provides services and products for

d. the team and individuals the team relies on to do its work or impacts through its work

At a minimum, stakeholders external to the organization include the six key stakeholder groups:

a. customers or clients

b. suppliers and partner organizations

c. employees and contractors

d. investors, funders, taxpayers

e. communities in which the organization operates

f. the 'more than human' world of the wider ecology

We would argue that unless an organization is co-creating beneficial value for all these six groups, it will not be sustainable in the long term. We strongly believe that all organizations need to be moving towards becoming 'Net positive organizations' (Polman and Winston, 2021). These are defined by Cooperrider and Godwin (2022: 40) as: 'An organization that improves the well-being for every stakeholder it touches, including employees, suppliers, communities, customers, and even future generations and the planet itself.'

To evaluate value creation, we propose seven methods, each of which builds on the others, as well as focussing on different stakeholder groupings.

1. HIGHER ENGAGEMENT WITH AND FROM STAKEHOLDERS

Whether you are a commercial company, public sector service organization or a not for profit (better termed 'for benefit') organization, the first step in creating value is to achieve greater engagement with your stakeholders, both inside and outside the organization. Typically, the first group from where increased engagement is needed is the employees.

2. HIGHER APPRECIATION FROM STAKEHOLDERS: DESCRIPTOR ANALYSIS

One of the key lead indicators in organizational performance is how the organization is perceived by all its stakeholders. Many businesses invest significant time and money in collecting feedback from employees, customers, investors and other stakeholders and in analysing their press and media coverage. However, very few systematically integrate all their data to create a holistic organizational 360° feedback dashboard.

Multiple stakeholder perceptions, when combined, provide a valuable lead indicator of change in organizational performance and value creation. One method I, Peter, have developed to assist in this process is the 'Descriptor analysis' (Hawkins, 2021: 355–57). This can be carried out informally by asking stakeholders what words they would currently use to describe the team or organization today and what words they would like to be able to use in one year's time. The team coach can repeat this exercise by gathering follow-up feedback to track ongoing perception shifts over time. For an example of using this see the 3i example in Chapter 5. Descriptor analysis can be integrated into the stakeholder feedback questionnaire before and after team or team of teams coaching to assess whether the individual or team is differently contributing to the overall culture change and shifting towards more positive stakeholder perceptions.

3. RETENTION OF BEST EMPLOYEES, PROMOTION AND IMPACT

Measuring employee retention can be a broad and sometimes misleading metric, as an organization could be retaining its worst-performing employees and still be losing its best talent. However, it can nevertheless be a useful measure of an organizational benefit, as the cost of recruiting, inducting and training new staff can be very costly.

Some organizations have attempted to measure the retention of their best staff by using a 3 x 3 scoring grid, commonly known as the 9-box grid, which rates all staff on a 1–3 scale for both performance and potential for developing to more senior roles. This provides a foundation for measuring whether the team or organization is successfully retaining team members who fall into Box 9 (3 for performance and 3 for potential), and other high scorers. Additionally, it evaluates their ability to improve these ratings across their team members and accelerate the readiness for, and achievement of promotions. This approach highlights the critical role every manager and leader plays in employee development and retention.

4. INCREASE IN CUSTOMERS AS ADVOCATES

There has been a general shift from measuring customer satisfaction, to measuring customer retention, measuring customer's advocacy using 'net-promoter scores', and now measuring customer experience and engagement (Clerk, Harrison and Fenton, 2016). This shift has been driven by sectors that recognize that high short-term customer satisfaction scores can be misleading. For example, in the car dealership sector they discovered that high customer satisfaction at the point of purchase was not strongly correlated with the customer buying their next car from the same dealership.

Instead, the key influence on customer retention was their experience of how they were related to and engaged with, by both the seller and the manufacturer, not just at the time of purchase but afterwards. Increasingly, companies are relying on their customers as their 'unpaid sales force', advocating their products and services to family and friends and promoting their products through social media, on sites such as TripAdvisor and Trustpilot. Thus, a key measure of value creation is the increase in the percentage of customers posting positive recommendations and the decrease in those posting negative comments.

We have worked with several hospitals using a team of teams approach, helping them introduce processes to monitor and evaluate compliments and complaints from patient and family member feedback. This provides another valuable customer feedback mechanism that can be linked to evaluating the benefits of organizational development.

5. INCREASE IN REVENUE AND PROFITABILITY

Many organizations that invest in coaching and team coaching will ask about the return on investment, and how spending on the development of their people affects the bottom-line. Return on investment is traditionally defined as the earnings before interest, taxes, depreciation and amortization from an investment made, usually expressed as a percentage of the original total cost invested.

Several writers have used ROI in their studies of coaching and claimed ROI of between 600 and 700 per cent: McGovern et al (2001), Parker-Wilkins (2006) and Anderson (2001). Others (De Meus, Dai and Lee, 2009; Grant, 2012) have challenged whether ROI is an appropriate or useful way of evaluating coaching, and we would agree with many of their arguments. At the same time many organizations are keen to have this measured. The 6th Ridler Report (Mann, 2016) showed that only 14 per cent of organizations measured ROI, although 80 per cent said they would 'value being able to evaluate coaching in this way, were data available' (2016: 20). Where this is important or essential for a client organization, it should be done well and is only one aspect of the evaluation process, that is integrated with the other processes we have outlined.

While he does not use an exact formula, Marshall Goldsmith (2004, 2011, 2013; Goldsmith and Reiter, 2007) operates a 'pay by results' approach to coaching. At the start of an engagement, he asks for agreement on two areas:

- What are the key behaviours that will make the biggest positive change in increased leadership effectiveness?
- Who are the key stakeholders that can determine (6 to 18 months later) if these changes have occurred?

He goes on to say: 'We then get paid only after our coaching clients have achieved positive change in key leadership behaviours, and become more effective leaders, as determined by their key stakeholders.'

Return on investment in regard to team and team of teams coaching can be viewed simply in the following formula:

$$\text{ROI as a percentage} = \frac{\text{Programme Benefits} - \text{Programme Costs}}{\text{Programme Costs}} \times 100$$

Hawkins (2012: 170) developed a relatively simple way of calculating ROI for coaching:

1 For every team coaching contract, collect the issues addressed by the team coaching and for each, estimate the cost of not addressing that issue, and/or the costed benefit of a performance improvement: for example productivity rise in the team leading to efficiency savings over the year £300,000 + financial benefit from the reduction in staff turnover £450,000 + increase in customer contracts £750,000 = Total Benefit £1,500,000.

2 Multiply by the percentage attributed by the team to the coaching: for example the team estimates that 50 per cent of the efficiency savings was directly attributable to the team coaching, 40 per cent of the reduced staff turnover and 10 per cent of winning new work can be directly attributed to the team coaching. This results in figures of £150,000 and £180,000 and £75,000 = £405,000 for the benefit from the team coaching.

3 A more sophisticated measurement can be achieved by asking the coachee's boss and subordinates to estimate this and averaging the results.

4 Multiply by the degree of confidence in the estimation, for example, 80 per cent, which gives an adjusted team coaching benefit of £324,000.

5 Subtract the total cost of the coaching = £90,000, resulting in a net benefit of £234,000.

6 Finally, to calculate ROI, divide the net benefit (£234,000) by the coaching cost (£90,000), yielding an ROI of 260 per cent.

There are many weaknesses in the approaches that try and jump straight to measuring the ROI of their team coaching in monetary terms, without first building a more rigorous, systemic approach throughout all stages of the evaluation chain. It is often an inexact science, with a great deal of subjective judgement, and driven by the pressure to demonstrate value quickly in purely financial terms. It may ignore many other factors that may have contributed to the value creating improvement. In many cases it only shows an associative connection, rather than a causative link.

Michael West in his work on effective team development in UK NHS hospitals (West, 2012, 2013; West and Dawson, 2012; West et al, 2006), first demonstrated that hospitals with effective real teams had lower mortality rates (an associative link). He then went on to show that those hospitals that improved the number of their effective real teams subsequently saw a further reduction in patient mortality rates, indicating a stronger causative link.

We believe that the weakness in nearly all the attempts to measure ROI from coaching can only be addressed by developing a stronger involvement of stakeholders in:

- contracting and setting the purpose of the team coaching
- reviewing the team coaching and team of teams' process, throughout the journey
- evaluation methods of the team coaching inputs, outputs, outcomes and value creation, right along the value chain

6. INCREASE IN COMMUNITY CONTRIBUTION

It is important for all organizations whether public sector, NGOs or Commercial companies, to evaluate the net benefit they contribute to the wider society and communities where they operate. To do this, they first need to recognize the benefit they receive from the wider community in terms of public services, from roads and transport, police and emergency services, water, power lines and communication cables, schools, hospitals, shops, parks and public spaces, to garbage collection and sewage, and many more.

Next, the organization needs to evaluate what it gives back to the community, not just in taxes and payments, but the services they provide, donations they give and days of employees volunteering. Every company should evaluate how much it is a good citizen that gives more than it takes and is contributing to building a better society for future generations. Any organizational transformation programme should have increased its net-positive contribution to the wider society as part of its objectives.

7. INCREASE IN THE NET BENEFIT TO THE WIDER ECOLOGY

Alongside making a net-positive contribution to the human community, evaluation should include an increase it the organization's net-positive contribution to the 'more than human' world of the wider ecology. The ecology is always the biggest investor and contributor to every organization, and we should remember that ultimately the ecology can close down every business! We have collaborated with companies that started by measuring their carbon footprint, tracking energy consumption and the carbon costs of transporting products and employees, and then developed strategic plans to achieve carbon neutrality or even carbon positivity. Then they examined the ecological costs of their entire supply chain, from the ecological costs that go into building and furnishing their offices, their equipment and their raw materials. Then this can be widened out to look at the environmental impact of the complete supply chain.

For example, when we were working with Unilever, who had successfully completed a major change project to reduce the ecological cost of their tea supply chain, they then shifted focus to their downstream costs including those associated with retailers and consumers. To their surprise one of the largest ecological costs was in how tea drinkers overfill their kettles and many boil as much as twice as much water as they need for the tea. Boiling kettles uses large amounts of energy. What is the role of a producer in educating their consumers in responsible use of resources?

Increasingly governments and informed consumers are demanding that all organizations are working to be ecologically net-positive. We, like many, believe that this is fundamental to the survival of life on our planet.

Embedding evaluation into the systemic team and team of teams coaching process

Evaluation, especially in the learning and development space, is often limited to post-programme surveys that are focussed on satisfaction and short-term gains (the inputs and outputs in our five-stage model of evaluation). It can be difficult to measure the more impactful outcomes and value creation that can be ascribed to the development programme, given the dynamic context of a typical organization. Embedding evaluation frameworks that draw on human-centred design principles and systems thinking (e.g. Douglas et al, 2024) emphasize the use of data sources that can be multi-tasked for both monitoring engagement effectiveness and used within the engagement for iterative learning. By assessing where existing data may be used (e.g. business-related metrics) and thoughtfully adding new measures where needed (e.g. pre- and post-assessments), it becomes possible to evaluate the connections – how inputs lead to outputs, which contribute to outcomes, and even to value creation. The two case examples below all show how embedded evaluation strategies helped to tell the story of the team coaching process.

Measuring the impact of Systemic Team of Teams Coaching

When it comes to team of teams coaching, the complexity increases as the focus shifts to measuring the impact across multiple teams. Some additional areas that team of teams and organizational development work are often designed to support are:

1 **Collaboration:** Assess the effectiveness of cross-team collaboration. Metrics might include the number of cross-functional projects initiated or improvements in communication flow.

2 **Enhanced agility:** Measure the organization's ability to respond swiftly to changes. Track decision-making speed or the implementation of new strategies.

3 **Innovation:** Evaluate the level of innovation across teams. This could involve counting new ideas implemented, process improvements, or cost savings from team initiatives.

Case example: connecting outputs to outcomes

In a Systemic Team of Teams Coaching project done by Lucy Shenouda and Susan Douglas at Health Connect America (HCA), success was measured not only in leadership effectiveness but also in how well teams collaborate, innovate and adapt across the organization.

Lucy and Susan began their work with HCA by focussing on middle management, both a bottleneck and a crucial lever for change within the organization. Their organizational coaching design included individual coaching using 360° leadership assessments with key operations and corporate leaders, coaching state-level teams during 'business as usual' meetings, and supporting the formation and strengthening of a new 'team of teams' for the 12 operations leaders and nine corporate leaders. Over the course of nine months, the coaches facilitated two multi-level leadership 'team of team' gatherings, setting the stage for sustainable, systemic change. These gatherings included both middle-level teams of teams and all senior leaders, including their supervisors and the C-suite. In between the two gatherings, three community of practice sessions were held with the supervisors to 'harvest the learning' (Stage 1 as referenced earlier in this chapter). These meetings created opportunities to grow awareness of the challenges and benefits to the company of supporting cross-functional teams.

By embedding data collection, pre- and post-assessments, surveys and interviews into every phase of the coaching intervention, Lucy and Susan were able to demonstrate the tangible impact of their work. Their coaching design, which started with individual leaders and expanded to a broader team of teams structure, helped unlock leadership potential across levels. The result was not only measurable improvements in leadership behaviours and collaboration but also a more cohesive, aligned, and future-ready organization.

During the final phase evaluation, 92 per cent of leaders reported increased self-awareness, with many acknowledging significant behavioural shifts, such as becoming more open, vulnerable and willing to ask for help. The work initially focussed on helping middle managers, whose transformation became a foundation for broader organizational alignment. As one operations leader shared, 'We've grown into a more cohesive unit. We have more growth ahead, but now we have a roadmap we didn't have before.' This sense of direction and clarity trickled upward, with middle management acting as the catalyst for senior leadership to embrace more collaborative and transparent ways of working.

As the coaching progressed, the formation of the new 'team of teams' strengthened cross-functional collaboration across the organization. Leaders at all levels began to demonstrate greater openness to feedback, improved communication, and a clearer sense of shared purpose. The two leadership gatherings provided opportunities to align on strategy and address challenges collaboratively. One outcome was the 100 per cent agreement among leaders that cross-functional collaboration was critical to the company's success, reinforcing the value of Systemic Team of Teams Coaching in driving organizational transformation. In a follow-up meeting two months later, the HCA sponsors remarked on the continued change in leadership approach where they think first about cross-functional and project teams to address complex problems. This shift to a teaming culture was seen as a cultural shift for HCA, which is contributing to a growing sense of resilience that 'we don't have to know exactly where we are going when we get into [a challenge] because we can work through things together'.

Case example: measuring large-scale organizational transformation

In large-scale transformation projects, data and ongoing evaluation and evolution is essential for guiding, measuring, and sustaining progress. Tania Hodgkinson, a systemic organizational transformation coach, exemplifies how embedding data at the heart of her coaching process leads to successful transformations.

Data not only identifies areas for improvement and progress tracking, but it also serves as a driving force behind transformation itself. In projects that span multiple departments or teams, Tania ensures that data aligns the entire system, supporting informed decision-making and keeping transformation efforts on track and accountable.

A powerful example of this approach can be seen in the transformation project Tania led for two divisions of one of the world's largest car manufacturers. Faced with disruptive forces like electric vehicles, digital technology and environmental regulations, the company needed to adapt quickly to enable them to meet their central digital sales goals. Tania's data-centric coaching was pivotal in this transformation to future-fitness, helping track leadership performance, research and development metrics, and employee future readiness throughout the process.

Tania explains:

> Data is not just about measuring learning and progress; it's an integral part of how I create a shared language and understanding within the organization. It helps establish alignment and a clear, unbiased awareness of where we stand. It's also about using the business language that resonates with my clients, meeting them where they are.

Her data-centric approach enabled the company to pivot in real-time, aligning internal goals with the fast-evolving market. Data wasn't merely an evaluation tool in this transformation; it was a core enabler of the teams' ability to succeed.

The automotive industry's shift to digital-first strategies required the company to put digital at the heart of the business, not just the IT department, reimagine the customer journey, and realign its leadership and culture across 18 distinct market teams and the regional leadership. Tania's team of teams coaching, including 55 workshops involving 250 participants (CEOs and digital experts included), ensured that the company developed a unified digital transformation strategy, aligning local initiatives with broader digital sales goals.

Similarly, Tania's Systemic Team of Teams Coaching played a pivotal role in the Fraport Twin Star Airports' Fit4Future initiative. Charged with post-pandemic recovery, technological acceleration and systemic leadership development, Frank Quante, the Fraport new CEO, collaborated with Tania to design a comprehensive leadership and Systemic Team Coaching programme. Data was embedded at every phase, starting with workshops that gathered over 600 data points on future trends, emerging technologies, and new business models that help reimagine the future customer experience at the airports. These insights formed the foundation for Fraport's five strategic themes, the core of their innovation roadmap.

Throughout the Fit4Future initiative, data collected from teams, customers and partners guided leadership decisions and tracked progress. During five ExO (exponential) Sprints, data enabled 28 team members to develop innovative solutions in real-time, with support from 26 senior leaders. Over 9,000 hours were dedicated to this initiative, leading to deep, measurable impacts on the organization's future.

In both the car manufacturer's transformation journey and Fraport's Fit4Future initiative, Tania's data-driven coaching approach was a key success factor. By integrating data from the outset, she ensured that these organizations didn't just track and measure their progress, they used data to align, shift perspective, and become agile, adaptive and future-ready in response to rapidly shifting markets and emerging opportunities.

The CEO Frank Quante, who we interviewed as part of the research for this book, reported that 'regular data, encouraged us, the leadership, to keep going as they could see progress, but it also showed what more we, the leaders, had to do, where the feedback from both employees and customers was less than satisfactory'.

Conclusion

In this chapter we have explored how evaluation is a key aspect of Systemic Team Coaching and Systemic Team of Teams Coaching, at all stages of the journey. This is essential to:

- Demonstrate the value to sponsors within the organization.

- Ensure that teams continuously increase the value they co-create with and for all their ecosystem partners.

- Provide data that enables everyone involved to review the development journey and make necessary adjustments for improvement.

Team and team of teams coaches have a responsibility to be not only facilitators of change but also stewards of value. To do this, coaches must embed evaluation methods and metrics from the outset of engagements. They must challenge themselves to not just prove the value of team and team of teams coaching, but to maximize it, ensuring that every intervention they lead contributes to a brighter, more collaborative and innovative future for the organizations they support and their various ecosystem partners. Let's move beyond retrofitting success measures, and in future design evaluation and evolution measures and processes, from the very beginning.

08

What the research revealed: key themes and insights

PETER HAWKINS, CATHERINE CARR, NAYSAN FIROOZMAND
AND SALOME VAN COLLER

Introduction

From the outset, it was clear that the most effective way to conduct our research was by creating a team of teams. The research began in 2022, as a partnership between Professor Salome Van Coller of the University of Stellenbosch and Professor Peter Hawkins of Renewal Associates. Both organizations saw the urgent need to discover best practice in coaching and developing the team of teams in different types of organizations right around the world. Together they drafted a research plan, process and protocol, that was reviewed internally by both their organizations and went to the university of Stellenbosch Research Ethics committee for academic and ethical approval.

The research was then delayed owing to Salome's ill health. Her role, in late 2023, was taken on by Dr Catherine Carr. We, as researchers and authors, then formed a collaborative team, comprising members from Renewal Associates and the alumni of our Systemic Team Coaching training programmes. Each team member brought connections to networks of professionals actively involved in team development across diverse organizations. These networks served as a foundation for collecting data on the evolution of teaming cultures, Systemic Team Coaching and Systemic Team of Teams Coaching, and how they deliver value to stakeholders and ecosystem partners.

The key to successfully gathering such diverse data lies in the strong relationships we have built with our research partners and their collaboration with client organizations.

As practitioner-researchers, we outline the process and methods we used so that others can build on this research. We then share the data and analysis that emerged, followed by insights developed through discussion with both key organizations and our research partners.

Research process

The research process shown in Figure 8.1 is depicted as cyclical. While it followed a logical progression through all the five stages, insights from the questionnaire process refined the research design and informed key interviews. Ongoing dialogues with both organizations and research partners have informed every stage, with many individuals from both groups contributing feedback on the chapters of this book.

FIGURE 8.1 The research cycle

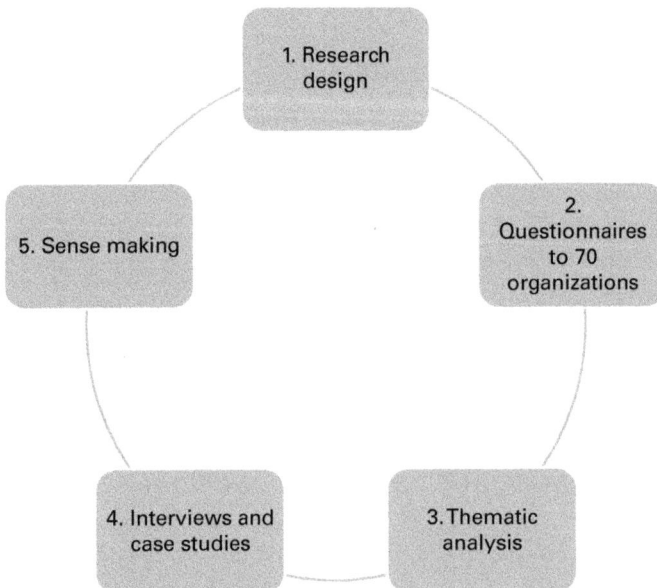

Research partner eligibility

1 Salome and Peter established ethical and robust criteria for selecting research partners. The two main criteria were: partners currently engaged in a team of teams project or able to propose such work within their organization.

2 Partners with prior experience in team of teams work, and with organizations willing to participate retrospectively.

Our research partners had an important responsibility throughout the process, which included ensuring that:

1 The organizations that had been involved in developing teams, and/or team coaching, filled in the questionnaire.

2 The potential organization could be an exemplar of one aspect of developing teamwork, teaming or team of teams.

3 If selected, they had the option to consent to a recorded interview about their work.

4 If there was consent, the coach(es) could contribute a 2,000–3,000-word case description or shorter vignette.

5 They would invite clients to the team of teams workshop that would share cross-organizational findings and practical applications (we wanted to give participants something tangible and timely).

It was important that our partners felt involved and that there was something meaningful and beneficial to them in the process. We committed to providing them with the following benefits:

- **Leadership in team coaching:** Be the Renewal Associates group of 'Team of Teams' coaches and research partners on the forefront of Systemic Team Coaching practices.

- **Early access to findings:** Stay ahead by receiving early access to emerging outcomes, staying informed about what we are discovering through this research on team coaching and teaming cultures.

- **Input and influence:** Be in a position to provide insights at key research stages, shaping the study's direction during questionnaire analysis and post-interviews.

- **Client relationship enhancement:** Leverage research findings to deepen client relationships, implementing insights for comprehensive teaming culture and team of teams development.

- **Acknowledgement and recognition:** Their contributions will be acknowledged in research reports, published papers and the resulting book, highlighting their commitment to advancing team coaching.
- **Complimentary book:** As a token of our appreciation, they will each receive a complimentary copy of the book.

Setting out a robust approach

Table 8.1 provides an overview of the key stages we undertook to communicate, collect data, brief and update research partners.

TABLE 8.1 Key stages in partner communication, data collection and research briefing

Date	Milestone
July–December 2022	Book proposal and research design
March 2023	Received research and ethical approval from Stellenbosch University and contract for the book
July 2023	Research project design
October 2023	Finalizing list of Team of Teams of researchers
22 December 2023	Finalized list of potential organizations and questionnaire. Drafted consent forms
1 February 2024	Questionnaire sent to participants
14 February 2024	Second meeting with the research group
May 2024	Questionnaire data analysed for themes and a second review for ethical dilemmas. Collective sense making stage 1.
June 2024	Selected organizations to interview and those invited to contribute case vignettes.
June–September 2024	Together with our research partners, we conducted client interviews and used that plus their organization's questionnaire data to draft a case vignette or illustration of key emerging themes and practices
September–December 2024	Submissions were reviewed. Stories were matched to chapter themes and topics and we did further sense making
September–January 2025	Coach research partners invited to review chapters and offer additional input to ensure alignment between their stories and chapter themes
December 2024	Chapters sent to research partners and their organizations for final approval and consent to publish

How respondents were selected

Our research partners identified organizations for the study and selected key individuals, such as CEOs or leaders, who acted as organizational coaching champions or sponsors within their businesses. The criteria required that organizations had engaged in some form of team development and expressed interest in advancing this work further. Most of the organizations contacted had specifically implemented Systemic Team Coaching (Hawkins, 2021) with one or more teams.

Once connected, the research partner provided the client with detailed information about the study, its purpose, and a consent form. The consent form explained that the research aimed to explore the relationship between teaming cultures and the delivery of value to stakeholders through team coaching.

It was important to us that contributors to this research also benefited from the process. We committed that they would:

- be the first to hear the emerging outcomes of the research
- receive feedback on their practice and how it compares to best practice
- get to discover what is best practice across the globe in developing a fuller teaming culture and team of teams development process
- receive a draft of how their case is written about in the book and will be asked to approve or change it and give permission for its publication
- have their contribution fully acknowledged in all publications
- be invited to book launches

What we asked

The questionnaire was designed to facilitate effective thematic analysis of the data while allowing us to identify the type of organization providing it. This enabled us to explore trends across organizations based on factors such as industry sector, geography, number of employees, teams engaged in team coaching, and team leaders who experienced leadership coaching without team coaching involvement.

The questionnaire consisted of 22 questions divided into 8 elements, enabling a deeper exploration of the conditions, benefits and limitations of

Systemic Team Coaching, Systemic Team of Teams Coaching and other team-related initiatives. These broad dimensions were:

1 How teaming shows up in the organization (documents, processes etc.).

2 Current experience of working with team development (past, current and future).

3 Needs and barriers to making team and team of team and organizational development happen.

4 Factors that make the biggest difference in team and team of teams coaching and what success looks like.

5 Factors that inhibit the effectiveness of team and team of teams coaching.

6 What the effectiveness of team and team of teams coaching has been and how it is measured.

7 Tools, methods or processes used in the organization in the support of team and organizational development.

8 How stakeholder partnerships are formed and/or used in team and organizational development.

How the data was analysed

We conducted a thematic analysis based on 'Grounded theory' (Charmaz, 2014; Glaser and Straus, 1967), a qualitative research method used to identify and analyse emerging patterns and themes across the data.

Familiarization with the data

The first step in our thematic analysis was immersing ourselves in the data by thoroughly reading and re-reading responses. Independently, we took notes and highlighted key points, building a comprehensive understanding to inform deeper analysis.

Generating initial codes

Next, we proceeded to coding the data, identifying and labelling segments relevant to our research questions. Using a manual process, we carefully examined responses and assigned codes to phrases or sentences capturing key ideas, such as 'culture', 'communication', 'support', 'impact' and 'stakeholders'.

Discovering themes

After completing the initial coding, we identified themes by reviewing and grouping similar or related codes. This involved independent analysis followed by collaborative discussions to ensure the themes accurately reflected the data. For example, codes like 'openness' and 'trust' were combined under the theme 'Psychological Safety and Trust'.

Reviewing themes

After generating initial themes, we reviewed and refined them to ensure they were coherent and distinct. This involved verifying themes against the coded data to confirm they accurately represented the responses, resolving over-laps or inconsistencies, and making adjustments as needed. Through this iterative process, we identified 10 core themes, each encompassing 2 to 10 sub-categories that captured the broader theme. We also identified ethical issues as a meta theme (separately covered in Chapter 13).

Defining and naming themes

After refining the initial themes for clarity and distinction, we verified them against the coded data, resolved overlaps or inconsistencies, and made adjustments as needed. This process resulted in 10 core themes, each comprising 2 to 10 sub-categories that encapsulated the broader concepts.

Writing up the analysis

The final step in our thematic analysis was documenting the findings. We summarized the themes and their relevance to team coaching, team of teams coaching and organizational development, linking them to our research questions and highlighting key insights. To add depth, we included direct quotes from respondents to illustrate the themes – many of which are featured throughout this book.

Follow-up, interviews and write up

Each coaching partner was provided with their organization questionnaire data and a semi-structured interview template. We discussed what we thought was unique or noteworthy in their questionnaire data and points where more detail was needed. We also chose to interview organizations that seemed to be carrying out best practice.

Ethical considerations

We ensured that all coaching research partners and participating organizations gave written informed consent before participating in each phase of the study. Additionally, participants were provided with opportunities to review and approve the case studies written about their organizations before publication.

The 10 core themes that emerged

We identified 10 core themes from the responses, each encompassing a range of sub-categories (between 2 and 8) that represented broader patterns within the data.

The 10 core themes and their associated sub-themes are as shown in Table 8.2. The various sub-themes represented positive (+), negative (-) and neutral (=) statements.

The written responses to each of the questions were very rich in data and as you can see from the table there is a wide variety of expectations and challenges identified within participating organizations that impact team and team of team coaching.

TABLE 8.2 Ten core themes and sub-themes

	Core Theme	Sub-themes
1	Senior level sponsorship	+ Engaging the CEO is necessary
		+ Having senior leader endorsement for team coaching
		+ Needing HR support
		+ Team development, seen as business as usual activity
		= Leaders need to develop themselves first/too
		= Greater awareness of the needs by leaders
		= Need to balance time and money (cost and earning for the business)
		− Organization needs to invest money and time into team coaching
		− Finding funds to support team development is hard
		− Changes in teams restrict activity
		− Many competing priorities

(continued)

TABLE 8.2 (Continued)

	Core Theme	Sub-themes
2	Alignment and cohesion within and across teams	+ A need for creating team cohesion + Working on common challenges + Working towards goals between sessions not just in team coaching + Creating a common language and tools − Absence of common purpose with the team − There is a need for more alignment and common goals − Misalignment causes barriers to team development
3	Stakeholder involvement	+ Awareness of stakeholders as a point of data + Increased awareness of how teams appear to stakeholders = Actively building engagement (and relationships) with wider stakeholders needed
4	Collaboration, and commitment in and between teams	+ Understanding why teaming within and across teams is important + Creating connections between teams + Realizing that collaboration is key to success + Having live coaching during meetings − The coaching highlighted that the organizational structure prevents effective collaboration − Not addressing differences and conflict − Mix of face-to-face and virtual not good − Lack of commitment from the team − Not making time to do things differently − People are just too busy
5	Whole organization involvement and learning	+ Team diagnostics and 360 excellent + Use of engagement surveys + Translating learning in teams for a wider systemic roll out + Sharing learning across the organization = Organizational alignment is needed
6	Strategic focus and results	+ Setting KPIs and OKRs that aligned across the business + Need to track results to demonstrate value − Lack of focus in the business (too much on team dynamics in the coaching) − Lack of consistent follow-up and support by coaches
7	Change and strategic innovation	+ Putting team development as a priority + Realization that the current system is stuck + Ability to challenge ourselves with tools and techniques + A strategy on teaming is needed = Feelings of being stuck − Resistance to change holds things back

(continued)

TABLE 8.2 (Continued)

	Core Theme	Sub-themes
8	Employee engagement and well-being	+ Team coaching increased employee satisfaction company wide – The system is in a regressive stress state – Overwhelm and overwork are common
9	Sufficient psychological safety and trust/conflict	= Leaders need to develop themselves first/too to build trust – Psychological safety and trust needs to increase – The culture is in survival mode – Not feeling safe enough to speak up
10	External support (consultants)	= There is a need for external not just internal support Both are helpful together as well – Sometimes bad fit between coach and team – Lack of role clarity

Factors influencing the effectiveness of team coaching

The response data highlighted a significant number of areas that specifically influenced the effectiveness of Systemic Team Coaching that team coaches could possibly action right away. Factors were categorized as positive (enabling team coaching to have a positive impact on individuals, teams and the organization), neutral or negative (hindering positive perception or impact on individuals, teams and the organization).We presented this list to our coaching research partners, who responded with enthusiasm and curiosity. In Table 8.3 is a summary of prominent factors that helped or hindered the application and impact of team, and team of teams coaching. We have ordered the table not in a ranking of most mentioned but in a logical flow of the unfolding team of teams process.

Our global coaching partners were particularly encouraged by the recognition of the value of external coaches while highlighting the importance of partnerships with internal resources. These collaborations enhance organizational knowledge, ensure follow-through, and secure senior leadership and organizational support, proving exponentially valuable at the team of teams level.

One key insight emerged from the responses: leaders often answered questions about their downline team and their own organizational challenges rather than on team of teams and network coaching. This observation

TABLE 8.3 Factors helping or hindering team of teams coaching

Factors helping team of teams coaching	Factors hindering team of teams coaching
Aligning with senior leaders who role model and endorse the process	No support from senior leader(s)
Working on common challenges	Absence of common purpose and goals in the team
Creating a common language and tools	Not feeling safe enough to speak up, let alone align
Working toward goals between sessions	Lack of consistent follow-up and support
Using team diagnostics and ongoing measures of success	Just relying on team members' views of what change is needed
Creating connections between teams as well as within teams	Not making time for the team coaching or to do things differently
Sharing learning across the organization	Learning and development staying within the teams
Addressing differences and conflict	Leaving differences and conflict unprocessed
Effectively using face to face and virtual approaches in effective ways to engage	Mix of face-to-face and virtual techniques and participation not effective
The use of external coaches	Not having external support
Ensuring coach-team-organizational alignment before engagement	Bad fit between team and team coach

is comparable to when senior leadership teams are asked to complete a survey and they default to answering based on their immediate teams rather than the broader leadership issues the survey was intended to address. It underscores how these larger systems are not as readily in awareness.

Furthermore, this confirmed for us that even among our most experienced global group of systemic team coaches, only a relatively small group are actively engaging in team of teams and network coaching at the level of organizational transformation. While there are numerous OD programmes and initiatives, few of these utilize a Systemic Team of Teams Approach, and only a handful of systemic team coaches have experience in how to coach systemically and effectively with and between multiple teams within an organization or network, and how to generate alignment and learning across the entire system. This insight validated the importance of this book and its contribution to advancing the field.

Interviews

Based on the research findings and discussion with our research partners, we selected 10 organizations for follow-up interviews. These were selected on the criteria that:

1 They had carried out team coaching with multiple teams.

2 And/or they potentially were an exemplar of one or more aspects of the team of teams process.

3 And/or they were linking their team coaching to the organizational transformation they were undertaking.

A number of these organizations are represented in the case studies that are included throughout this book.

We also undertook additional interviews with representatives of companies not included in the initial survey where there was an opportunity to expand the global reach and type of companies represented. These interviews also allowed us to explore the emerging themes and discover if they resonated with other organizations.

This led to a gradual development of three important and interrelated models that illustrate how systemic transformation unfolds in practice:

1 The 'best-of-the-best process model of the systemic team of teams journey' which is outlined and shown in Chapter 4.

2 The organizational life cycle that is outlined and shown in Chapter 5.

3 The core essentials and enablers which are shown in Figure 8.1 – which is a higher order synthesis of both the emergent themes of Table 8.1 and the enablers and derailers in Table 8.2.

Sense making one: reflections and insight on Systemic Team Coaching

This research also highlighted several immediate insights and applications for team leaders and team coaching practitioners. We will highlight a few here and note where we have expanded on these themes in this book.

First, external Systemic Team Coaching is highly valued in team and team of teams coaching. The barriers that organizations identified are also ones that they hope the team coaches will help them find a way to navigate through. Factors such as not organizing priorities, allocating time, not fully committing to the team coaching work, and a lack of consistent follow-through on agreements showed up in our research, as resoundingly verified by our research partners. These are classic issues for teams.

A common resistance we encounter is: 'We can't afford the time and/or cost.' We then need to address with them the cost of not doing the work and addressing key issues. The world around the team will continue to change and pressures will increase. We look to the waste inherent in doing the same thinking and behaviour and expecting different results or trying new things without thinking it through systemically. This kind of conversation can be an opening to contract in stages and phases – to offer team coaching in bite-size chunks. Just watch you don't end up with team(s) only eating crumbs – for example an hour here and there of team development that stays disconnected from their work proper.

In Chapter 14 on tools and methods, we describe contracting around commitment. The team coach needs to remember that they are there in service of the work the team's stakeholders, now and in the future, need from them. The team coach needs to hold a resolute focus on the initial remit, the planned coaching activities, and the resultant teamwork, but not lose sight of the desired outcomes. For while there is often initial hope that the team coach and coaching will miraculously help, the culture and patterns often settle back in like a low-pressure weather system. A coaching inquiry to unpack this includes exploring what are the drivers that can create an updraft or where are there exceptions and examples that are not the normative pattern and perhaps are not being heard or actioned? The coach needs to not do the work for the team, but neither can they hang back and hope the team figures it out with the right question. Systemic team and team of teams coaching is an active process, where the team may not have figured it out yet, the coach won't know exactly what will work, but together they can create something new. In Parts 3 and 4 we offer approaches and methods along these lines.

A critical factor in building the business case for team and team of teams coaching is establishing a clear and measurable connection to tangible business outcomes. Team coaching cannot be a 'nice-to-try' service; it must be integral to the organization's strategy for driving change and delivering results. Systemic Team Coaching interventions enhance vertical development and leadership effectiveness, build aligned teams and foster innovation, directly impacting organizational performance. When leaders recognize how coaching improves productivity, employee engagement and bottom-line results, it transitions from being seen as an optional activity to a strategic imperative. This clear line of sight between coaching efforts and business outcomes not only secures senior leadership buy-in but also ensures sustained investment in team of teams coaching as a vital part of organizational success.

Another interesting theme centres on the dynamics of buy-in and disconnection. Either the client thought that the team and coaches were a mismatch or the value and power of the coaching was diminished by lack of senior buy-in. Coaches may jump too quickly to say yes to an assignment rather than spend enough time at the outset to contract well and contract powerfully. This includes needing access to one level higher than the team or team of teams. Sometimes the team leader you are directly coaching will say that they don't need to involve the higher leader, or they are too busy. Sometimes the team coach is nervous pursuing that further, however, consider where this might be an issue down the road. For senior leaders, this work represents an invaluable opportunity to pause, reflect and truly 'invest in their investment' – unlocking the systemic potential across their teams and organization(s).

Psychological safety and trust emerged as one of the most frequently highlighted themes in our research. We suggest that you need just enough psychological safety to directly address issues of mistrust and hold the necessary difficult conversations. It is clear from the research that when teams have created a collective purpose and have learnt to address conflict systemically rather than personally, a good deal of interpersonal conflict melts away. Trust, in this context, is not a prerequisite but a result of intentional, collective action. We reframe the focus on psychological safety to collective relational and psychological safety (Hawkins, 2024b).

Addressing root issues, particularly with leadership and at the organizational culture level, is critical. Organizations must commit to deliberate, consistent and persistent actions over time, 'walking the talk' in alignment with their values and goals. At the leadership level, leaders often encounter a gap between their intentions and the impact of their actions. Coaching conversations should bridge this divide, kindly normalizing what is common, exploring what is unique and directly addressing what appears as problematic. If the coach is curious, and committed to learning and growth, the leader(s) will be well supported to do the same.

Sense making two: the essentials and enablers for Systemic Team of Teams Coaching

From the analysis of what helped and hindered team coaching, we explored this further in the interviews and went on to focus on what was essential and what enabled team of teams coaching across and beyond organizations. From this we developed a new model of what were the essentials and enablers for systemic team of team coaching and developing an effective teaming culture (see Figure 8.2). This model builds on the important work done by Ruth Wageman and colleagues (2008) with their research on senior leadership teams and the 'Six Conditions' necessary for them to be effective. Our research takes this template and outlines the necessary conditions for establishing an effective 'team of teams'.

ESSENTIALS:

Business centric: This is the overarching condition that connects the other three essentials. Creating a team of teams must be seen as a business essential and not as 'a nice to have'. It must be driven by what is necessary for the organization to be 'future-fit' and co-create value with and for all its stakeholders and ecosystem partners.

Senior sponsorship: In successful organizations we interviewed, creating a team of teams was a key organizational priority. It needed to be sponsored, led and role-modelled by the top team. Senior leaders made it clear to leaders across the organization why this was essential for the organization to succeed.

Organizational alignment: Team of teams development supports and contributes to greater organizational alignment by helping teams discover how to connect, create synergy and contribute both horizontally across the organization and vertically within it.

Stakeholder engagement: Every team must clearly identify their key internal and external stakeholders, understand what these stakeholders value about them, and determine their future needs. Teams must also actively engage these stakeholders to develop them into ecosystem partners.

ENABLERS:

A strong supported process: This is the overarching condition that links all the enabling processes.

FIGURE 8.2 The essentials and enablers of Systemic Team of Teams Coaching

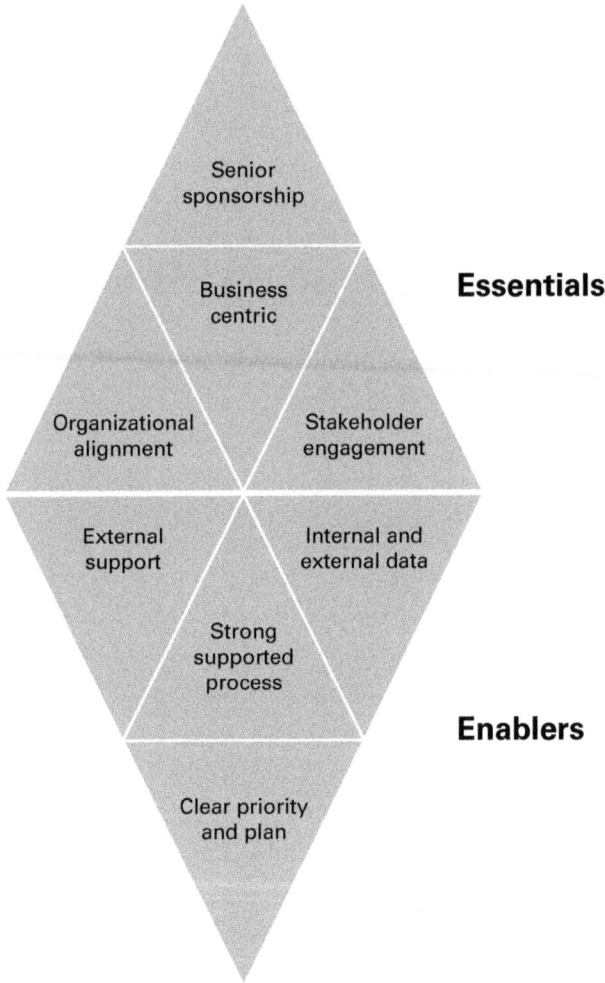

Essentials

Senior
sponsorship

Business
centric

Organizational
alignment

Stakeholder
engagement

External
support

Internal and
external data

Strong
supported
process

Enablers

Clear priority
and plan

Clear priorities and plan:

The process requires a clear design that includes:

- An assessment of where the organizational strategy, culture, leadership and teaming are currently.
- Where these key organizational elements need to be in two to three years' time for the organization to be future-fit.
- A roadmap for the journey.

- A steering group to oversee the journey, with regular reviews that measure and evaluate progress, what is working and not working, and who then evolve and upgrade the process and plan.
- Clear contracted roles and expectations for all the key internal and external players.

Externally supported: The research showed that this process is much more effective if supported by professional organizational consultants and systemic team of teams coaches. But it is essential that they are well chosen, partner well with the internals and gradually train up internal systemic team coaches and consultants to increasingly take on their work. It is extremely rare for organizations to have all the requisite skills, with the right level of authority and impact, to carry out all the roles needed in this process, and it is extremely hard to see the culture, when you are immersed within it and your perceptions and mindset are a symptom of the culture.

With ongoing internal and external data: Assessing the starting state, defining the desired destination and planning the route requires high-quality internal and external data. Successful companies emphasized the importance of a well-developed diagnostic tool to gather insights from both within the organization and external stakeholders. Examples of these can be found in Hawkins (2021).

Conclusion

In this chapter, we detailed the research process and the themes and patterns that emerged from the questionnaire data, interviews and case studies. This allowed us to co-create clear guidance on the factors that help or hinder Systemic Team Coaching and the essential conditions for a successful team of teams process. This work has led to the development of a new model, which we and others aim to trial, evaluate and refine in the future.

Looking forward, we hope this research and book inspire readers to take what they've learnt and apply it within their organizations, while also considering further practitioner-based research of their own. By embracing these insights and contributing to the evolving field, we can collectively enhance the practice of systemic team and team of teams coaching. This work is critical for creating sustainable change across systems, a vital necessity in today's complex and challenged world.

PART THREE

The contribution of a Systemic Team of Teams Approach to other levels of development

09

Coaching the connections rather than the parts

Introduction

In Chapter 3 we quoted a CEO of a global insurance business saying:

> I have lots of coaches who coach my people and lots of consultants that consult to different parts of my organization, but that is not where our challenges lie. All our significant challenges reside in the connections – not only between individuals but between teams, divisions, countries, and between us and our stakeholders.

He went on to give this challenge: 'Where are the coaches and consultants skilled in coaching these connections?' (Hawkins, 2017).

This chapter delves into the intricate web of these connections, examining their various forms, perspectives and the nuanced ways they can be enhanced through Systemic Team of Teams Coaching (STOTC). E M Forster, the Edwardian English novelist, in his novel *Howards End* (1910) wrote: 'Only connect... and human love will be seen at its height. Live in fragments no longer.' His call to transcend fragmentation resonates deeply today, echoing in the more contemporary thoughts of Douglas Rushkoff, who advocates for viewing humanity as 'one big, interconnected team' (Rushkoff, 2019: 11).

We start by showing how to develop a relational perspective, learning to listen to the spaces between individuals, teams and organizations. Then we will explore many different types of connections and disconnections, and describe different methods for coaching these, with illustrative examples. Before concluding we will share a short case vignette, of a Brazilian company that developed from a top-down hierarchy to a collaborative and interconnected team of teams.

Shifting our perspective: from individuals to relationships, and parts to flows

Our modern discourse often leans heavily on atomism and individualism, where connections and relationships are seen merely as constructs of individual parts. This view, while dominant in much of today's global dialogue, is relatively new and culturally specific. Yet, another way to look at the world is one that sees relationships as the foundation, with individuals unfolding from these relationships, always living and acting from within an interwoven meshwork of relationships, human and more-than-human.

From a biological standpoint, this relational perspective is vividly evident. We emerge from the intimate relationship of our parents, develop within the nurturing environment of our parental mother, and depend entirely on relationships for survival post-birth. This biological interconnectedness serves as a powerful perspective for understanding the deeper nature of collective human interaction and creativity.

In previous work (Hawkins, 2025), I, Peter, explored how creativity is inherently born from relational dynamics. This insight extends beyond the creative arts into every facet of human endeavour, suggesting that our most profound achievements are not solely individual triumphs but the fruits of collaborative interaction. Expanding on this theme, I delved into how beauty – and indeed love – is not merely an attribute of objects or a perception in the viewer's eye but arises from the profound relational connection between them.

> Beauty lies not in the viewed or the viewer, but in the viewing; not in the musical score or the listener, but the playing and hearing that co-create each other. Beauty is always relational; co-created by the eye and what it sees, the ear and what it hears; the touch, taste and smell, and what they are awakened by and awakened to.

This echoes the sentiment of the Chinese French philosopher Francois Cheng who, in his analysis of Cézanne's painting, illustrates that beauty manifests through relational essence (Cheng, 2009: 26). For Cézanne, beauty results from encounters on all levels. On the level of represented nature, it is the encounter between the hidden and the revealed, between the moving and the fixed; on the level of the artistic act, it's the encounter between brush strokes, between the colours applied. And beyond all this, there is this decisive encounter of the human spirit and the landscape at a privileged moment, with something trembling, embracing, unfinished in that interval, as if the artist has made themself the repository or host, awaiting the coming of some visitor who knows how to inhabit what is captured, offered.

This interconnected view challenges us to rethink our approaches to leadership, coaching and organizational development. By adopting a relational perspective we can develop a deeper appreciation for the fundamental role of relationships in shaping our world, we can enhance our ability to work more effectively together, elevating our collective capacity for innovation, empathy and understanding.

In both coaching and leadership, listening is a key competence. However, there are many levels to listening (Hawkins, 2025; Hawkins and Smith, 2013). We can listen with our ears to the words of another and even accurately play them back, but this is very different from being able to listen with our whole body to the emotions and feelings beneath the words allowing ourselves to attune with their emotional resonance. To listen with 'wide-angled empathy' (Hawkins, 2019; Hawkins and Turner, 2020), is to listen with empathy and compassion, not only for the storyteller who is present with us, but with equal compassion for everyone in their story.

To coach connections we need to develop yet another level of listening, which is to listen to the spaces between people and not just what each is saying, but the rhythm, movement and harmonics of the interplay between them. In Japanese culture there is a beautiful concept of Ma, which is the silence between the notes, the stillness between the movements, and the space between the branches of a tree, or the limbs of a dancer. Tom Frengos (2024), a Canadian who lives and coaches in Japan, has written a beautiful book on Ma in life, leadership and coaching. He describes listening not just to the people, but the spaces between them, not just to the agenda items but the space between the issues. To be a systemic team coach, you need to be able to listen to the spaces between team members, the quality of the relating in the space between them. To systemically coach a team of teams, you need to discern the quality of the relational dance between teams, between departments, and between the organization and all it stakeholders.

Then there is another level of listening, seeing and sensing. To listen through what is said and sense and perceive the patterns that underlie and influence what is emerging in the words, feelings, dynamic and interplay on the surface. In Daoist and Neo-Confucian training they distinguish between Qi (sometimes spelt in the West as Chi) which is the energy of what is manifest, and Li, which is the underlying patterns that lie behind what manifests on the surface. We can study the Qi or energy of the waves of the ocean, and we can study the Li of how this energy emerges from the tides (including the lunar and seasonal influences), the currents and ocean streams. For Daoists, the Li is the intermediary realm between the manifestation of things, people, events etc. and the Dao from which everything emerges.

To learn to listen through what is happening to the Li of the patterns that are creating it takes many years of training. We need to sense the patterns beneath the behaviour of individuals, to the family and team patterns these emerge from. These team patterns are, in turn, shaped by the broader 'team of teams' and organizational dynamics, and how these are part of a larger human dance. This dance manifests through political, economic, social, legal, technological and ecological patterning. These human Li unfold within the ecological and evolutionary Li-patterns that have been unfolding over millennia on our planet and within the wider cosmos.

The nearest we come to it in modern Western thinking is Gregory Bateson's (1972, 1979) 'pattern that connects'. 'Gregory Bateson has been blessed, and cursed, with a mind that sees through things to a world of pattern and form that lies beyond' (Keesing, 1974: 370). Bateson developed a rich ecosystemic thinking which encompassed couple and family dynamics organizational patterns, natural systems and the meta patterns that connect across the many systemic levels. Eventually he sensed, like the Daoists that it was the patterns which connect us-one to another, and between the human and more-than-human worlds.

As leaders and coaches, we need to sense how the pattern of interpersonal relationships in teams often emerge more from the pattern of inter-team and inter-function dynamics in the organization, and how these, in turn, emerge from the pattern of different stakeholder interests. We must also recognise how the patterns of relating are shaped by the culture we are born into and live within. The culture we cannot see, as it is the water we are immersed within, yet forms our ways of perceiving the world (our worldview), shapes the way we think, through the language, grammar, metaphors and narratives we think within, and shapes how we act and relate through cultural norms, unwritten rules and mores.

Many types of connections

In today's rapidly evolving business landscape, the ability to effectively manage and enhance formal connections within an organization is more crucial than ever. These formal connections structure the interactions that occur within the defined organizational hierarchy and serve as the backbone of an organization's operations. They facilitate the flow of information, dictate the allocation of resources and define the pathways of influence and decision-making. As such, coaching leaders and teams on how to optimize these formal relationships can lead to significant improvements in organizational efficiency and effectiveness.

Let's now explore specific types of formal connections and identify 10 crucial areas where targeted team of teams coaching can profoundly impact organizational performance. By understanding and refining these connections, organizations can ensure that their structured interactions are as effective and strategically aligned as possible.

- **Relationships between team members:** Fostering strong connections among team members while addressing any points of disconnection is essential for building a cohesive unit.

- **Inter-team relationships:** Ensuring effective communication and alignment between different teams can prevent silos and enhance collaborative efforts.

- **Cross-cultural connections:** In diverse organizations, understanding and bridging cultural differences is vital. Exploring connections and disconnections across cultures can enhance team and organizational integration and effectiveness.

- **Agenda connections:** Examining how issues on the team's agenda are interconnected or remain isolated can reveal underlying patterns of communication and priority setting.

- **Functional integration:** Connections and disconnections between various functions within the organization can impact operational efficiency and cross-departmental collaboration.

- **Hierarchical interactions:** Addressing how different levels of the hierarchy connect or fail to connect can help in smoothing information flow and decision-making processes. This importantly needs to be focussing on the clarity of commissioning of the team, from the teams above, including the purpose of the team, the key expectations of what it needs to deliver, by when, as well as what resources will be made available. There also needs to be a good two-way flow of information, communication, feedback, suggestions and challenges.

- **Regional and global dynamics:** For organizations spread across multiple regions or countries, nurturing connections while managing disconnections is vital for maintaining a unified organizational identity and purpose.

- **Organizational stakeholder/ecosystemic partner relationships:** Building and maintaining robust connections with stakeholders while identifying any disconnections can align organizational goals with stakeholder expectations and needs.

- **Stakeholder/ecosystemic partner interactions:** Understanding how different stakeholders are connected or disconnected from each other can provide deeper insights into external influences and pressures.

- **Temporal connections:** Reflecting on how the organization's present actions connect with its past experiences and future aspirations can help in shaping a forward-thinking strategy while honouring its legacy.

By paying close attention to these aspects, we can better support organizations in achieving a more integrated, effective and forward-looking approach. This focus on both connections and disconnections not only aids in immediate problem-solving but also in strategic planning and fostering long-term resilience. Often you will have teams with several lines of disconnection. The next section illustrate this.

Coaching connections within the team

This requires team coaches to shift their focus from listening to individual team members, to attending to the spaces and relationships between them. When sitting in on a team meeting, the team coach can listen, observe and tune in to the flows between the team members: who speaks to whom; where the eye-contact is directed; whose comments get built on and developed; whose ideas are disagreed with; and whose suggestions are ignored.

There are several ways to map the connections between team members. Socio-mapping and picture sculpts (Hawkins, 2021) are visual techniques for coaches to analyse and map the relationships, interactions and communication patterns within a team or organization. Coaches plot team members or groups as nodes and use lines or distances to represent the strength and frequency of interactions. This helps identify collaboration gaps, communication silos and relational dynamics, providing insights to enhance team effectiveness and systemic performance. This technique provides ways of both playing back a variety of psychometric personality differences in a team and real-time socio-mapping the way they are enacted in meetings (see Hawkins, 2021: 361–63 for an example of how to constellate the Myers-Briggs personality assessments across a team). Such approaches can help teams better understand the richness of diversity they contain, and what forms of diversity are missing from their group, that may be necessary to bring in. It can also help the team see where team members are competing for the same space, or where interpersonal antagonism is due to different ways of seeing and experiencing the world.

There are also a number of methods for mapping the connections (and disconnections) between the team of teams, as well as the organization and its stakeholders. Examples of these are included in Chapter 14.

Coaching difficult relationships

Sometimes we are asked to coach a difficult stuck or conflictual relationship within a team. Our starting point is to explore what this relationship is carrying for the wider systemic levels it is embedded within. Often their relationship is carrying a polarized disconnection that exists in the team, the organization or the wider stakeholder ecosystem. One may be holding the need to focus on stability and continuity, the other the need for change and movement. One may be holding the need to reduce costs and the other the need to expand into new products or markets. One may be voicing the needs of the investors or funders, and one the needs of customers, suppliers or employees. Once the systemic nature of the conflict is surfaced, we can coach the pairing in how they might take this polarity back to the team and invite them collectively to explore how to find a third place that connects both systemic needs, without being a transactional compromise.

The other important intervention that we learnt from both having provided counselling and therapy for couples and families in the past, is to ask them what the team and the wider organization need from their relationship, and not to start from a transactional inquiry of what they both need from the other? This helps by establishing a joint purpose that requires them to work better together, in the same way that we do for teams.

Coaching the networked connections between teams in the organizations

No team is an island on its own, its internal dynamics are continuously shaped by, and in turn, influence, the interactions with other teams within the broader network.

Pittinsky (2009: xiii) writes how team cohesion 'can exact a price. Classic research by sociologists and psychologists has identified a general tension between internal cohesion… and external conflict… which I refer to as the "in-group/out-group trade-off", [which] can be either a boon or a trap.'

Over-focussing on coaching the connections within a team can build internal cohesion at the price of a decrease in external connectedness. Focussing on external connections, before there is collective responsibility inside the team, can lead to a team of fragmented unconnected activity and work. The internal and external connections need to be developed and evolved in sync with each other. At times, as team of teams coaches, we have to resist the team's demands to just focus on one or the other, or to completely address one dimension before even attending to the other.

In Systemic Team Coaching a common way for the team coach to increase this awareness with the team is through mapping their internal and external stakeholder relational field. This can be done either visually, by the team drawing a picture sculpt, or by an enacted network sculpt or constellation.

Mapping external connections in a team meeting

When attending a team meeting, the systemic team coach can also listen for the external relationships that are mentioned or invoked. We have found it useful to have a check list of potential internal and external stakeholders/ecosystemic partners and to mark down which are mentioned within the meetings or workshops. Those that are talked about can be scored on a scale:

1 mentioned but in a derogatory way

2 mentioned by one person but not responded to by other

3 discussed by several team members

4 discussed and ways of engaging them more effectively are planned

5 a team member speaks as the stakeholder/ecosystemic partners bringing their perspective live into the room, and the team find new ways of responding to the that person/entity

6 a representative of the stakeholder/ecosystemic partners attends the meeting and is listened to, and new ways of partnering are developed

7 there is two-way representation with someone from each team or group attending the other's meetings

Over several meetings this starts to show where external relationship flows are strong or weak, and where the stakeholder group is out of awareness.

The connection with visitors to team meetings

We have attended many leadership team meetings where representatives from other teams and groups, both within and sometimes outside of the organization, are invited to present. Often, we have seen instances of 'guests' being kept waiting, well beyond the time they were told they would present, sometimes with no apology. We have witnessed the team leader fail to welcome guests introduce them, or clarify why they were invited and what joint outcomes the engagement needs to achieve. Often they also neglect to summarize what has been agreed outline next steps, before thanking them for attending the meeting.

To address this, we often invite the team to reflect on how they imagine visitors feel when attending one of their meetings, and what changes might improve how they engage with guests. Over time we have seen an enormous shift in the engagement with those invited to attend team meetings. In one team they agreed that for every team visitor they would assign a team member host, who would take responsibility for bringing them in, ensuring a welcome and introductions, and providing the frame for the two-way engagement and ensuring that a summary and next steps happened before thanking the person for attending.

Nudging cross-team collaboration

Many teams become so over-focussed on their immediate and internal issues that they forget that they are one part of a team of teams, and that many other teams are resources they can learn from, partner with, and through whom they can access expertise and connections. These are also teams that may need to receive their learning, innovation and resources. Cross-team collaboration needs constant nudging from both team leaders and team of team coaches.

In Chapter 14 we include the team of team nudges I, Peter, developed for team leaders, coaches and team coaches to stimulate global networking and cross-boundary teaming. We have successfully implemented these in two large global organizations such that they have begun to change the conversations in ways that have stimulated more, and better, networking connecting and partnering. Every team leader should have these front of mind in every team meeting.

Coaching the connections between agenda items and initiatives

Most of you will have attended team or board meetings that have an itemized agenda of separate atomized and seemingly disconnected items, often with different people leading and speaking on each issue. This atomization creates a culture of every issue being a separate problem to be solved in isolation, with team members only engaging if they think it is directly relevant to their role. It also has the consequence that critical interdependencies and unforeseen knock-on consequences are often not noticed or addressed.

With one board, I, Peter was very aware that the non-executive members had no real sense of the interconnections between different issues and proposals and would just engage the executive member who was primarily responsible for that area. This had the effect of increasing the silo working in the organization and the lack of collective ownership by the executive leadership team. Having explored this with the team, they decided that every agenda item would have a top sheet on the presented paper, showing in diagrammatic form its connections with other strategic items of the organization. They gradually developed a common template that looked something like a subway, metro or underground train network, showing all the cross-links between strategic plans, initiatives and issues.

In another large organization, I, Peter, was called in to coach the top executive team of 17 people. Not only was the team large, but the agendas were enormous! When I started, I was struck by the team having five large strategic change initiatives: one led by marketing, one by the strategy department, one by HR, one on core values and purpose, and one on structure! I very quickly picked up that this was creating competition for time and prominence on the weekly agenda, confusion among the employees and was in danger of unnecessary duplication of effort.

We spent time exploring and capturing on a large chart, the purpose and hoped-for outcomes for each initiative and for which stakeholders each initiative created value. Then we put all five charts on a large wall, and I asked the team to look at how they were interconnected and to draw these connections across the charts.

Very soon they concluded they needed one change initiative for the organization with a small number of interconnected sub-sections. When the wider organization heard this they breathed a sigh of relief!

Coaching inter-team connections

We use the term inter-team coaching specifically for coaching the relationships between teams inside an organization, which could be either across vertical or horizontal connections. By vertical, we refer to coaching a team with either the team hierarchically above it, or with the teams that report into it. By horizontal, we mean coaching the relationships between teams at the same level. Sometimes we will work with both dimensions. Both inter-team types are examples of team of teams coaching 'team of teams' coaching.

In vertical inter-team coaching, one of the most common approaches is to focus on the inter-relationship between the team and the next senior team above them. Often the work of the team is sub-optimal because they do not have a clear commission from their bosses. Just asking for more clarity, direction, expectations or resources rarely delivers what is necessary. Many senior teams cannot provide full clarity of what is required from the teams that report into it. They can often only spot what is missing, when it is not delivered, but find it much harder to describe what 'good will look like' ahead of time. This can lead to a great deal of frustration.

To overcome this oft-repeated pattern, we will suggest a workshop bringing both teams together (this could also be an executive team and a board). At this workshop we will often start by having both teams collectively co-create the necessary outcomes for the workshop. This can be done by having them all individually contribute to boards that are titled:

- This workshop will be a success for our joint relationship if…
- This workshop will be a success for our organization if…
- This workshop will be a success for our joint customers and suppliers if…
- This workshop will be a success for our joint employees if…
- This workshop will be a success for our joint investors (or community partners) if…
- To achieve that success what we need from each other and from our team coaches is…

Once we have a joint co-created agenda, we can sense whether we can go straight to co-creating a better future interconnection or whether we need to first do work on the current relationship. If the former, we could ask all those present to complete, by themselves, the sentence, 'if we had a much better value-creating partnership in a year's time, we would be doing the following…' using between three and five bullet points. Then we can do a collective build (see Hawkins, 2021: 371–72) to co-create together a collective list that can then be prioritized. This provides a clear jointly created vision of what good collaboration and partnering would look like, feel like and sound like. We can then ask small groups, drawn from across the two teams, to take a specific area and work out the steps that will provide the roadmap, and necessary steps, to travel towards the desired destination.

If the team has too much resentment, frustration or antagonism towards each other, then we might choose to do a more foundational inter-team exchange. A simple framework for this is to ask each team to separately create the top three things that they:

a. appreciate and value about the other team

b. find difficult about the other team

c. request from the other team

After a reasonable period of preparation, we would invite the team to come back together and first share their responses to a, then b and finally c, alternating who goes first.

Coaching connections in individual coaching

When coaching individual team leaders or team members one can also bring a relational perspective to the coaching. When they tell you about their difficult customer, or terrible boss, you can simply play back the situation, not as a problem but as a challenge which is in the relational connection. When they tell you: 'The board never adds any value', you reply: 'I understand that you have not yet found a way of getting value from your board.' When they say: 'This member of staff is so resistant', you reply: 'I hear that you have not yet found a way of engaging them that they will respond to.' In each case you are not locating the problem in either them or the other but locating a challenge in the connection or relationship. We have found this far more productive and makes for a quicker route towards a way forward.

It is also possible to use the team of teams nudges (see earlier in this chapter and Chapter 14) in one-to-one coaching, inviting the coachee to focus on the resources, opportunities and needs in the wider network.

Here is an example of the journey from team coaching to 'team of teams' coaching, beginning to focus on coaching the connections.

Leveros case study: coaching the connections: a multi-year journey

Leveros, a Brazilian family business in the Heating Ventilation and Air-Conditioning (HVAC) sector, faced a pivotal moment in its growth journey. While the organization excelled at operations and innovation, its leadership team struggled with fragmentation. Decision-making was overly centralized, communication lacked structure and trust among leaders was low. Tiziano, the CEO, recognized the need for a shift from a command-and-control approach to a more collaborative and connected organization. His vision of 'One Leveros' became the driving force behind this transformation – a vision of fostering shared leadership, interdependence and purposeful connections across the company.

BUILDING THE FOUNDATION (2021–2022)

The journey began with coaching the leadership team. The team coaches facilitated candid discussions to surface the team's challenges, including unspoken tensions and a lack of alignment. Through guided exercises, the team articulated a shared vision, creating a charter that defined their purpose and the value they aimed to deliver to stakeholders.

Crucially, the CEO confronted his own role in the dysfunction. Recognizing his tendency to centralize decisions, he began stepping back, allowing his team to take ownership of their areas. New communication rituals, such as regular alignment meetings, created a rhythm of collaboration. Gradually, trust began to rebuild, and the team moved from fragmented operations to a more cohesive, purpose-driven unit.

One of the turning points came when the leadership team collectively realized the importance of balancing operational demands with long-term strategy (see Sharpe, 2020). This was the first step in preparing the team to act as stewards of the company's future, rather than mere managers of its present.

DEEPENING LEADERSHIP AND EXPANDING COLLABORATION (2023–2024)

As the leadership team matured, the team coaching expanded into team of teams coaching, to encompass mid-level leaders who were essential for cascading the cultural transformation. Individual coaching sessions helped these leaders gain clarity on their roles and develop their capacities for strategic thinkers, and team coaching fostered collaboration among teams that previously operated in silos.

A significant milestone came when the leadership team successfully developed Leveros's first three-year strategic plan – a process that required not only clear thinking but also a high degree of trust and shared purpose. For Tiziano, this shift was profound. No longer the sole decision-maker, he transitioned into the role of orchestrator, empowering his team to take the lead.

The restructuring of the leadership team was another pivotal moment. Reducing its size to a more focussed group enabled faster decision-making and more meaningful connections. With a smaller, tightly aligned top team, Leveros began to operate less as a hierarchy and more as an interconnected system.

TRANSFORMING INTO A TEAM OF TEAMS (2024–PRESENT)

With foundational shifts in place, the next phase centred on creating a 'team of teams' structure throughout the organization. The coaches guided the leadership team to map stakeholder ecosystems (see Chapter 14) and clarify the interdependencies between functions. Offsite workshops became spaces for connection, where teams not only aligned on strategic objectives but also explored the cultural shifts required to work as a unified system.

One powerful moment came during a two-day event where functional teams presented their revised team charters. These charters outlined their vision, purpose and key objectives, fostering a shared understanding of how their contributions aligned with the organization's larger goals.

The cultural transformation was not without its challenges. As Tiziano reflected, 'Giving autonomy is a chaotic process.' But this process ultimately equipped leaders with the skills and confidence to collectively lead and make better decisions, fostering an environment of agility and mutual trust.

OUTCOMES

The multi-year journey transformed Leveros into a more cohesive, connected organization. Tiziano's evolution as a leader-coach set the tone for a culture of empowerment and trust. Silos dissolved as teams embraced their interdependencies, and the organization's vision of 'One Leveros' became a tangible reality. Leveros now operates as an ecosystem of partnerships, with stronger internal and external networks, a unified strategic direction, and an enhanced ability to create value for all stakeholders.

FINAL TAKEAWAY

Coaching the connections is about creating intentional linkages – between individuals, teams and the larger organizational system. Across all phases, the focus should remain on fostering alignment, trust and collaboration, while equipping leaders to navigate the complexities of shared leadership and interconnected ecosystems. Coaches who guide teams to embrace this interconnectedness can help organizations move from fragmentation to thriving, purpose-driven systems.

Conclusion

In this chapter we have offered many ways and examples of coaching connections, in teams, between teams, and between the team of teams, and between the, wider organization and its stakeholders. However, the work begins not with new tools and methods but with new ways of attending, focussing where we look, how we listen, and what we reflect back to teams and networks. Our modernist education encourages us to see, name and analyse separate atomized things and entities, leading us to live in a world of individuals, rather than an evolving meshwork of interconnected relationships and systems.

To coach connections rather than parts requires a paradigm shift, in our perception, thinking, doing and being. We relate within an interconnected world, where no part can be understood fully, apart from its relational context and wider systems. We must also recognize that the world we see is not static and networks and connections are not fixed, but always evolving and becoming. By the time we have mapped and analysed those connections they have become something new. While mapping is often necessary to reveal the patterns of interconnection, we should never confuse the map with the territory, or the territory with the ever-changing ecology of becoming.

10

Every team is a team of teams: the contributions of Systemic Team of Teams Approach to Systemic Team Coaching

Introduction

Individual executive coaches are beginning to wake up to the realization that they are never coaching an individual, but rather are addressing the development needs of teams, organizations, stakeholders and the future world. Similarly, as team coaches, we must recognize that we are never coaching a singular executive team. To be a systemic team coach is to understand that our goal is not just to enhance a team's internal efficiency and performance but to partner with a team in continually co-creating greater value with and for all stakeholders.

Most teams in organizations, aside from front-line teams, consist of members who also lead other teams. Therefore, these members naturally bring the needs and perspectives of their own team into other teams where they are a member. In an executive team, for example, the Sales Director represents the sales function, the Chief Financial Officer (CFO) represents finance, the Chief People Officer represents the HR function, and so on for other members. Even the CEO is typically a member of a more senior team, whether it's the company's board or the executive team of the group holding company. Thus, the executive team functions as a team of teams.

As a systemic team coach, except for front-line teams, you are always coaching a team of teams. Understanding this dynamic is crucial for effective team leadership and Systemic Team Coaching.

Building the Baptist Integration Centre: a team of teams transformation

The Baptist Integration Centre (BIK) operates as a vital branch of Baptist Aid, a close-knit ecosystem in Hungary with a profound societal impact. Baptist Aid employs around 3,000 people across three main pillars: international rescue operations through the Baptist Aid Foundation, site management providing shelters for people in crisis, and a robust network of primary and secondary schools run by the Baptist Church. These legally distinct yet interconnected entities share a unifying leadership board and a commitment to reducing prejudice, mental distress and inequality.

Within this ecosystem, the BIK focusses on sheltering homeless individuals and families in crisis across six locations in Budapest. Its five individual shelters and a dual-institute family shelter, known as the Transitional Home of Families (CsÁO), serve as lifelines for vulnerable populations. However, the leadership team faced a significant challenge: how to collaborate effectively across sites while addressing the unique demands of each location. With site managers deeply committed to their local missions, the organization struggled to align on collective priorities. The BIK leadership began an ambitious journey to transform into a cohesive team of teams, striving to balance autonomy with unified action and foster a culture of collaboration across its operations.

This tension mirrored a broader organizational shift within Baptist Aid, a sprawling charity network addressing education, disaster relief and homelessness. Baptist Aid's leadership recognized that fostering alignment across its interconnected operations was essential to achieving its purpose of inclusive support for vulnerable populations. The Systemic Team Coaching process became the catalyst for this transformation, enabling the BIK leadership to embrace their dual roles as both independent leaders and part of a larger collective purpose.

The systemic team of teams coach, Beata Barkoczi, not only coached the connections across the teams and organization, but also the connections to the global challenges. She worked within the wider Baptist Integration Centre (BIK) to clarify their purpose and align their work with the United Nations Sustainable Development Goals (SDGs). BIK identified its impact on seven key SDGs, while the broader Baptist Aid organization also addressed global challenges such as the climate emergency, zero hunger and quality education. This alignment helped the Centre ground its mission in a global framework for sustainability.

During the coaching process, the leadership team assessed their strengths using the Inner Development Goals (IDG) Framework, which supports sustainable action tied to the SDGs. They identified inner compass, empathy and compassion as key strengths while noting opportunities to build skills like communication, perseverance and long-term visioning. Team coaching interventions focussed on these areas, helping the team strengthen their collective capacity to lead for systemic change.

Mapping the complexity: why understanding the system was critical

The systemic team coach began by tackling the team's sense of fragmentation. Using stakeholder mapping, the coach guided the team in visualizing their connections within and beyond BIK. This exercise revealed significant interdependencies – such as how decisions at one site impacted resource allocation at another – and illuminated areas where collaboration was either missing or fraught with tension.

To dig deeper, the coach introduced empathy mapping, a tool that helped the team step into the shoes of their key stakeholders, including site staff, residents and external partners. By understanding the needs, challenges and emotions of these groups, the team began to see their work not as isolated efforts but as part of a shared ecosystem. One site manager reflected, 'We always thought we were just doing our best for our site, but now we see how what we do here affects everyone.'

These exercises helped the leadership team acknowledge that their silos weren't just operational barriers – they were obstacles to fulfilling their shared purpose. The team realized they couldn't achieve their broader goals without acting as a cohesive system.

Clarifying roles and priorities: the turning point

With a clearer understanding of their interconnectedness, the team needed a framework for moving forward. The coach facilitated a workshop using a method for mapping 'Circle of Influence' (Covey, 2013), challenging the team to distinguish between the areas they could control, influence or needed to accept. This shift in focus was pivotal; instead of fixating on external limitations like funding or policy constraints, the team concentrated on actionable priorities within their sphere of influence – such as improving communication across sites looking for synergies and service improvement initiatives in three time horizons.

This clarity of focus led to the creation of a shared leadership charter, outlining the team's collective purpose and defining their roles as part of a larger team of teams. The coaches emphasized that the charter was not just a document but a tool to guide decision-making and foster accountability across the group.

The breakthrough came during a leadership gathering, where the systemic team coaches introduced systemic mapping to highlight the 'spaces in between' the teams. These were the areas where the most significant opportunities for collaboration – and potential friction – existed. Using this approach, the team identified several practical initiatives, including resource-sharing, cross-site problem-solving sessions. In addition, the team created a five-year strategy plan for the organization for the first time.

A key moment of transformation occurred when site managers took turns representing the perspectives of their peers, exploring how decisions at one site affected another. This exercise fostered a new level of empathy and trust among the team. As one leader noted, 'I used to think my challenges were unique, but now I see how similar we all are – and how much stronger we can be if we work together.'

The team began to embrace a team of teams identity, recognizing that their individual success was tied to the collective's ability to collaborate and align. This shift from independence to interdependence marked the turning point in their journey.

By the end of the coaching engagement, the BIK leadership team had transformed into a cohesive collective they called the 'BIK Collective'. They had implemented several systemic practices, including:

- **Collective strategic lens:** This involves utilizing a stakeholder-informed, future-back and outside-in perspective to collaboratively design a cohesive and impactful strategy.
- **Cross-site initiatives:** Collaborative problem-solving forums to address shared challenges and sharing training and resources across sites.
- **Feedback loops:** Regular check-ins to ensure alignment with the leadership charter and purpose.

The Systemic Team Coaching intervention not only strengthened the BIK leadership team's internal dynamics but also positioned them as a model of collaboration within Baptist Aid. The team's ability to act as a team of teams rippled outward, inspiring other teams within the organization to adopt similar practices.

Using a Systemic Team of Teams Approach to address team conflict

Teams will often personalize issues rather than learning how to hold and work with this complexity (see Chapter 2, 'It's not personal!'). This often results in teams having too little conflict rather than too much, but the conflict that does arise is often personalized instead of being addressed systemically. I, Peter, developed the Law of Requisite Conflict, which states that: 'A team should have neither more nor less conflict than exists in the wider system it leads and the stakeholder ecosystem that it works within' (Hawkins, 2021).

This principle highlights the importance of addressing conflict in a systemic manner, considering its broader implications and context, as well as seeing the team, not as an island, but also as a holographic fractal of the wider systems it is nested within, and which in turn lives and breathes within them.

From a systemic perspective, every team member carries wider stakeholder needs and perspectives into the room and the coach needs to understand how to work with all the players' needs that are not actually in the room but in some ways are. The Sales Director will have absorbed the needs of the customer, the Chief People Officer the needs of the employees, and the CFO the needs of the investors, auditors and regulators. In our many years of working with senior teams, much of the conflict that emerges interpersonally in teams stems from the roots of each person carrying different systemic needs and pressures. These needs are often expressed and heard as personal opinions and then opposed by other team members who are carrying different stakeholder needs and pressures.

Handling the tension of multiple membership

Some senior teams try and manage these tensions, by the CEO asking their team members to make this executive team their number one team and leave their other team memberships and identity outside the team meeting door. In our experience in most cases this is impossible as much of what we are carrying is outside of full conscious awareness. It is part of the sub-culture we are immersed in, and as we have previously defined, 'culture is what you stop noticing when you have worked somewhere for three months' (Hawkins and Smith, 2013). Sub-cultures, like cultures, become part of your ways of seeing issues, hearing others, framing problems, reacting and responding.

There is another danger in trying to leave your other team identity outside the room, in that this can lead to a form of vertical organizational splitting, and the team member, leaving their membership of the senior team outside the door, when they are part of the team they lead. This can be seen in the case example below.

Another way teams and team coaches address tension is to try and build psychological safety and collaboration, by focussing on areas of agreement and alignment in the team and leaving areas of systemic conflict outside the door of the team meeting. The members act as fully signed up and aligned members of the top team, for the time they are all meeting together. The team coach thinks things are going really well! But then as soon as they leave the room, they stop being a member of the top team and become members and leaders of their own functional team. This then creates conflict and silos between the different areas they each separately lead.

A government executive team becoming a team of teams

A large government department asked me, Peter, to coach their senior executive team, comprising leaders of their three main operational divisions and the heads of the main central functions (Finance, HR, Policy, IT etc.). They invited me to attend their weekly executive team meetings and explore how they could work better as a team. Their meetings were extremely well run with a supporting secretariat, every item timed to the minute, and all team members fully engaged and committed. There was very little conflict or disagreement despite the department being under enormous pressure. It was undertaking a major organizational transformation, to reduce its workforce by 25 per cent, while simultaneously facing increased demand for its services, and both service users' and politicians' rising expectations that it raise the quality of its services.

I imagined that as the team meetings were so smooth and non-conflictual the pressure must be hidden under the waterline. Very soon I discovered there was significant tension and conflict two levels down within the organization, with competing silos unable to collaborate effectively together and competing for limited resources. What became clear is that every member of the top team was a fully committed top team member on the Wednesday morning they were together but ceased their top team membership the moment they walked out of the door and went back to leading their own team and department.

I was reminded of my own early experience of leading a key organizational department and being on the national executive. In their own ways each side of this vertical divide asked me: 'Are you part of them or part of us?' It took me some time to be able to say: 'Both and neither – I am committed to what has to happen between both teams for us to partner better together.'

With the government department they had to discover together how to bring the systemic conflict into the senior team meetings, without the conflict becoming interpersonal or competitive. Instead, the aim was to create a space where the whole team could hear and take responsibility for the different conflicting needs of the various functions and divisions, and more importantly, their stakeholders. The service users and recipients needed and wanted better quality services; the taxpayer less taxes; the politicians a service they could show they had improved while reducing costs; and the regulator clearer reporting, documentation and audit trail of decisions, actions and spend.

Only when the senior team could move beyond listening politely to each other, and systemically listen through the individual to the team, function and stakeholders that they belonged to, and were responsible for, could the team begin to take collective responsibility for discovering how to weave together the seemingly conflicting needs and create a 'win-win-win' for all stakeholders.

Systemic Team Coaching one team, using a systemic team of teams perspective

It is easy to either get pulled into the immediate team dynamic or trying to find a resolution yourself to emerging issues, rather than come alongside and partner with the team. To do this, we must develop the four key systemic aspects of perceiving, thinking, being and doing, beyond the current level of the team and those they serve. This four-step process of developing systemic awareness is described in detail in Chapter 12.

Conclusion

Many leaders today are members of multiple teams, including the team they lead, the more senior team they are a member of, as well as cross-functional teams, innovation teams, client-facing teams, or external teams in partnerships, professional bodies, or the wider community. We have worked with some senior leaders who were members of over 20 different teams. To be a fully committed member of so many teams and manage the different team identities and loyalties is an enormous personal stretch. In this chapter, we have argued that it is necessary to go further and be responsible for developing the effective connection and partnership between these various teams. This requires us to find effective ways of carrying each team identity into the other teams we enter while not defaulting to just being a representative spokesperson or delegate of that team but a full member of both teams and a bridge and connector between the two.

In this chapter we have shown how every team, other than front-line teams, are also, in essence, team of teams, with team members coming from other teams they lead or are a member of. This requires every senior team leader and systemic team coach to view the team, not as a bounded discreet entity, but as a fractal of the larger team of teams and develop ways of attending to the larger systemic dynamics as represented through the individual team members, as well as the systemic relational dynamics between them. This requires all team leaders and team coaches to adopt and develop a systemic approach to leading and coaching teams.

11

Coaching the inner team: the contributions of a Systemic Team of Teams Approach to individual coaching

Introduction

The theories, models and approaches of Systemic Team of Teams Coaching, can provide guidance on insight, not only to work with whole organizations, but also for coaching and mentoring individuals. For as Jean Boulton (2024: 185) points out, the individual themself 'is a complex, interwoven, relationally shaped "becoming"'.

The individual, like the team and the organization, is not a fixed entity but a constant becoming, and neither are we singular, for each of us have multiple 'I's. Jean Bolton goes on to show how we are:

> constituted through the relationship with our environment, and impacted by the people and pets and possessions that surround us. We are shaped by our past, shaped by our present – yet always becoming. In some ways, we can feel caught in patterns – or behaviour, of expectations, or social norms – from which, at times, it can feel, there is no escape. At other times, we adapt, transform and surprise ourselves. (Boulton, 2024: 185)

In 2023, I, Peter, wrote an article entitled 'Is your inner team more than the sum of its parts' in which I said:

> The most essential teams we must coach is the 'inner team' that each team member and coach need to lead. We believe that integrating the inner team not

only transforms individual coaching but also leads to us being more effective contributors to external teams, whether as systemic team coaches, team leaders or team members.

> Each person is part of many teams – their immediate team, the team below, beside and above, committee teams, external teams, family and community teams and that of the natural world around them. How do they hold all those teams in every team interaction they are in? The more integrated someone is within themselves, the better they can serve the various teams they are on. (Hawkins, 2023a)

In this chapter, we will first look at different approaches to understanding our internal team of many roles and sub-personalities, and how a STOT approach can help us coach the inner team in others.

The concept of the inner team

Each of us has many different roles which are matched by different sub-personalities. We think we have just one 'I', but we have many 'I's. Sometimes these different parts of us complement and support each other: other times they disagree and fight with one another.

Wilson (2023) questions the assumption that there is one true and unified self. He argues that the self is multi-faceted and sometimes these different aspects of self can be contradictory. The spiritual teacher Gurdjieff (Ouspensky, 1950) described how the 'I' that goes to bed committed to getting up early, is not the same 'I' that wakes up in the morning. He also wrote:

> Man has no individual I. But there are, instead, hundreds and thousands of separate small 'I's, very often entirely unknown to one another, never coming into contact, or, on the contrary, hostile to each other, mutually exclusive and incompatible. Each minute, each moment, man is saying or thinking, 'I'. And each time his 'I' is different. Just now it was a thought, now it is a desire, now a sensation, now another thought, and so on, endlessly. Man is a plurality. Man's name is legion. (quoted in Ouspensky, 1950: 59)

Some theorists and psychotherapists including Jungians (Jung, 1966), psychosynthesis writers (Assagioli, 1993) and object relations writers (Winnicott, 1965), argue that maturity comes with having an integration of one's different identities and sub-personalities. This integration is guided through the developing of a core inner self that can act as a witness or a stage director, or team leader, to the various self-identities.

Roccas and Brewer (2002) developed this further with their concept of *social identity complexity* where different identities conflict with one another. Daniel Goleman sums up this paradox when he writes: 'no one has just one fully integrated self-image, a single harmonious version of the self. Various points and stages in life accrue overlapping selves, some congruent, others not' (Goleman, 1998: 102).

This multiplicity of selves is not only psychological but deeply emotional. Research in neuroscience, psychology and behavioural economics show that emotions influence a substantial portion of our choices, from everyday decisions to major life changes. While we like to think that we make rational, logical choices, emotions often serve as the underlying force that guides our thought processes. In the workplace, this emotional influence emerges in how we make decisions under pressure, manage relationships and navigate conflicts. For instance, a manager may unconsciously favour one team member over another based on emotional rapport and 'likeness', or employees might resist change because of prior experiences and underlying fears, or anxieties, even when logic supports the decision.

Several therapeutic models help us understand and work with these inner dynamics. The Internal Family Systems (IFS) model (Schwartz, 2023) describes some of our internal family members as inner critics, protectors or exiles. Each part has a purpose and all are important in some way, albeit sometimes exaggerated versions of themselves.

Similarly, Gestalt psychotherapy and coaching (Parlett, 2024; Perls, 1969) views the person as a whole made up of fragmented parts that need to be interconnected. Allowing oneself to surface and experience the full range of emotions, thoughts, images and sensations in the present moment fosters integration and wholeness. Transactional Analysis (TA) offers a model of how our inner team may have sub-personalities that act from different familiar roles, or ego states, and they focus on those of 'Parent, Adult, and Child'. Our inner Parent may come across as overly controlling or authoritative or be overly supportive and protective of others. Our Child state might respond with adaptive or rebellious behaviour.

Our times increasingly require us to develop a *protean self* which has high flexibility and adaptability to the flux of our times.

> We are becoming fluid and many-sided. Without quite realizing it, we have been evolving a sense of self appropriate to the restlessness and flux of our time. This mode of being differs radically from that of the past and enables us to engage in continuous exploration and personal experiment. I have named it the 'protean self', after Proteus, the Greek sea god of many forms. (Lifton, 1993: 1)

To develop coherence, maturity and what the Chinese call Ren, or heart-mind wisdom, we need to develop a personal coherence. Our protean self must also have a rich coherence where, like players in the orchestra, the inner team can co-create a depth of music that no sub-personality could ever create alone.

Developing and integrating the inner team

We can start developing our inner team by discovering more about each of the team members. Each of these is co-created in the space between us and the worlds we inhabit. In Hawkins (2023a) I described some of the members of my own inner team:

> I have in my team, a teacher, writer, organizational consultant, coach, gardener, husband, father, and grandfather. Then there are the less prominent members, such as an avid reader, one who loves good food and wine and entertaining, the humorous one, the meditator, the one who loves young children, a poet, friend, walker, and the one who watches cricket and sport. Then there is the integrating and orchestrating 'Self', who witnesses these different roles and sub-personalities and who needs to play the role of the team leader.

In coaching sessions, I, Catherine, invite coachees to draw, name and characterize the members of their inner team and how they are connected. Later they might consider whether it is time to update their drawing to include or recontract with inner team members to support what they need now, versus what served them in the past. Just as we teach leaders to transcend either/or polarities, into a third possibility, one can do this with competing inner roles. This can help create balance and healing in the inner team by understanding and validating the truth within the needs and fears of each part and aligning to higher order values and purpose.

I, Catherine, worked with a leader who was cycling between sharing contradictory messaging to the team around modernizing operations. It sounded like the leader was committed to this new bold corporate direction, but also to a counter commitment of keeping the peace and status quo. Jobs were at stake and people were worried. Those on this leader's team expressed confusion, frustration and over time cynical resignation about real change.

Together we mapped the leader's various inner team members or 'parts'. One member (Daring Driver) wanted to do the right thing and drive the team towards bold new goals, another (Cautious Caretaker) wanted to go slower and take more care. The leader felt overwhelmed and stressed. Through coaching conversations the leader discovered two other parts including a 'Fearful Critic' that was convinced that they would fail if they tried. This third part feared people would hate them for it, confirming core beliefs that they were ultimately inadequate as a leader and person. A fourth part, 'Centred Self', could facilitate a dialogue between the other three. This internal kind of conflict is common, as many leaders believe they need to appear strong and so are quick to state their desire to move forward then privately get knotted up in indecision and inaction, representing what Kegan calls having one foot on the gas and one on the brake (Kegan and Lahey, 2009).

Together we (virtually with a whiteboard) explored the leader's and team's purpose, vision and values, then mapped the various conflicting parts within the leader. By being curious, and listening deeply, the leader was able to able to express concerns and desires. They could see where every part had played an important role for them in their life, but were not integrated and working effectively together. Once the leader listened to all their 'internal team members' they could see what life drama they were re-enacting, saw it was no longer a play they needed to be in, and were able to progress forward. Their Centred Self ensured that all team members got updated job descriptions!

The five disciplines of the inner team

I, Peter, have developed and refined the model of the 'Five Disciplines of High-Value Creating Teams' over the last 20 years (Hawkins, 2011b, 2015, 2018, 2021, 2022b) and in this book we have developed a new model of the 'Five Disciplines of High-Value Creating Team of Teams' (see Chapter 6). In this chapter we will outline a new model 'The Five Disciplines of High-Value Creating Individuals'. Each of these models uses the same starting framework and the belief that all living organisms of whatever size need to be co-creating beneficial value with and for all their stakeholders, and for all the larger systemic levels they are nested within. The same five disciplines are reflected in each level of the system, but how they are lived and developed changes for each level (organization, team of teams, team, individual), in the same way that family therapy and individual therapy may share the same psychological foundation but have different frameworks and methods.

We will now outline methods for working with each of these five disciplines, which you can do for yourself, and then also use to support the development of people you lead or coach.

1. Purpose

Purpose involves discovering who and what the life and work of the individual serve and what this wider network appreciates and needs different from them in the future. I have for many years used my favourite purpose question: 'What can you uniquely do that the world of tomorrow needs?', not only for organizations and teams (Hawkins, 2021), but also in coaching individuals (Hawkins and Turner, 2020). This is a great place to start in discovering your inner team's core purpose.

One of the methods going deeper in exploring this question with individuals is Ikigai, which we have learnt from our colleagues in Japan. According to the Japanese, everyone has an Ikigai, which can be roughly translated as a reason for living or a raison d'être. This model has helped many Japanese people plan and live a happier, more focussed, meaningful, and longer life. It is a model to help you first clarify and then integrate:

a. what you love

b. what you're good at

c. what you can get paid for

d. and what the world needs (Garcia and Miralles, 2017)

Japanese elders who have developed their Ikigai, rarely retire (both authors are past retirement age and have no plans to retire). They remain active and work at what they enjoy, because they've found a real purpose in life, that all parts of their inner team can contribute to.

Once you or your coachees have addressed the strategy question and carried out your Ikigai mapping exercise, you can address the question: 'Who does their work and life serve?' These stakeholders and partners can be drawn on a large flipchart or whiteboard. This is done by putting a small version of your Ikigai plan in the middle and then clustering all your stakeholders and ecosystemic partners around the page. These may include family, friends, colleagues, employees, bosses, funders, groups and communities and importantly the wider ecology.

Then you or your coachee are ready to undertake a co-inquiry process with all these stakeholder groups of key representatives. The purpose of this inquiry is to discover what they currently value receiving from you, and what is the contribution they need different going forward. For each stakeholder, you step into their shoes, adopt their way of being, either standing or sitting, and speak back to the place representing your inner team, each saying:

- this is what we continue to value about your contribution
- this is what we need different from you in the future
- this is how we think you could make a bigger beneficial value contribution

Now all these 'future-back' perspectives can be reviewed and either we, or our coachees, can develop our personal purpose, from the one we developed using the 'Ikigai' model, to a richer purpose that is connected to the changing needs of our ecosystem.

2. Clarifying

Having developed a personal purpose, we then need to develop a plan to fulfil this purpose. To do this we need to create a clear personal charter, that includes:

- objectives you have for fulfilling your purpose, both medium and long term
- a road map for achieving your objectives, including a timeline and immediate actions
- what you need to start doing, stop doing, and continue doing to increase your impact and accelerate your journey in the planned direction
- the key members of your inner team you need to centrally engage on this journey
- what each of these team members can best contribute to achieving the objectives and furthering the journey

3. Co-creating

Having created your inner team charter, you can now turn to synergistically aligning your inner team so it can be more than the sum of its parts. One of the best ways we have used to coach people in this process is to use an adapted version of Peter's 'Team Contribution Grid' (See Chapter 7 in this book as well as Hawkins, 2021: 376–77).

Each inner team member (sub-personality) reflects on their contributions to the overall self and whole team. This grid can be divided into four sections for each role:

TEAM CONTRIBUTION GRID

1   Three ways I best contribute to the team...

2   Three ways I could contribute more to the team...

3   Three ways I receive value from the team...

4   Three ways I could receive greater value from the team...

Once they have all been completed, then you can put each separate inner team member on a different chair. Next, imagine them all sitting there and one by one giving feedback as you stand in the middle representing the whole team. Picture how they are sitting, their expression, clothes, gestures, words and emotional expression.

If this is not possible, stick them all up on a wall or whiteboard. Arrange them in clusters with those who get on well together, close to each other and those who are disconnected at a distance. Think and sense into how they would respond to each other.

Having listened to all the inner team members, as your own team leader you can explore where you need to facilitate better connections between members; which team members need more attention and time in the spotlight; and which need to be less prominent and move into more of a support role.

Now, as the team leader (Self) composes the message you want all your team members to hear and take on board, complete the following seed sentences:

- Our biggest collective challenges, which requires help from all of you are...
- Together we could achieve so much more in... by...
- To achieve that, the help I need from all of you is...

Once you have written this, try reading it out loud imagining all the different team members in different places in the room. Then compose individual messages for each of the individual members.

- What I value about your contribution is…
- What I find diffcult about you is…
- The difference I need from you going forward is…

In response to each of these, write the commitment that you need each of these roles and sub-personalities to make. Try and be as specific as possible. Hear their responses back and negotiate until you have mutual agreements.

As our own team leader, we need to love and appreciate every member of our inner team and not be ashamed of any one of them. If there are any we really cannot value, we need to find ways of developing them to change or help them successfully leave the team. Our biggest challenge is to help the inner and outer team to be aligned to collective purpose and key future challenges.

4. Connecting with the wider network

We now return to the outside-in perspective that we began in discipline one. You can revisit our stakeholder and partner mapping, and the co-inquiry process we carried out with our stakeholders. You may wish to update this. On the whiteboard or flipchart map of all your stakeholders and partners; you can use different colours and symbols to show the nature and quality of the connection. For each you can show:

a. how much is a one-way or two-way reciprocal relationship
b. where you are on the continuum of becoming a true partnership where together you co-create value for the wider world that you could not do apart
c. which have high levels of mutual respect, trust and commitment, and which have high levels of constructive conflict
d. which energize you and which drain energy from you

You can stand back and look at your network map and notice where there are current or potential connections across your network. Draw these inter-connections. This will help create a more complex meshwork. Your wider world has many interconnections that do not happen just through you.

Now consider which relationships and connections you need to focus on to improve the quality of partnering, and which you need to be less focussed on, to more fully fulfil your purpose and achieve your objectives. This meshwork picture will also help you look at how other interconnections can help you in this process and ensure you do not atomize and create a siloed stakeholder and ecosystem partner world.

5. Core learning

For your inner team to be an effective learning team, you will need to make space in your calendar for regular team reviews. We recommend scheduling such reviews every three months.

These should include:

a. successes you have achieved in fulfilling the purpose and achieving the objectives that you need to celebrate

b. what has worked and not worked on the journey so far

c. what you need to amend, change and develop in your purpose, objectives, actions and inner team working in this next quarter

d. the competencies, capabilities and capacities you need to learn, practice and develop in this next period to be more effective

It is helpful to develop these into clear new habits and disciplines, as it takes strong new habits to replace and let go of no-longer-helpful and ingrained personal habits.

Other helpful models for working with the inner team

To deepen the coaching process, several psychological and leadership models offer invaluable insights. These include:

1 **David Kantor's roles** (2012): Kantor's structural dynamics identify four roles: 'Mover, Follower, Opposer, and Bystander'. I, Peter, have developed a progression of these roles to 'Challenger, Inquirer, Contributor and Implementer' respectively (Hawkins, 2023b). These roles can apply to both inner and outer teams, allowing coaches to recognize patterns in their clients' internal conversations.

2 **Above and below the line roles:** Being above the line (open, creative and committed to learning) or below the line (closed, defensive and committed to being right). Above is responsive and below is reactive (Dethmer, Chapman and Klemp, 2015).

3 **The Drama Triangle** (Karpman, 1968): Clients often unknowingly assume roles of 'Victim, Persecutor or Rescuer' in their inner dialogues. The coach's task is to help clients shift to the more constructive Empowerment Triangle roles: 'Creator, Challenger and Coach', within themselves (Luetz, 2014).

4 **Systemic Awareness:** Understanding inner and outer systems allows us to see how internal dynamics shape external relationships. Coachees can begin to recognize how their internal conflicts mirror outer team dynamics (see Chapter 12).

5 **Vertical Development** (Torbert, 2004): This framework emphasizes the growth of emotional and cognitive capacity, allowing individuals to handle greater complexity. This is essential for those whose inner team must navigate complex environments, both personal and professional (see Chapter 12).

Team coaching check-ins

For many years we have been asked by trainees whether you can combine individual coaching with Systemic Team Coaching. We have responded by providing guidance for when this might be helpful and unhelpful; how you cannot unknow what you have been told by individual in one-to-one coaching and this can interfere or skew how you see the team as a whole; and how if you are co-coaching you cannot provide confidentiality in individual coaching sessions.

Recently two of our faculty colleagues (Dr Hilary Lines and Tim Chapman), provided a clearer framework, describing how if you are systemically coaching a team, it is useful to have two or three touch points with each individual team member, but that these are better referred to as team coaching check-ins, where the focus is on coaching the connection between the individual and the team, and are not personal sessions just for the coachees (see Chapter 9 on coaching the connections). They suggested the following areas of joint focus:

- how they are experiencing the team at the moment
- what they see changing
- what the stakeholders need the team to address next
- what is currently left unsaid

- how they could bring more of themselves to the team
- what that might look like
- then how they might do a fast forward rehearsal of this

Conclusion

To bring coherence to our inner team, and help those we lead, or coach others to do the same, we need to shift from a 'reactive mind, focussed on fixing problems, staying safe and with a tightly held identity: to a 'creative mind' (Kegan, 1994), which harnesses collective potential and focusses on the future. When the inner team aligns around a shared purpose and vision, the creative mind is activated, enabling more constructive and empowered responses and choices, and more inner and outer harmony.

Murray's (1951) famous words, 'Until one is committed, there is hesitancy, the chance to draw back, always ineffectiveness…' capture the essence of this transformation. When clients commit to aligning their inner team, providence, whether we interpret this as luck, opportunity, or grace, begins to favour them.

PART FOUR

Developing the field of Systemic Team of Teams Approach and its practitioners

12

Development and supervision of systemic team of teams leaders, coaches and consultants

Introduction

In this chapter we explore the architecture and core elements needed to train, develop and supervise a systemic team of teams practitioner, whether they are leaders developing their own organization, internal or external coaches, HR professionals or consultants in organizational transformation.

The evolution from Systemic Team Coaching (STC) to Systemic Team of Teams Coaching (STOTC) represents a paradigm shift in how organizations, leaders and coaches approach complexity, collaboration and systemic transformation. While STC mostly focusses on enhancing a single team's capacity and value contribution, STOTC extends this lens across interconnected teams, or 'teams of teams'. This requires a sophisticated integration of coaching, consulting, organizational development (OD) and organizational transformation (OT). We will start by addressing how to train and supervise coaches in this important and demanding work and then look at how to bring STOTA into leadership development.

Transitioning to STOTC requires a significant evolution in both practice and perspective. Our research with over 70 global organizations (as noted in Chapter 8) highlights that coaches working at the team of teams level must combine coaching expertise with a strong foundation in OD and OT. This blend is essential for addressing complex challenges such as building effective networks, overcoming siloism, fostering clear and transformational goal alignment, enabling cultural change and realigning longstanding power dynamics.

The development of architecture

To develop a team of teams in a way that helps transform an organization to being net positive and future-fit cannot be taught didactically or learned solely from books like this. It requires a sophisticated action learning design. This should cycle through the following stages:

- **Thinking:** learning the key models and elements in theory
- **Practising and planning:** practising the key tools and methods, with feedback from trainers and fellow participants
- **Doing:** action learning by coaches and consultants with organizations that the learners either work in or with
- **Reviewing:** built-in evaluation and feedback (see Chapter 7)
- reflection that integrates the above four phases and helps the learner mature their approach (supported by journalling and supervision, see later in this chapter)
- arriving at a new learning edge, with new inquiry and questions for the next cycle

FIGURE 12.1 The STOTA learning and development cycle

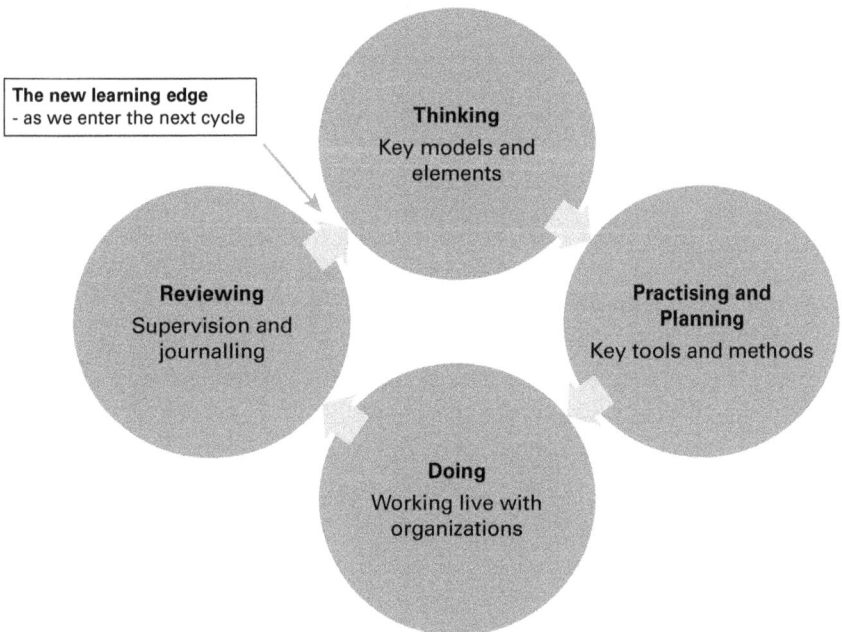

The key elements

Below we outline seven of the most important key elements that need to be focussed on, through the action learning cycles mentioned above.

1. Systemic awareness

As we have indicated throughout this book, systemic awareness is foundational and is both broader and deeper than 'systems thinking'. While it draws on the key developments of systems thinking in the 20th century (Bateson, 1972, 1978, 1979, 1991; Capra, 1996; Hawkins, 2021, 2022b; Prigogine, 1997) and ecological, evolutionary and complexity theory of this century (Boulton, 2024; Capra and Luisi, 2016; Kauffman, 1993, 1995; Lent, 2021), it also draws on indigenous, spiritual and psychological practices that develop our innate abilities in sensory, intuitive, empathic and embodied knowing (Hawkins, 2025). It requires practitioners to go on a journey of personal vertical and horizontal development (see later in this chapter) and also develop the four key systemic aspects of perceiving, thinking, being and doing, beyond the current level of the team and those they serve (see Figure 12.2). This development should be seen as circular, spiral or helical rather than linear steps.

FIGURE 12.2 The spiral of systemic awareness

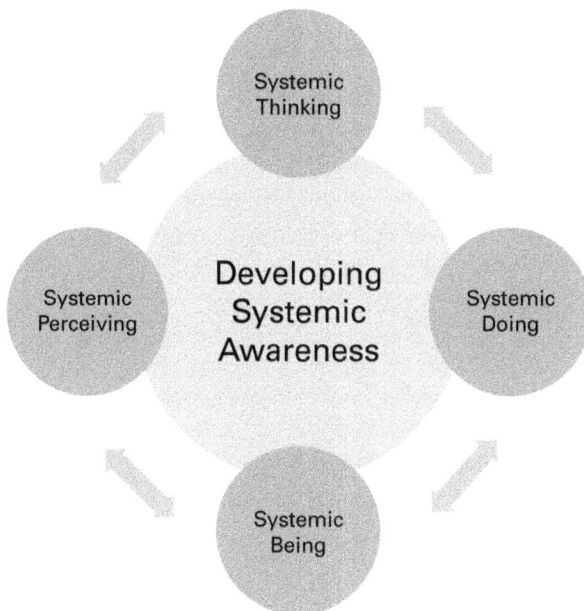

SYSTEMIC PERCEIVING

Once we adopt a systemic lens and see any senior team as a team of teams, our perspective as a systemic team coach begins to shift. We develop our listening skills from focussing on each individual person to listening through the individuals to the different organizational and wider systemic needs they are carrying and giving voice to. We move from empathy and compassion for every individual within the team to 'wide-angled empathy' (Hawkins, 2019a) for their direct reports, their colleagues and bosses, and for everyone in their stories, as well as for everyone in their communities and the wider ecology. Systemic perceiving is an essential step for coaches committed to impacting the wider social and environmental challenges in their work (Whybrow et al, 2023).

Our perceiving also needs to shift from looking at, listening to and empathizing with each separate individual, to looking and listening to the connections and sensing the spaces between people, and the spaces between the team and its wider systemic web. We need to sense the interpersonal, collective and systemic flows, eddies, blockages and divergences in the connections. As I, Peter, regularly suggest (Hawkins, 2021; Hawkins and Smith, 2013; Hawkins and Turner, 2020), we need to constantly ask ourselves: 'What is disconnected, that needs connecting?' The work of systemic team coaches and systemic leaders is to unblock what is impeding life's natural flow.

Imagine a senior social services team where there's a recurring problem with communication issues. We have worked with countless teams with this challenge. One team member, Robin, consistently feels left out of important discussions and decisions. They might start to feel that their colleagues are purposely ignoring or excluding them or discounting their input. Robin takes this personally, feeling disconnected, angry and unappreciated. They distance further as a result, increasing the outcome of not being included.

If we view this situation systemically, we may discover wider systemic elements that need addressing. This team has a long-established cultural pattern of resolving issues informally as they occur in their very crowded workdays, discussions that unintentionally leave some members out. In this case, the root cause of Robin's feelings of exclusion is not animosity from colleagues but rather a habitual pattern within the team. Robin may still need to address the issue and bring themselves more forward, however, what they are experiencing represents a team issue to address. This team explored their team pattern and came to collective agreements of what should be resolved informally and what needed to come to team meetings where everyone is involved.

Often the team members cannot see beyond the personal and interpersonal levels. We naturally focus with our left hemisphere brain on what we see in front of us, and in the short term.

SYSTEMIC THINKING

It takes time to develop systemic thinking, both for the team coach, as well as the team leader and team members. It involves learning to see the team not as an island unto itself, working on its internal performance, processes, and dynamics, but as nested within many larger systems, that are not just external to the team but flow through it and are often enacted between team members.

Through the predominant modernist individualistic lens of industrialized economies, we tend to think of teams as being created by the team members. The team dynamic is seen as formed interpersonally and originating primarily from the personality, psychological needs and preferences of the individuals within the team. When we shift to a systemic way of thinking, we see the team as not created by the team members, but by the collaborative purpose it is there to fulfil. Indeed, if there was not a purpose that pre-existed before the team members arrived the team would have never been created. As I, Peter, wrote in my earlier Systemic Team Coaching books (Hawkins, 2021, 2022b): 'It is the purpose that creates the team, not the team members that create the purpose.'

Additionally, the team dynamic and culture are shaped by various factors, including:

- the history of the team
- the legacy and influence of past team members
- anticipation of the future and those coming after current team members
- the relationship with the teams above and beneath, upstream and downstream of the team, and connections represented by multiple team memberships
- the wider organizational culture (see Chapter 2)
- all the stakeholders the team serves and ecosystem partnerships
- the wider political, economic, social, technological and legal changes
- the ecological changes and their impact on climate, resources, human conditions, migration and all aspects of the environment in which the team operates

Our systemic thinking helps us recognize that the purpose of a team is always made up of meeting what are unmet needs, both beyond as well as within, the specific team and the organization. As in the public sector case above, the unmet needs often emerge in conflict with one another. In a commercial organization: investors may want a higher return on their investment; customers may seek a cheaper and higher-quality product or service; suppliers or partner organizations may desire better rewards for their contribution; and employees may want better pay, working conditions and fewer demands.

To these we can add the wider stakeholders who are most often ignored. First is the wider community that provided all the infrastructure that makes the organization able to function – the schools, hospitals, roads, sewage system, rubbish collection, water and energy supplies – and want a better contribution from the company. The second and even more fundamental stakeholder that is often ignored is the 'more-than-human' world of the wider ecology, which provides everything that makes life possible, from the sun that provides the primary source of all light, energy and photosynthesis; the wind and rain that are essential for providing the water necessary not only for our own consumption, but essential for all life and everything we eat; to the billions of microbial beings that turn dead matter into new life-producing earth.

The team of teams coach who works systemically can help them perceive issues and conflicts as systemic, rather than personal and interpersonal, and understand how wider organizational dynamics are being played out within the teams (see Chapter 2). Then the Systemic Team Coaching can work with the team to map the wider stakeholder ecosystem and understand how the contending needs of different stakeholders need to be held, connected and reconciled by the whole team together, rather than causing competition and conflict within the team.

For instance, a team coach might help the team to develop clear team agreements around their collective ways of working. Carr and Peters (2012) found that establishing these agreements on their ways of working together – what the team will do and not do, in service of their collective work, was crucial for enhancing team effectiveness. Examples include ensuring everyone's voice is heard for team decision-making. Another example from I, Catherine's, team coaching came from a highly politicized senior public sector team. They adopted an approach they called 'all 52 cards on the table'. This was agreed upon to prevent holding back resources, including keeping the best staff from being poached, and safeguarding ideas they wanted to lead and get credit for.

SYSTEMIC BEING

Having added a systemic lens to our forms of perceiving through all our senses and shifted our conceptual thinking and our epistemological ways of framing our knowing into a systemic understanding, we can now begin to develop a systemic way of being. This is often a greater challenge, as our way of being is part of who we have become, and our habitual ways of showing up, and reacting to situations.

The foundation of systemic being is first being present to ourselves and others without judgement or reactivity. If we operate from stress and distress, we no longer connect to patterns in the room. Our brain becomes wired to survive not thrive, to reduce risk, by narrowing our focus to solve immediate problems, or escape because we are overwhelmed. To stay calm in the storm, resolute on acting on the important and not reacting to the urgent, we need to develop and model our own self-care practices to unplug, rebalance and restore. Only then can we support team leaders and members, teams and organizations to become more systemic and resilient. Employees are then more capable, creative and connected in an embodied way that enables deeper thinking, sensing and action. There is an economic argument as well. As Brassey et al (2023) wrote in 'Working nine to thrive', 'better aligning employment with modifiable drivers of health could unlock years of higher-quality life and create trillions of dollars of economic value'.

Systemic being entails training ourselves not to react based on our personality or ego. This means not taking comments made about us or what has been happening personally, for 'The quickest way of falling out of systemic awareness is to take things personally' (see Chapter 2). We also need to learn not to make judgements about individuals in the team, not to the individual, privately to the team leader, nor even inside our own head. Then we need to learn how to not take sides in any disagreement but see each person as holding a partial truth and representing a part of the bigger whole that the team needs to acknowledge and find a way of connecting (See polarity mapping in Chapter 14.).

Our newly acquired or deepened systemic thinking and perceiving need to permeate our whole being and our presence, from the moment we enter the room, and even before that in how we prepare for the engagement. This 'being' preparation is not just in our cognitive minds, but needs to be embodied in our heart, gut and whole being.

The systemic team coach needs to develop greater systemic being than the team to guide them beyond their current abilities. I, Peter, have developed an ecosystemic (and some would say spiritual) practice, called 'Opening the

Seven Levels', that coaches and leaders can use to accelerate their development. This practice opens them to the dance between the nested systemic levels prior to engaging with a team, a larger internal event or an engagement with stakeholders (this practice is included in Chapter 14).

SYSTEMIC DOING

The quality of an intervention, according to former Hanover Insurance CEO Bill O'Brien, depends on the interior condition of the intervenor. This includes 'doing our work' to integrate our own internal systemic parts – the parts of ourselves that we like and those we don't like, those we are aware of, and those others help us to see. Without acknowledging our shadow aspects and integrating all parts of our being, we cannot fully access all of our own knowing and abilities and tend to align with only parts of a team or wider system that resonate with us, rather than hold space for the whole.

Our ability to make effective systemic interventions rests on this inner work of self development. It is what enables our systemic thinking, perceiving and being. When we are more at peace with ourselves, we are less attached to our own ego and more able to see and work beyond this level in service of the whole. Systemic interventions are not directed at individuals but at the whole team as a whole. They aim to open up new perceptions, ownership and engagement with the 'patterns that connect' (Bateson, 1972), both inside and outside the team.

2. Self as instrument and vertical development

Our current strengths can become ingrained patterns and habits – trusted ways of working. Often, we have to unlearn what has made us successful at one level of development and practice, before we can fully step into a higher order way of working.

We invite all those we train in organizations and on our open programmes, to expand their ranges of ways of engaging and partnering with multiple teams, ability to hold multiple different perspectives, and alignments, and not to be on the side of any one person or team, but there to support the needs of the systems they are all nested within. This requires practitioners to expand their range of 'wide-angled empathy' (Hawkins, 2019) and emotional engagement (Hawkins, 2011b) to come alongside different teams and to coach the connections.

One of the key frameworks we use to help leaders, coaches and consultants deepen and expand their systemic awareness, is vertical development – a process that enhances their capacity to navigate complexity, broaden perspective and operate with greater systemic insight (Braks, 2020; Hawkins and Smith, 2013; Petrie, 2014; Torbert, 2004). This builds on earlier work on adult ethical development frameworks about how we can expand our world view to embrace greater complexity. We need to start by exploring our own dominant mindsets that frame what we focus on, ignore, how we sense make, and how we react.

Many leaders, coaches and consultants start their training with us, with a *technician/expert* mindset, wishing to acquire new expertise, and more efficient tools and methods. They are eager to get the correct 'inputs' mastered (see Chapter 7). Their attention is on immediate problems and issues, and the best way to solve them.

Then they move to an *achiever* perspective, more focussed on the outputs and outcomes – starting with the end in mind. Here they learn to begin to think 'future-back' and 'outside-in' and move from focussing on what individuals, team and organizations want, to what is required and necessary, for all of them to thrive in tomorrow's world.

In the next stage of *redefining* they develop the capacity to listen through the presenting issues and what is discussed to the deeper systemic and cultural patterns that are behind these narratives (see Chapters 2 and 10). They move from listening to individuals, to listening to the relational and team dynamics. Then from listening to the internal team patterns, to sensing the wider organizational dynamics, and then beyond this, to sense the even wider ecosystemic patterns that all these levels are nested within and which flow through them.

Only when we develop to the *transforming stage*, do we become able to not only sense this meshwork of interconnecting systemic dynamics, and perhaps comment on it, to being able to intervene in a way that creates a fundamental shift across these levels. This requires the abilities to:

- **Enable co-creation of shared purpose.** Leaders need to see their issues in a new light and create a path between their current and future state, embrace polarities and find ways forward that transcend the current thinking.

- **Facilitate new generative dialogue** in and between teams and organizations.

- **Continually reframe** not only issues but relational discourse – often changing the frame to a larger systemic level.

- **Enable different wider stakeholder perspectives** into the discourse.
- **Shift the emotional tenor and generate new active hope.**

The final stage of vertical development, *alchemist*, is beyond the scope of this book, but is where we are no longer in partnership with any individual, team or organization, but in partnership with what life is requiring and becoming.

3. Five disciplines framework

At the heart of all our training is the five disciplines framework. This was originally developed for Systemic Team Coaching (Hawkins 2011b, 2021, 2022b), but in this book (Chapter 6), we have extended and deepened the model to create a new STOTC model of the five disciplines that can be used to work with organizational transformation. We have also created a 'five disciplines' approach and methodology, that can be used in coaching individuals on their internal team (Chapter 11).

4. Organizational types, transitions and transformations

It is important for all those working with a Systemic Team of Teams Approach (STOTA), to adapt the approach, for different:

- types of organizations
- life-cycle stages (see Chapter 5)
- and for the transformation that the organization's wider ecosystem requires

In this book we have quoted examples from our research of global commercial companies, international partnerships, early-stage growth companies, government sector organizations and non-profit and charity organizations. Understanding the different context, structures and challenges of each of these is important.

In Chapter 5, we have provided a model and guidance for how STOTA can be used for some of the most common life-cycle transitions and transformational challenges.

Throughout this book and particularly in Chapter 6, we have shown how to work with organizations to discover what their future ecosystem is requiring of them.

5. Navigating the process journey

Based on our organizational and literature research, in Chapters 4 and 6 we show the major stages of the STOT journey, and some of the leading, coaching and consulting skills and capabilities that are needed for each stage. In Chapter 14 we provide some of the tools and methods needed for each stage.

Among the core capabilities that run through the whole journey are the following:

Scoping and contracting. Scoping and contracting the work is not just something that happens at the beginning of the journey, but throughout. ABC: Always Be Contracting-as the journey unfolds, and the context and needs constantly evolve. The complexity of contracting in whole organization work is much greater. It often involves contracting with the board, the senior executive team, different regions and functions, as well as internal partners such as those in HR function, learning and development and internal coaches.

Collaborative inquiry. To build a collective sense of what is needed from all key parties, at different levels and across the organization, as well as key stakeholders and ecosystem partners, and from this multi-dimensional data and feedback, facilitate the mapping and sense making of the key connecting themes and patterns.

Designing the process. Collaboratively working with key individuals and groups to design the roadmap and process to address the current challenges, build on the current strengths, and create a journey plan to what the future requires.

Evaluation and iterative evolution of the process. In Chapter 7 we laid out the key skills in continually evaluating progress on the journey and evolving the approach, in line with what has worked and not worked, and the changing circumstances.

6. Designing and conducting large-scale events

In STOTA, there is often a need to bring together teams and senior leaders from across the organization. Designing and conducting such large-scale events requires not just being taught the skills and practising them, but apprenticing with someone skilled in this complex capability and capacity. These whole organization workshops need to move beyond information sharing, presentations and discussions, to whole organization generative dialogue that creates not just new quality thinking, but embodied change in the room (see Chapter 14 and examples earlier in the book).

7. Handling ethical dilemmas

In Chapter 13, we will outline some of the more complex ethical dilemmas that emerge when engaging in team of teams coaching and provide some guidance. But more important than this, guidance is growing our ethical maturity, as we will always encounter new ethical challenges as the work develops. This needs to be a core element that is weaved throughout every training and development process.

Supervision

In the team of teams context, supervision is not merely a supportive function – it is a catalyst for transformation. It enables STOT leaders, coaches and consultants to move from isolated interventions to integrated, systemic impact. Just as leaders need support to think beyond their thinking, so do coaches. Effective supervision helps coaches see themselves, and their client teams and team of teams, in a new, strengthened and interconnected light.

It requires trained supervisors, who themselves are systemic and trained and experienced in working with whole organizations and a team of teams approach. The supervision needs to balance the three core supervision functions:

- **Qualitative:** ensuring the quality of the work is the best possible and it is delivering value for all those involved and their stakeholders.
- **Developmental:** growing the capability of the supervisees, and generating new learning for the field.
- **Resourcing:** ensuring the supervisees are adequately resourced.

The seven-eyed model of supervision (Hawkins and McMahon, 2020; Hawkins and Smith, 2013) provides a systemic framework for attending to all aspects of supervision. This was extended to include all the wider systemic levels that the work is nested within (Hawkins and Turner, 2020; see Figure 12.3). This was further extended into the ten-eyed supervision model (Hawkins, 2021) to address the greater complexity of team, and team of teams coaching (see Figure 12.4).

FIGURE 12.3 Extended seven-eyed model

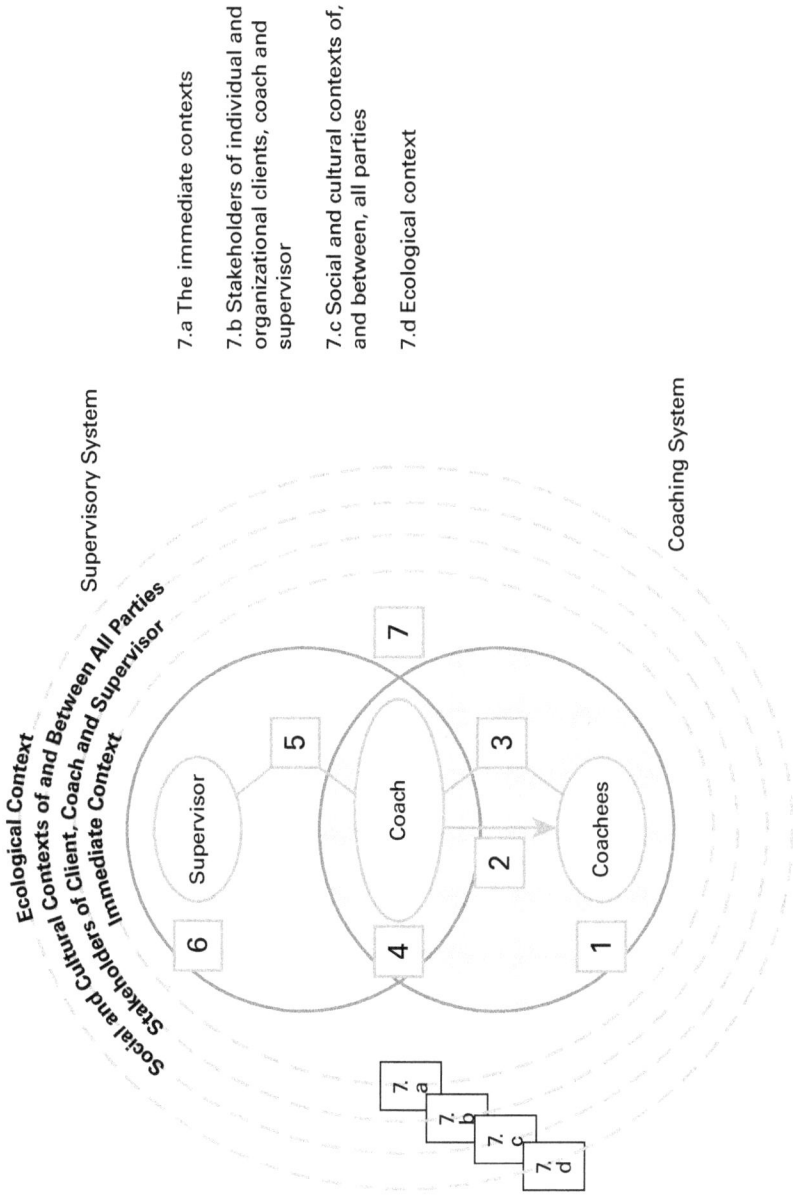

7.a The immediate contexts

7.b Stakeholders of individual and organizational clients, coach and supervisor

7.c Social and cultural contexts of, and between, all parties

7.d Ecological context

Ecological Context

Social and Cultural Contexts of and Between All Parties

Stakeholders of Client, Coach and Supervisor

Immediate Context

Supervisory System

Coaching System

Supervisor

Coach

Coachees

FIGURE 12.4 The ten-eyed model of supervision

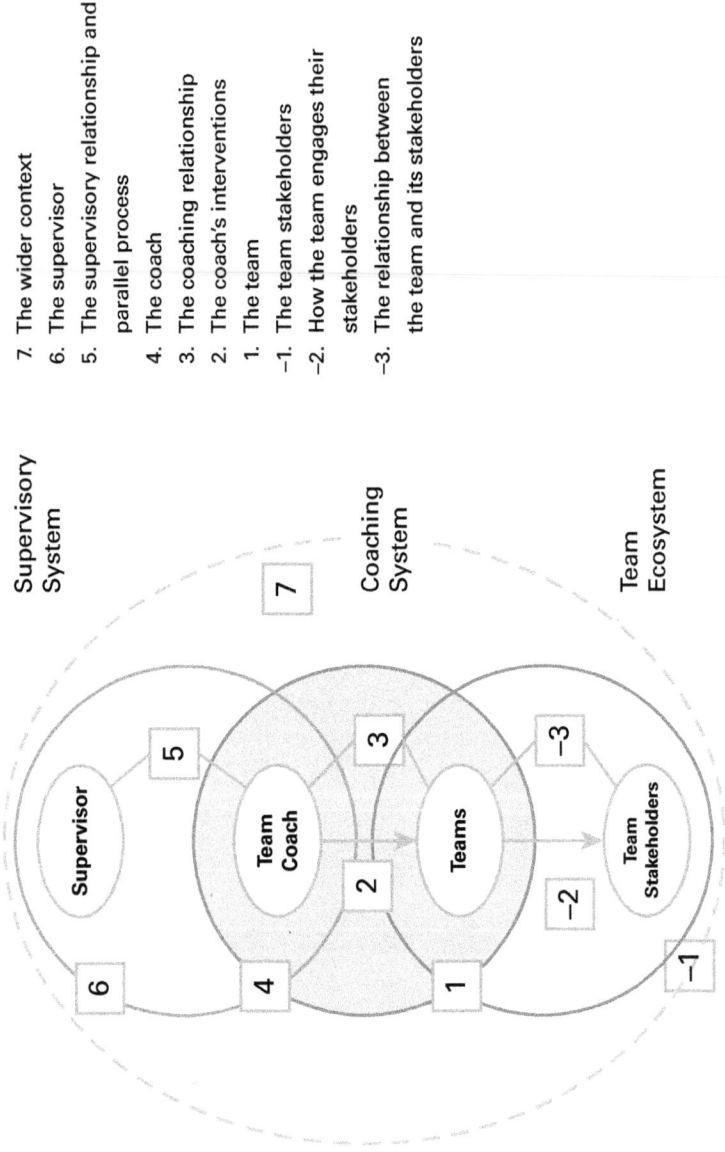

Supervisory
System

Coaching
System

Team
Ecosystem

7. The wider context
6. The supervisor
5. The supervisory relationship and parallel process
4. The coach
3. The coaching relationship
2. The coach's interventions
1. The team
-1. The team stakeholders
-2. How the team engages their stakeholders
-3. The relationship between the team and its stakeholders

SOURCE Hawkins (2022)

There are three other key ways that STOTC supervision is significantly different from other forms of team coaching, which we will now explore.

1 **Supervising co-coaching.** We encourage coaches to work as a team when doing Systemic Team Coaching. Co-coaches are a team themselves. Supervising them requires a balance between supporting their own teaming work and focussing on their practice.

2 **Supervising a team of team coaches.** When supervising a whole team of team coaches, there are always elements of needing to systemically coach them as a team themselves. This includes ensuring they have a clear team purpose (discipline 1); clear aligned objectives, roles and processes (discipline 2); that they are attending to their own co-creation and team dynamics (discipline 3); that they are effectively partnering with all the different individuals and teams across and beyond the organization (discipline 4); and that they are constantly learning and growing their collective capacity (discipline 5).

3 **Addressing the parallel dynamics within the team of team coaches.** The dynamics within the team of team coaches is not just created by the participants, but also by the conscious and unconscious assimilation of the organizational and team dynamics they are working with. The coaching team become a collective resonance chamber, through which we can more fully sense the team and organizational dynamics. Supervision needs to surface these dynamics as they are crucial ways of understanding the more hidden dynamics, processes and culture of the organization.

Here is an example from Catherine's supervision practice. Leaders were experiencing a top-down directive to cut costs and were caught within a dynamic of internal resource competition. As a result, they began disengaging, acting cooler towards their peers and sharing less. In the supervision, I, Catherine noticed that the coaching team felt reticent to share and disconnected, and had different ideas about where to go next. I commented on this dynamic and explored with the team how their reticence and disconnection might be paralleling the disconnections in the organization. This not only freed up the co-coaches energy, but opened up new ways of attending to the interconnections between the teams and ways of intervening.

Our supervision also incorporates forward-focussed rehearsals, where coaches actively experiment with potential strategies or interventions rather than simply discussing them. This experiential approach bridges theory and practice, helping coaches build confidence and refine their ability to navigate complex systems effectively. This is no different when working with one team or many. What is different is managing complexity and working with core dynamics and 'flows' that can create a ripple effect of change.

Conclusion

When people ask me, Peter, how long it takes to become proficient in Systemic Team of Teams Coaching, I answer: 'Well I have been doing it for over 45 years, and I still have a great deal to learn.' It is a long and exciting journey, which involves a great deal of learning and unlearning along the way.

The journey we have outlined in this chapter involves continually being taught; engaging in many hours of practice in training groups; applying learning with teams and organizations; reflecting on our individual and collective practice through journalling and supervision; and staying in constant inquiry and experimentation.

The field itself is still emerging, and we are all part of creating its future. In doing so we are contributing to a much wider and deeper learning process: the great work of growing human collaborative intelligence, to address the urgent challenges of our time (see Chapters 1 and 15).

13

Ethical challenges and dilemmas in coaching a team of teams and organizations

PETER HAWKINS AND VLAD DUȚESCU

Introduction

As we have shown throughout this book, team coaching is becoming increasingly common in organizational development contexts for team development at different levels, from boards and C-level executive teams to departmental levels, cross-functional, cross-cultural, and project-based teams. There is a better understanding of teams' role as fundamental units of organizational learning (Edmondson, 2023; Hawkins, 2021; Senge, 2006). Additionally, systemic awareness is increasing, with a shift towards what I, Peter, refer to as the fourth level of Ecosystemic Team Coaching (Hawkins, 2017, 2021). These levels represent an evolution from coaching individual teams, to coaching the entire organization and its broader stakeholder ecosystem.

Individual coaching, team coaching, Systemic Team Coaching and Systemic Team of Teams Coaching, all bring different ethical challenges and dilemmas. Hawkins and Carr (2023) offered five examples of ethical challenges from a systemic ethical perspective, drawing parallels between individual coaching and team coaching ethical challenges. However, ethical codes in the major professional coaching bodies are still mainly focussed on individual coaching and little has been developed about how these need to be both adapted and developed for the much more complex worlds of team, and team of teams coaching.

The role of ethics

Ethics is often described in general textbooks and in many professional associations as the study of what is right and wrong, focussing on the principles of good conduct by individual humans or individuals acting in a professional capacity (American Psychological Association, 2017; ICF, 2021; Singer, 2011). The International Coaching Federation (ICF) defines ethical coaching as the adherence to a set of standards and guidelines that guide coaches in their behaviour and practices.

Different professional bodies have varying perspectives on ethics. Some, like the European Mentoring and Coaching Council (EMCC), Association for Coaching (AC) and Association for Professional Executive Coaching and Supervision (APECS), view ethics as a set of guiding principles rooted in shared values that shape behaviour. Others, such as the American Medical Association (2020) see ethics as a framework for addressing moral and professional dilemmas encountered in one's work.

Ethics can be understood along a continuum, ranging from *descriptive ethics* – which describes how people actually behave – to *normative ethics* – which outlines how people ought to behave. This normative approach is reflected in the works of many philosophers, from Plato and Confucius to John Stuart Mill's (1863) theory of Utilitarianism.

Ethics can also serve as a method and a tool for fostering coherence within a community whether this be historical examples, like Moses defining the Ten Commandments for the Jewish people crossing the Sinai Desert, or modern professional bodies setting out standards. Ethics becomes a key element in creating a shared culture, complemented by a common purpose, values, language, practices and rituals. In communities of practice, codifying ethics can help shape a collective identity and establish clear boundaries regarding who qualifies to belong to that community.

While ethics can provide clarity of identity and boundaries, serving as a stable foundation for communities of practice and professional bodies, it can also lead to rigidity. This rigidity may restrict professional communities from evolving and adapting in response to their changing contexts.

Living in a time of rapid, complex and interdependent change, all communities and professional bodies must evolve and adapt continuously, including a constant evolution of ethical values and codes. Anthony de Mello (1982: 199) tells a lovely story: 'There were rules in the monastery, but the master always warned against the tyranny of the law. "Obedience keeps the rules," he would say, "but love knows when to break them."'

From our supervision and research, we have discovered that many coaches and team coaches, and indeed supervisors, describe ethics as: a) keeping to the rules, b) the behaviour of individuals, and c) knowing the difference between right and wrong (see Dartnall, 2012). When asked what ethical dilemmas they had encountered, some said 'I have not had any ethical issues'. We would contend that every coaching, team coaching and organizational consulting relationship involves ethical issues, and every intervention is an ethical choice. McGilchrist (2009, 2021) says that: 'Attention is a moral act.' He also suggests that attention changes the world, for the world we experience depends on how we perceive it, and how we perceive it depends on where we put our attention. There is a myth in coaching that the coach can be objective and non-directive by using open questions and clean language. Although both approaches at times can be helpful, what the coach asks about, and what the coachee experiences the coach as being interested in, has a directive influence on what the coachee does. Silence is an intervention.

There is also a coaching myth held by some, that if you only get the contract right there will not be ethical challenges or dilemmas. This is rarely, if ever, the case. One cannot anticipate everything that may emerge in a relationship. We therefore advocate the ABC of coaching – 'Always Be Contracting' – and recommend that contracting should be a continuous flow running alongside any form of development contract.

We believe that ethics are most healthy, when rooted in, and grown from the earth of experience, rather than cut and pasted from abstract theory. They are healthiest when they are developed in dialogue with all players involved in the field, including clients and customers. Following this principle, to develop this chapter, Vlad Duțescu in early 2024 came as scholar in residence (supported by the Renewal Foundation), to spend six weeks working and dialoguing with Peter Hawkins, exploring the following inputs:

- ethical guidelines and codes of the major coaching bodies
- main literature on coaching ethics, team coaching ethics and organizational transformation ethics, including published case studies
- both of their wide experience as practitioners of team coaching, Systemic Team Coaching and Systemic Team of Teams Coaching, organizational transformation, as well as from their many years of supervising practitioners in all these fields
- case material emerging from the research for this book on coaching the team of teams

From these explorations, the key ethical dilemmas that every systemic team of teams coach faces emerged. These build on previous work by Hawkins and Carr (2023) on the main ethical dilemmas emerging in Systemic Team Coaching.

Before we share these dilemmas, we also thought that it was important for us to be clear about different ethical terminology and how we are using it. Thus, we first have a short section on key ethical distinctions.

Key ethical distinctions

It is important to distinguish between the following:

- **Ethical codes of practice:** These define the ethical standards and rules that professionals are required to stay within. They provide the basis for carrying out an inquiry following an ethical complaint and then arriving at a judgement on whether professional standards have been maintained. Thus, they are necessarily based on the individual behaviour of a professional and only focus on areas where there are clear distinctions between good and bad practice.

- **Ethical principles:** These are the underlining principles that stand behind and inform ethical codes of practice. They are essential in training and supervising professionals in ways that grow their ethical maturity (see below) and the ethical quality of their practice.

- **Ethical dilemmas:** Often people assume that ethical issues only occur where there are breaches of ethical codes, but we would contend that all choices, interventions and behaviour within professional practice have an ethical dimension. Both what we do, and what we do not do, are ethical choices. Religious writing on morality focusses on both sins of omission, as well as sins of commission.

- Most ethical issues do not fall into the area of a clear right and wrong judgement, and practitioners are daily faced with complex ethical dilemmas. As we move from individual coaching, to team coaching, to Systemic Team Coaching, Systemic Team of Teams Coaching, to coaching whole organizations and networks of organizations, these dilemmas become ever more complex.

- **Ethical maturity:** Focusses on the development of the practitioner's capacity to embrace the complexity of moral choices and engage with ethical dilemmas from multiple perspectives and different systemic levels. Ethical maturity is central to all adult development and essential for all forms of coaches and consultants. Coaches need both good ethical training and skilled supervision that can constantly utilize emerging ethical dilemmas, to accelerate the ethical maturity of all parties, coachees, coaches and supervisors. There is a lot of good literature on ethical maturity in: leadership (Kohlberg, 1981; Loevinger, 1976; Torbert, 2004); the helping professionals more generally (Carroll and Shaw, 2013; Hawkins and McMahon, 2020); and in coaching (Hawkins, 2011b, 2021: 321–23; Hawkins and Smith, 2013: Chapter 2; Hawkins and Turner, 2020: 171–73; Turner and Passmore, 2019).

Ethical dilemmas

Ethical dilemmas are not problems, but challenges that can often take us to our learning edge and provide the opportunity to develop our ethical maturity. Ethical dilemmas are sometimes a form of colliding perspectives (Petrie, 2014), where we are faced with two beliefs, or two ways forward that are both important but cannot be reconciled within our current ways for thinking and acting.

As Jean Boulton (2024: 197) points out: 'There is no logic based algorithm, no left-brain method that can be programmed to make such nuanced judgements, as to what constitutes ethical behaviour, and what is fair.' To this we would add that there is no ethical code or pre-formed coaching contract that can pre determine what might be right in all the possible situations that may arise in the work.

Ethical dilemmas require the practitioner to pause and reflect, rather than attempting to quickly resolve the issues at hand. Ideally, the practitioner would also bring the dilemma to supervision. In Systemic Team of Teams Coaching, supervision is even more critically important than in individual or Systemic Team Coaching, as the complexity increases exponentially. This approach involves many more people and ecosystem partners across various organizational levels, divisions and aspects.

When addressing an ethical dilemma, whether through self-reflection, peer reflection with co-coaches, or in supervision, it is essential to view the situation within its broader systemic context, considering the many different parties and interests involved.

Our first principle is to always locate the challenge within a connection rather than assigning it to an individual or a specific part of the system (Hawkins, 2025). Secondly, consider a range of possible responses, avoiding polarized 'either-or' choices or compromises. Instead, aim to discover a way forward that creates value and learning for all key parties involved. I, Peter, describe the 'Heart of Systemic Ethics' (Hawkins, 2024a), by defining systemic ethical behaviours, as that which is in service of, and creates benefit for all the systemic levels the individual, team, organization, country or species are nested within. I describe unethical behaviour as any attempt to optimize one's own self, group or species benefit, at the cost of the wider systemic levels that the system or species is nested within. Later in this chapter we offer several examples of such unethical behaviour.

With this systemic approach we can see how we are all contributing to and/or colluding with, unethical behaviour and dynamics. Systemic ethics provides a clear framework for addressing collective unethicality and can act as a guide for all those working with developing teams, team of teams, organizations and networks (see also Chapter 7 on 'Evaluation and evolution').

Here are eight ethical challenges that we believe will help practitioners and team coaching supervisors in developing ethical awareness, capacity and maturity for all participants and ecosystem partners involved in systemic teams-of-teams' coaching projects.

1. Collusion versus misalignment

To support a system, you must engage with it. Coaching an individual requires empathic entry into their world; coaching a team demands partnering within the 'team coaching system'. Observing solely from the outside limits understanding, but becoming absorbed obscures the broader context. There is a traditional Sufi saying that a 'Sufi should be in the world but not of it', and we believe the same applies to all levels and types of coaching. Such professionals are paid to bring an external perspective, drawing on their experience of having seen multiple occurrences of similar patterns and dynamics. On the other hand, to be effective, the coaches need to partner closely with the coachees and feel aligned to their joint purpose. Coaching, team coaching and coaching the 'team of teams' require a focus on what the coach(es) and the system being coached can do together that they cannot do apart. We need to share a joint purpose of helping the system we are coaching to flourish and co-create greater value, with, and for, all their stakeholders and ecosystem partners.

In supervision, we are often asked: 'What should I do if my values differ from those of the team I've been invited to coach, or if I don't feel aligned with the team's purpose?' Alongside this, there is the opposite challenge of becoming overly identified with the team, which can lead to losing the necessary separateness.

In such cases, coaches may risk entering a collusive groupthink with the team. This reduces our ability to step back and see the bigger picture, potentially missing opportunities to bring fresh perspectives and constructive challenges to the team.

To transcend this polarity, we recommend two principles:

1 Good work does not arise if you cannot find a joint love and commitment to a joint purpose. True partnerships survive through both good times and bad, but only when partners are aligned in purpose and values.

2 It is important to feel committed to what the team needs to become, rather than colluding with what it is today.

During the early inquiry and exploration phase of team of teams coaching, it's not always apparent what differences may exist in the values, beliefs and ethical conduct of the individuals and businesses involved. As time progresses, and as more people and events put the organization or meta-system under pressure, the level of intimacy and depth of exposure increase exponentially.

In Romania, there is a saying: 'Real character is revealed in both great achievements and great challenges.' In today's polarized world, even close friends and family members can find themselves on opposite sides, sometimes without a bridge to reconnect.

Some ethical decisions are straightforward. For example a vegan team coach may not want to work for a meat factory. However, some ethical dilemmas are more complex. For instance, imagine an armament producer asking a coach to help them both become a more effective team today and develop a strategy to transition to a war-free world for the future of the company. If you are a committed pacifist, would you accept such a project? Could you focus on future development without being triggered by past and present conflicts?

A second situation presents a more delicate challenge. I, Vlad, am accustomed to conducting thorough research before making a proposal or getting involved in a programme, particularly for longer programmes that require multiple team coaches. To avoid potential conflicts in values, I explore how well I resonate with and can connect to the company's vision, purpose, objectives and values.

A recent request from an IT company illustrates such a scenario. This global organization sought a programme to run across three continents, involving several countries, about 2,000 employees and multiple team coaches and consultants. Three of us collaborated on the proposal, conducting interviews and briefings. The client appeared to be very clear in communicating their purpose, vision, mission and values.

However, when I looked one level deeper to understand the broader context, I discovered that the company was part of a larger group facing numerous legal challenges and operating in an industry that many team members would not resonate with. We decided to withdraw from submitting the proposal, realizing it would have been far more challenging if we were already in the middle of the project when these issues came to light.

During a team of teams programme, which can last for several years, we will often have enough exposure and opportunity to find out about:

- their collective and individual ethical and relational maturity, business conduct and even legal governance
- the collective and individual transcultural capacity
- the use of power within and outside the organization

It's easy to understand our point if you search the internet for corporate scandals over the past 10 years. Some of you may have worked with teams from those organizations before, during or after the scandals took place. Often, you may have had no connection to what caused the issues, yet still found yourself affected by association.

Even if you haven't worked with any of those organizations or their close ecosystem partners, you might feel disturbed by what occurred and bring it to supervision. After reading the following challenge, you may want to take some time to reflect on how you would prepare for such situations, should they arise.

2. Being in the team and organization but not of it

Coaching an individual or a team involves both entering their world and allowing their world to enter you through empathic and embodied listening. As a coach or team coach, it's easy to become immersed in what individuals want from other parts of the system.

Here are some examples. A senior sponsor of the team coaching may complain to the coach about how the team never delivers reports on time. A team leader might disclose that one team member is at risk of losing their job if they don't improve collaboration with colleagues. Several team members might confide that they feel pressured or bullied by the team leader but are too afraid to speak up. Additionally, you may receive confidential information about an upcoming team restructuring, even though the team hasn't been informed yet.

Once you've been told something, you cannot 'unknow' it, and this knowledge inevitably influences how you engage with others and the lens through which you perceive what happens.

Even in individual coaching, a coach may get entangled in the differing agendas of the coachee, the coachee's boss (who is sponsoring the coaching), and the HR department. We have often supervised coaches who find themselves acting as 'go-betweens', attempting to bridge disconnections between internal parties (Berne, 2010; Hawkins and Carr, 2023; Hay, 2009).

As supervisors, we help these coaches explore ways to facilitate necessary, difficult conversations directly, encouraging parties to engage in multi-stakeholder contracting (see Hawkins and Turner, 2020: 74–76).

The same principle applies in team coaching, where the team coach must avoid being the 'go-between' carrying messages or needs from one part of the team to another. Again, the team coach needs to focus on enabling the necessary conversation to happen directly between the key parties, either with the whole team, or in a facilitated smaller meeting.

In a team of teams context, I, Peter, have many times found myself in the space between an executive team and their board, each telling me about the failings of the other. In one such instance I persuaded the two parties to have a joint workshop, in which each group met separately and prepared feedback to the other, stating:

a. What we appreciate about you collectively is...

b. What we find difficult about you collectively is...

c. What we would request differently from you is...

Rather than let either group do their full presentation, we alternated the live feedback, hearing first the appreciations from each team, then the difficulties and then the requests. This was followed by cross-group small teams of two to four people working on inter-team protocols and agreements that would greatly increase the quality of their co-working.

As mentioned earlier, the Sufi mystic is trained to be 'in the world, but not of it', meaning they must be fully engaged in normal life without retreating to a remote monastery; but also avoid being swept along by life's tides and currents by maintaining a well-anchored, reflective witness to what is happening around them.

Similarly, the Sufi is trained to view every issue from at least two perspectives. For the team and team of teams coach, it is crucial to recognize that whatever they hear from one part of a system is inevitably just one story and one partial perspective. It's important to hold all perspectives lightly, respecting each one and the needs it represents, while always remembering that it is a story and never the whole story.

We are reminded of the tale of the four blind men and the elephant, each of whom is asked by the king to go and discover what an elephant is. One of them puts their arm around the elephant's leg and reports back to the king that the elephant is like a strong tree trunk with a leathery bark. Another who had felt the ear, told the king that it was like a very thick leathery sail on a boat. Another felt its trunk and said it was like a strong thick snake, while the fourth grabbed its tail and said no, you are all wrong, the elephant is like a flexible rope. As a team of teams coach, we must realize that every part of the system is unable to see the whole picture, but also respect their story as being true, from their partial perspective.

3. Confidentiality and integrity

Benjamin Franklin (1732) wrote in *Poor Richard's Almanac*, 'Three may keep a secret, if two of them are dead.' All codes of ethics from professional coaching and mentoring bodies include clear references to confidentiality and integrity.

Even in one-to-one coaching, confidentiality can never be absolute. If the coachee shares something that indicates they are a danger to themselves, their organization or others, the coach may need to, or be legally required to, disclose this information. Every coach should understand the legal requirements that apply in the countries where they work. Professional coaches also need to be transparent with coachees about how issues that arise may be discussed in supervision.

Many coaches we have supervised have encountered difficulties by promising absolute confidentiality to the coachee, only to face situations where they cannot keep this promise. I, Peter, tell my coachees that I will not take anything beyond the boundaries of our relationship without first discussing it with them and explaining why and how I would communicate it. I also clarify that while I attend supervision, the focus is not on individual coachees but on my own actions and what I need to do differently.

In Systemic Team Coaching there are always at least three or even more parties, including several team members, the team leader, the sponsor and the team coach (and sometimes two co-coaches). At this level, relationships grow exponentially complex, requiring team coaches to continuously (re) contract to maintain trust and a safe environment to foster team capabilities.

I, Peter, often meet with the team leader between team coaching workshops and live coaching of the team, in their team meetings. I consider the team leader as a key coaching partner, who needs to continue the team coaching between my engagements, and after I have finished working with the team. I always need to make it clear that I will not pass judgement on, or make assessments of, their team members, or comment on who they should promote or remove from the team. I need to reinforce this boundary, for effective team coaching means that I cannot coach a team and be part of the assessment and selection of individuals.

It is also important to be clear with all team members that as a team coach, you are not there to support, or be on the side of, any individual and that your focus is on helping the whole team increase the value it co-creates with, and for, all its stakeholders. Thus, anything an individual shares with a team coach may need to be shared with their co-coach and, in time, skillfully with the whole team. We regularly use the phrase: 'How can I help you share that with the whole team, or the individual concerned?'

When we work at an organizational level, using team of teams coaching, team coaches often face even more complex situations. These include:

- Hearing gossip and complaints about other parts of the organization.
- Receiving negative feedback from one team about the team coaching received by another team.
- Discovering complaints from multiple teams regarding senior leaders' bullying, discrimination, or interpersonal boundary issues such as inappropriate sexual behaviour.

STOTC requires the following ethical principles:

- Viewing the problem as not residing in an individual or part of the system, but locating the challenge in the connections between teams.
- Avoiding being a message carrier or go-between.
- Facilitating appropriate conversations between the people and teams that need to address emerging issues.

- Being clear and transparent about your own role, boundaries and codes of practice.
- Being clear that as a team of teams coach, you are not there to be on the side of any one individual or team, but there to serve the collective transformation of the organization.

4. Working with a competitor or a very close stakeholder

We have both experienced the situation where an individual within a client organization has gone on to work for a competitor and has invited us to work with their new organization. Our practice is to let organizational clients know from the beginning of our work that we will be transparent with them if we are approached by any other organization in their sector or one that could be a significant stakeholder for them. We will follow any non-compete contract clauses, and only proceed with the new organization if we have their agreement. This sometimes requires us to agree with both parties how we establish the appropriate boundaries of confidentiality between separate teams of coaches working with one client and those working with the other. As the work progresses, we may be in the position to revisit this contract and suggest that we bring two or more organizations that we are working with together, to facilitate potential exchange of learning and possible partnering opportunities.

5. Managing the team of teams project

When we have multiple systemic team coaches working with different teams in an organization, it is necessary to attend carefully to the dynamics that emerge within our own coaching team. A level of competitiveness is common, and at times this can be helpful, spurring everyone on to do better work. However, at other times it can be counterproductive.

Team coaches may feel the need to showcase how successful they've been with 'their team', which can make it harder for others to openly share their own struggles or vulnerabilities. This tendency can be intensified if team coaches feel they are competing for future team coaching opportunities within the organization.

We have found the following principles helpful.

1 Being clear that whichever teams we are working with, we are all there to serve the whole organization and their stakeholders, and share the purpose, vision and the changing priorities of the organization.

2 It's essential to be clear about how work is allocated and the criteria used for assignment. For example, in one project we specified that in assigning, coaches would consider geographical proximity to reduce ecological and financial costs, along with relevant business experience in the team's specific area of work.

3 Having clarity on the budget for the work and how this is allocated, how and when people will be paid, and what they can and cannot invoice for.

4 Meeting regularly with the whole coaching team, and spending time to build the purpose of the coaching team, its team charter, protocols, how it will become a 'learning team' (Hawkins, 2021: 129–34) and a map of all the key stakeholders and ecosystem partners in and around the client organization. Thus, we are applying the 'Five Disciplines of High-Value Creating Teams' to our own coaching team (Hawkins, 2021 and see Chapter 12).

It is important that the team of coaches has supervision as a whole team and is therefore able to attend to the connections between the various strands of work, aid collective insight and learning, help address the coaching team dynamics and explore 'parallel process' (see Hawkins and Smith, 2013: 196–97). Parallel process in this context is where the inter-team and organizational dynamics of the organization are unconsciously replicated by the team of team coaches.

We would recommend that ideally the supervision is carried out by two supervisors, one who is leading the project and carries the organizational overview and one who is external to the project and has no alignment or vested interest, thus free to focus on what is emerging live in the team.

How an external supervisor is funded as well as how the systemic team coaches are paid (or not) for attending the team of teams' supervision, needs to be clear and contracted upfront. We have found some client organizations are willing to pay for this and others are not. Some co-coaches are happy to do this supervision unpaid, as they see their reward coming from the learning they receive from their peers and the supervisor, others may not be so willing.

6. Being on the learning edge

Operating at the forefront of an organizational transformation project is anything but psychologically safe as everything is in flux and under intense scrutiny. It requires collective psychological and relational maturity

(Hawkins, 2024). In this challenging environment, it's essential to avoid the comfort of complacency and remain adaptable, ready to address emerging complexities without relying on familiar safety zones (Duțescu, 2024).

I, Vlad, as a medical doctor, uphold the Hippocratic oath, 'First, do no harm', yet I acknowledge that decisions, whether for physicians, leaders or team coaches, are rarely simple or straightforward. Hawkins and Smith (2013) highlighted the complexities executive coaches face when shifting from one-to-one to one-to-many coaching, particularly given the diverse learning styles and varying rapport-building approaches required.

Consider how the organization's culture and meta-system interact with the culture and meta-system of the team of teams coaches. To support the organization effectively, team of teams coaches must first learn and go through the Fourteen Steps model developed by Peter and Renewal Associates (Hawkins, 2024b), to assess their collective psychological and relational maturity. Ethical maturity is crucial and includes sensitivity, acuity, awareness, decision-making, and consistent ethical reflection and supervision. Fostering ethical growth involves allowing time for open dialogue, holding space for constructive conflict, and searching for what may not be immediately apparent.

Like organizational leaders and managers, who often must make decisions with limited information and under pressure, team coaches face similar challenges both during and between sessions. I, Vlad, often think of Formula 1 racing, where a single mistake can derail an entire project or even an organization. Hawkins and Carr (2023) emphasize the importance of behaviour, intent, disposition, ecosystemic and global ethics, values and reverence for life.

7. Supporting a system without sub-optimizing a larger system

When coaching systemically using a team of teams approach, we often work with the whole organization, while also partnering closely with specific teams. This creates a tension between helping individual parts of the organization achieve success, while ensuring they don't pursue local success at the expense of the wider systems of which they are a part (see above and Hawkins, 2024a).

For example, an individual executive may use organizational time and resources to promote themselves as the best candidate for a future CEO role, even when this comes at the expense of the organization as a whole. At the team level, a team may strive to become the most successful team within the organization by taking more than its fair share of collective resources. This pattern, which we have observed in many companies, can also occur between regional offices and larger divisions within the organization.

At an even larger level, an organization or professional body may attempt to dominate a sector in ways that hinder the sector's evolution and adaptation to future needs. Similarly, species can prioritize their own needs and survival to the detriment of the ecosystem they are part of, by exploiting resources in ways that harm other species or the entire ecosystem. This exploitation may also involve using non-renewable resources, compromising the well-being of future generations of their own and other species. Currently, much of the human species – especially in economically richer countries – can be seen as acting in a systemically unethical way.

As a systemic team of teams coach, one must serve the teams they are directly supporting, but in ways that co-create value for: a) the teams above them, beneath them, upstream and downstream of them; b) the whole organization; c) the wider human communities it operates in and with; d) the wider ecosystem of which it is a small, wholly dependent, and intrinsic part.

As Bateson (1972) pointed out, sub-optimization of one's own local part is ultimately self-destructive; any species that destroys its ecosystem ultimately destroys itself. The same principle applies to teams within an organization. A team that undermines the wider organization for its own gain is ultimately harming itself. If, in the pursuit of a larger share of resources, a team damages or reduces the overall 'pie', their benefit will eventually decrease as well.

8. Working with complex diversity and power

In our research, many companies that completed the questionnaire and participated in interviews highlighted the importance of systemic team of teams coaches in enhancing the organization's capacity to address Diversity, Inclusion, Engagement and Belonging (DIEB), as well as managing power differentials.

All systemic team of teams (STOT) coaches need to continuously reflect, receive feedback, and learn about their own unconscious biases, which often influence who they pay the most attention to and how (see McGilchrist's concept of 'attention is a moral act' mentioned earlier in the chapter). This bias can be seen in whose views and comments they attend to or validate and with whom they are seen to align or partner.

Developing a healthy leadership and organizational culture requires not only recruiting the necessary diversity but also valuing, listening to and utilizing that diversity within teams and across the organization. This includes gender, age, ethnicity, personality types, neurodiversity, abilities, gender identities, sexual orientations and more. I, Peter, defined 'requisite diversity' as having at least as much diversity within the organization as exists among the stakeholder communities it serves (Hawkins, 2021).

The STOT coach also has a responsibility to notice who might be excluded, overlooked or not respected and to facilitate more inclusive and healthier engagement. It is essential to foster a sense of belonging at multiple levels, within the team, the region or division, the organization, and the broader stakeholder system, helping people experience, recognize and feel connected across these systemic layers.

DIEB considerations involve supporting those with nominal authority, such as senior leaders at the team, division and organizational levels, while also empowering those with less power. This includes challenging the status quo and inviting unheard voices, both within the organization and from the broader ecosystem, into conversations and ensuring they are heard.

Early in my career, my mentor advised me (Peter) to always support both the nominal authority (the team leader) and the biggest risk-taker, the voice of challenge, when working with teams. Both carry significant responsibility and risk and need empathy, compassion and support. In doing so, we aim not to uphold fixed authority and stability or foster chaos, but to create dynamic kinetic stability, a balance that allows for continuity through the necessary constant change.

Conclusion

In this chapter we have explored eight of the most common ethical dilemmas that we have both found, and indicated ways each of these dilemmas could be worked with and learnt from.

Beyond these individual dilemmas, we found that true partnership in team of teams coaching projects is fostered by a shared passion for the organization's purpose and its vision for the future. Without shared love, true partnership, strong teaming and learning at the edge, long-term successful team of teams projects are impossible. The organization and the team of teams coaches who work with the development and transformation of the organization must have a joint love for the purpose of the work and for working together to develop the future of the organization, that the wider world needs. This is a love to partner with organizations on the journey to being 'net-positive', thus co-creating beneficial value, with and for all its stakeholders and ecosystem partners.

At the joint learning edge, where both coaches and organizations are learning, we both can see a window and a mirror: a window through which we can see the work that is necessary and essential, and a mirror that reflects what both parties themselves must change to be in service of this work.

14

Tools and methods for Systemic Team of Teams Coaching

Introduction

Throughout this book we have included a number of tools and methods for Systemic Team of Teams Coaching (STOTC) and for transforming organizations. In this chapter we bring together some more tools and methods that we have found to be very helpful in our work in these areas, as well as those that emerged from the research.

We start by exploring the methods and tools for contracting, both with the organization and the team of team coaches (both internal and external) to create a strong foundation for the work to progress. Then we move to the inquiry and sense-making stage, assessing what is already working well in and between teams, and what needs to change, for the organization to be future-fit. This includes tools and methods for mapping both the network of teams and the meshwork of many flows and interdependences between teams and their wider stakeholder ecosystem.

The next section provides a summary of some of the most useful tools and methods for each stage of the team of teams journey. These include approaches we have developed in our own work, as well as those generously shared by organizations and other practitioners, during our research.

The preparation: starting with yourself

Throughout this book we have mentioned how the most important tool or instrument you have is yourself and this instrument needs constant developing and tuning. Every engagement we do is an opportunity for learning and development of our systemic awareness, vertical development (see Chapter 12) and our ethical maturity (Chapter 13). So, we begin with a core practice, I, Peter, developed for training inter-faith celebrants and then brought to the development of systemic team coaches. Every team coaching session is, in some way, a rite of passage of a shift from one way of thinking and being, to another way. So, this is a practice leaders, coaches and consultants can do before each important meeting (Hawkins, 2021: 308–09).

Opening the even levels

Picture the team you are about to coach, listen to their voice and sense their presence in your imagination. Recall the journey they are on and their context.

Centre and connect with yourself through some deeper breaths and longer exhales. Sense into your body. Soften and let go of tension. Feel your feet connecting to the earth. Centre your attention on your out breaths and in breaths deep in your abdomen.

1 The first level is to open to the individuals on the team and picture them with loving kindness, compassion and openness.

2 Then, refocus on the relational connections within the team. Who is closer or more connected to whom? What is the quality of these relational flows? Sense the feeling or mood. What colour or music would describe the spaces between them?

3 Open to the wider community of immediate stakeholders, including employees, customers, suppliers, investors and communities. How does the energy shift? What are you sensing?

4 Move your focus to those who are often ignored, such as future customers and organizational partners, future employees and wider future generations. What voices do you hear from them about this team's work? Whose voice is needing to be heard?

5 Now, zoom out and shift your attention to the whole interconnected human family, all eight billion of us that share this planet. How is this team contributing to our wider connected human family, and moving us to a more inclusive and equitable world?

6 Move your attention to the more-than-human world of all the sentient beings that surround us, and the elements that support and flow through

us in the air we breathe, the food and drink we take in and live from, and the non-renewable resources we consume. Sense the deep connections of this team to the Earth we are part of and which supports us every moment of every day. Hold this expansiveness in your awareness.

7   Finally, sense opening the door to the mystery of oneness and inter-being – that which connects everything, beyond time and space, beyond words, and certainly beyond our own limited comprehension. Feel the deep interconnection – how you and the team are joined with all that is, has been and will be.

Now please come back down through the levels, sensing how the wider systemic levels live in and flow through those that are more immediate and local levels.

What we know from the experience of many practitioners who have experimented with mindfulness practices like this one is that when you open to some new awareness within you, even though you never mention it, others start sharing at that same level, as though they had only been waiting for our readiness to hold space with expanded awareness, and listen more deeply, spaciously and systemically.

Sponsorship and contracting methods

When asked how I sell Systemic Team Coaching, I, Peter, reply that I never do. The process begins by talking to senior leaders about their current and future challenges, and then where they think the organization needs to travel towards, for it to flourish in the future. We then explore the journey that is necessary, and I share my experience of what most enables such a journey. Before we begin a complex team of teams journey, we nearly always need to speak with a least three key sponsors. This is often, but not always the CEO, HR director and Chair of the Board. From the outset, the work needs to involve collaboration across levels and teams.

Sometimes the organization is ready to contract for a full organizational transformational journey (Chapter 6), but often they will start by contract-ing the first stage (Chapter 4). This may be Systemic Team Coaching of the leadership team, or a wider organizational inquiry and evaluation.

If, and when, they are ready for working across several teams or trans-forming their organization, it is wise to create an 'Organizational Transformation Steering Group' that represents key sponsors, HR and internal developers, and a diverse mix of team leaders.

The coach or consultant should share insights from other successful STOTAs and common pitfalls (see Chapters 4, 6 and 8) with this group. Establishing this kind of steering group or advisory board during the early planning phase is ideal. While setting it up later can still work, early planning helps build momentum, generates greater value and enhances the likelihood of success.

Collaborative inquiry and contracting

The co-inquiry should be done by the steering group and the systemic team coaches in partnership to understand an organization's:

- stage in its life cycle (Chapter 5)
- strengths (see appreciative inquiry in Chapter 3)
- aspirations
- current and future challenges
- perceived impact and role within its ecosystem
- evolving stakeholder expectations and their future needs

STOTA coaches use a variety of assessments and methods including our 'High-Value Creating Team Questionnaire', 'Team Maturity Assessment', 'Descriptor Analysis' (all three are in Hawkins, 2021) and Vertical Development Assessment (see Chapter 12).

Sense-making methods and designing the process

Having carried out a co-inquiry process, then it is important to have a 'Co-discovery' workshop, either with the senior leadership team or the steering group. There are a number of sense-making methods that can help distil the collected data into a clear understanding of where the organization is currently, where it needs to get to, and a possible roadmap for the journey.

Setting the scene and contract for the session

We also start the sense-making workshop by encouraging participants to leave their roles, judgements and solutions outside the door and become like curious visitors and anthropologists to their own organization. We ask them what are the most important questions that they want the data to help them answer. First, they write these down individually, then share and refine them through a 'collective build' (Hawkins, 2021: 114–16, 371–72). This enrols them as curious inquirers, helping them see the data as a resource and not a judgement. We then contract for what we need to have achieved by the end of the workshop, and the process for getting there.

Fishbone analysis

In Hawkins (2021: 93–96) I, Peter, outlined the fishbone method that we have used with many teams and organizations for this collective sense making. On a very large sheet (or Miro or Mural board if working virtually), we:

1 place the key current strengths and challenges at the fish's tail
2 place the vision of where the organization needs and aspires to be in two to three years' time, at the head
3 collectively plan the journey from then, back to now, along the fish's spine
4 develop these key spine stages into processes, project or events on the appropriate rib coming from the spine

Doing this with moveable Post-it notes, with everyone working together at the chart, creates a journey plan that everyone owns.

Systemic Team of Teams network analysis

There are many ways of mapping teams and team of teams, organizations, and their wider ecosystem. We have built on the work of Barabási (2016), Carboni and Cross (2020) and others, to develop our own approach to mapping networks.

Network Theory focusses on the patterns of connections and relationships in any system - whether: mechanical, such as a train or telephone network; technological, such as a computer system; physical, such as relational patterns between particles in an atom; biological, such as an ant colony; medical, such as the blood flow system in the body, or the neuronal networks in the brain, heart and gut; or human, such as social networks in communities, or innovation networks in and between organizations.

A key concept in network theory is the study of nodes and links. In mapping, networks entities are represented as nodes (or vertices), and their relationships are represented as edges (or links). If we look at a team as a network, then the individuals are nodes and the connections between them are edges or links.

If we look at an organization as an internal network, then the various teams are nodes, and their relationships, including the exchanges of services and resources, are edges or links. If we look at an organization's stakeholder ecosystem, then each stakeholder grouping becomes a node and we can map the different types of connections between all the stakeholders, as well as the links to different team nodes within the organization.

In our systemic network analysis, we carry out a picture sculpt of the team of teams and then analyse each node via four elements:

- **Degree centrality:** The number of connections a node has.

- **Connecting centrality:** How often a node acts as the main connector between two other nodes.

- **Closeness centrality:** How close a node is to all other nodes in the network.

- **Influence:** A measure of a node's influence on its neighbouring nodes. This is similar to what is referred to as 'Eigenvector Centrality' (Freeman, 1979), which assesses a node's influence by considering both the number of connections it has and the significance of the nodes to which it is connected.

Network mapping, measuring and analysing has a number of important benefits in being able to see a team, organization or ecosystem as a living system that is made up of relationships. However, it mainly focusses on the horizontal connections within a system, such as how particles relate within an atom, and usually ignores the systemic vertical relationships between parts and wholes.

It also comes from a paradigm of seeing nodes as primary and links as secondary and of seeing relationships as created by the relata. Even the words node and edge imply the node is primary and the edge derives from it.

So increasingly, we have incorporated meshwork theories and approaches (Ingold, 2007, 2011) into our work. This perspective helps us to clearly see:

- the web of interconnected flows and practices and relationships

- the relationships as equally, if not more, important than the nodes

- how the relationships are dynamic and fluid, constantly shaping each other
- the meshwork as an open and unbounded system, connected to other meshworks, which create a larger meshwork of meshworks
- how meshworks adapt continuously to other systemic levels they are nested within
- the movement and change within meshworks, and how interactions shape their structure and dynamics

Visualizing systems

I, Peter, described how to do detailed picture sculpts of teams (Hawkins, 2021: 378–79), and enacted psychodrama sculpts and team and organizational constellations in Hawkins and Presswell (2022).

All of these methods can be adapted for working with team of teams, where instead of constellating or portraying individuals and their connections, the process draws or portrays the teams and the connections between them.

Team of teams picture sculpt

No team operates alone – its success depends on how it engages with other teams and groups. This exercise helps teams visualize their network, uncover hidden patterns and identify where connections need strengthening. By mapping relationships symbolically, teams gain insight into their interdependencies and evolving landscape.

1 Each team to draw, on large piece of paper a symbol that represents their own team along with metaphorical symbols for all the other teams they need to engage with in order to do their work. Teams that are most closely connected to them should be drawn nearer and those that are less connected further placed away. It is also helpful to do internal teams and groupings in one colour and external groups in another, even if some of these external groups are closer in proximity.

2 Then symbolically draw the quality of the connections, e.g. a two-way flowing river, an intermittent signal, full of barriers and walls, etc.

3 Stand back and see the bigger picture and ask:

a. What groups have been missed out?

b. What new groupings may come into the picture in the next two years?

c. How is the landscape changing?

d. If this was a picture, a landscape, a piece of music, what would it be?

e. What is in flow and harmony, and what is blocked or discordant?

f. What connections in the meshwork need changing or developing?

When a number of teams have completed this exercise, they can create a gallery of their picture sculpts. Each team leaves one or two members to explain their map, while the remaining members visit other teams' displays, to see how their team and connections are represented in others' pictures. Then they can return to their team, with the insights from these multiple perspectives, and explore how they might amend their picture. Next, they create a development plan in the light of this feedback.

Now it is useful for each team to share with the others:

a. Three things we appreciate about our network connections with you are…

b. Three ways we will be strengthening our connections with you are…

c. New ways we could partner with other teams, to serve third parties are…

Following this sharing, teams can form joint agreements and commitments to strengthen important connections, as well as address key blockages.

Polarities and paradoxes

In the world of increasing complexity, there are very seldom straightforward solutions to key challenges. A key skill for all leaders and coaches is to avoid either-or debates and generate systemic ways of navigating through them.

In Hawkins (2025: 80), I lay out 'The four laws of either-ors'.

- **Law one:** If you are having the same 'either-or' debate for the third time, you are almost certainly asking the wrong question.

- **Law two:** Both solutions are inadequate and incomplete and likely to sub-optimize one part of the system at the cost of the wider system. Or as Peter Senge (1990) pointed out, simple solutions get us out of one problem, but leads us into the next one.

- **Law three:** Each solution represents important systemic needs that must be addressed in order to move forward; yet we have not found a way of connecting these currently disconnected needs.

- **Law four:** The way forward is not a compromise between the two opposing 'either/or' solutions, for that would in effect combine two wrong solutions. Rather, what is needed is collectively to find a creative third position, that transcends the limited frame of thinking, from which the 'either/or' debate emerged.

There are four levels of responding to polarities (Price and Toye, 2017). If we take a very common polarity, 'should we centralize or decentralize?', we can explore these four levels.

Level one is to choose one answer or the other, or swing between the two possibilities. For instance, the organization decides to decentralize, and let all regions and functions self-determine. Then in a year or two they discover that every region and function have developed their own central functions like finance, technology and HR, creating extra costs, misalignment and confusion, so they begin recentralizing (This is win-lose thinking).

In level two the organization looks for a compromise and decides what functions to centralize and what to have self-determined locally, with rules on delegated authority. But so often compromises lead to the worst of both worlds and endless debate on what the compromise should mean in practice (every approach half loses).

At level three, the organization adopts 'both-and thinking', aiming to achieve the full benefits of both approaches. It seeks to maintain consistency while allowing local flexibility, striving for a win-win solution.

Only in level four do we begin to work systemically, moving beyond dualistic thinking to triangulated thinking (Hawkins, 2025), aiming for a 'win-win-win'. The third win starts by asking who we serve, what is the value we create for them, and what do they need from the solution. Here we begin to consider how we meet the needs of customers for reliability and choice, the funders' need for efficiency and return on their investment and employees' need for feeling they have some autonomy in their work. We start to design a way forward from both 'outside-in' and 'future-back' perspectives.

There are a number of tools that can help such as:

1 **Reframing** the polarity in a wider systemic context.

2 **Bringing in the stakeholders' perspective:** Ask who the solution needs to serve. This can be done through data, by having team members 'stepping into the shoes' of different stakeholders, and speaking as them, or bringing stakeholders into a team workshop.

3   **Balancing and integrating competing priorities** into a virtuous cycle of benefit.

4   **Starting future-back:** Asking how we will know in five years' time that we have navigated the right course through this?

5   **Causal loop mapping:** See Senge (1990), Senge et al (1994).

6   **Polarity management:** See Johnson (1992), Hawkins (2025: Chapter 13).

Nudging the team of teams connections

In the Renewal Associates work with GHD described earlier, Peter designed 'nudges' that could be used by all 11 Renewal Associates, and all 30 GHD internal, systemic team coaches, when leading or coaching teams.

This was designed to help teams adopt the mindset and habits of global networking and cross-boundary teaming.

Team of team nudges

1   When the team is faced with a challenge internally or externally, ask: 'Who has already addressed this issue at GHD and what could you learn from them?'

2   If they respond, 'I have no idea' then ask: 'How could you find out?'

3   Ask them how many people they have working for their team? If they answer with the number on their team, respond by saying: 'No, you have several thousand, but you have not yet found how to get them to partner with you.'

4   Ask them which areas they are most trying to develop their work in, and then ask: 'How are you leveraging the global experience of GHD to accelerate this development?'

5   Explore what are the top three dream projects they would love to be working on within the next two years. Then ask: 'How could you use GHD's global network of contacts and global expertise to make that happen?'

6   Ask: 'What has been your best success and best failure in the last three months?' Then ask: 'How have you shared the learning from both, with other relevant teams?'

7 Ask: 'What is your best experience of teaming beyond your own region/function?' Then: 'How can you build on this elsewhere?'

8 Ask: 'What is your best experience of teaming with client organizations and other partners, in doing good work? How can you build on this in future projects?'

Lands work across teams

Another method we draw on is 'Lands Work' (Rod and Fridjhon, 2016). We have adapted this method for team of teams work, for building inter-team understanding, empathy and alignment.

Each team is given either their own space within a large room, or if working virtually, a breakout room and share of a joint Mural or Miro board. They are given 20–30 minutes to arrive at a joint portrayal of their team as an 'Island nation' complete with its own:

a. landscape

b. weather

c. flag

d. anthem

e. beliefs

f. rituals and celebrations

g. behaviours

h. industries

i. trading partners etc.

We encourage teams to move beyond conceptual language and create pictures, songs, maps, and use whatever is around to give us a full experience of their world.

Then the whole group reassembles, and in turn visits each team's land. We encourage them to be curious tourists or anthropologists and leave judgements and reactions at home. Once they have been taken around the other team's island, they are invited to ask curious inquiry questions to draw out a deeper understanding, in themselves and in the team presenting. Commenting on the presentation is not allowed.

When all islands have been visited, the whole group is invited in the middle of the room or Mural/Miro board, to create 'Our Land', the land that belongs to, and is the responsibility of, all the teams. This defines the joint purpose, area of collaboration and joint responsibility to which all the other teams contribute. All the elements used to create the separate team lands earlier are now used to create 'Our Land' – anthem, flag, rituals etc.

In this process it is important to pay attention to:

- whose voices are being heard, whose are missing, and how to ensure all teams and stakeholders have representation and influence in the system
- where energy, information or resources flow smoothly across the system and where blockages (e.g. silos, misalignment) are disrupting progress
- how individual team goals align with the shared collective purpose and where fragmentation exists, prompting collective alignment across the ecosystem

It can be helpful to have a collective hub space for:

- shared emerging themes
- emerging issues that the team of teams need to attend to

Teaming externally

In STOTC we have facilitated many workshops between teams and external teams and groups that they need to team with, for both mutual benefit and to co-create a better way of meeting all their joint stakeholders needs. Here is an example.

Peel Police's transformation journey

In Hawkins (2022) we included a case study of the systemic team of teams work in the Peel Police in Canada. This was led by the Police Chief Nish Duraiappah and coached by Heather Clayton. This foundation positioned Peel Police to move beyond developing its internal culture and team of teams to teaming across its boundaries with various parts of its wider community. These included ecosystem partners like Boys2Men (supporting at-risk youth), and the Intimate Partner Violence Unit. These partnerships reflect a deliberate cultural shift towards collaboration, co-creation and shared responsibility.

A powerful example of this shift emerged when Peel Police responded to a call about a young man agitated and wandering his neighbourhood in his boxers. Officers, unaware of his context, used a Taser and handcuffed him. His father later explained that the young man had severe autism, and the incident left the family traumatized.

Although the officers were exonerated, Peel Police chose reflection over justification. They asked: '*What could we do differently?*' This pivotal question marked the start of a restorative, coaching-led response:

1 Community engagement: Leveraging existing relationships, Peel's Division Mobilization Unit (DMU) invited the young man's father to share his story.

2 Collaborative learning: Listening deeply to the family's lived experience, Peel Police launched an 'Autism Collaborative' that brought together:

 a. families and individuals with autism

 b. officers with personal connections to autism

 c. partner organizations advocating for autism services

Through these conversations, Peel Police applied Systemic Team Coaching principles like deep listening, alignment and co-creation to develop meaningful next steps. Initiatives included tailored programmes to strengthen relationships between officers and the autism community and proactive safety measures to support vulnerable populations.

Recognizing the need for systemic consistency, Peel Police embedded coaching principles into front-line operations. A *designated officer* now reviews call recordings flagged with autism-related keywords. This ensures that individuals or situations requiring support receive the necessary interventions, further integrating their learning into day-to-day practices.

Peel Police's transformation earned them the Community Safety and Well-Being Award from the Canadian Association of Chiefs of Police. This recognition affirmed their commitment to systemic change and amplified their impact, inspiring other police forces across Canada. Peel Police leaders have been invited to share their journey at national conferences, spreading their innovative approaches.

By teaming and partnering across the organization's boundaries, with both families and organizations, Peel Police turned a crisis into an opportunity for inclusive, sustainable solutions.

Conducting large team of teams workshops

I, Peter, was meeting with a senior leader in organizational development in a very successful American-led global organization. They were telling me how they had introduced director forums for the 75 directors in the region, who were the vital engine room of their business. The forums were well attended, and they were led and organized by the directors themselves. The senior leader was keen to explore how they could get more value from these events, given employment costs of tying up 70-plus leaders for a couple of hours, as well as the opportunity cost for the business.

If you are going to bring your best brains and key leaders together either virtually or in person, start by working out what the cost is for your organization, and how you are going to get a measurable high return on that investment. Then start with the end in mind and work out what you need those attending to leave thinking, feeling, saying and doing differently. Then ask: how can the event itself embody the message and model the new culture we aim to create for the future?

I shared with him some of our top advice based on over 45 years of helping organizations make their leadership meetings and conferences and town hall meetings more impactful and value creating.

1. From topics to current challenges

The senior leader shared how the directors chose the topics and agenda items for the next forum. I suggested they change the language and instead of discussing possible topics, ask the working group of directors what were the top challenges that this group could collectively impact.

2. Focus on challenges that can be only dealt with by this group of people

We then explored what were the challenges that these middle leaders was best placed to address, rather than waiting for senior leaders to decide, or dealing with them in their separate silos. Most of these were challenges concerning horizontal partnering and learning across the business. Barry Oshry (2007) points out that the top leaders need to focus on the external and the future, while the middle leaders take responsibility for joining up and integrating the organization. We teach how this middle cadre of leaders are key to creating a 'team of teams' across the middle layers of an organization.

3. Facilitate real-time strategizing

A good leadership forum should engage all the brains and creativity in the room, and the best way to do this is to focus on real collective challenges for the organization that require new collaborative thinking. Senior leadership needs to articulate why these challenges are important for the future of the organization and ask for help from everybody in finding a new original response. There are a number of methodologies that can be used for doing real-time strategizing in large groups, face to face or online, such as Open-space technology (Owen, 2008), Real-time strategic change (Jacobs, 1997), Future-search (Weisbord and Janoff, 2010), World-café (Brown and Isaacs, 2005) and Hackathons (Hawkins, 2021: 236–37).

4. Be mindful of unconscious bias – yours and everyone's in the room

Leadership needs to stay mindful of unconscious bias, power and privilege – who is silent or being silenced through discounting or turning away? What patterns emerge in the group dynamic that limit the empowerment of all members to feel valued, heard and respected? It is essential to begin with a clear intent to create space for all voices – across roles, levels, tenure and diverse representations. However, setting an initial intent is not enough. Leaders must anticipate that bias will creep in and be prepared to name it when it does. Thoughtful self-disclosure, when done well and at the right moment, can be a powerful tool in this process.

5. From breakouts as discussion groups to task groups with well-defined outcomes

It can be useful to split a large leadership forum into small working groups, but it is important that each group is not just given a topic to explore, but is commissioned with a clear outcome that they are asked to bring back to the main plenary.

6. Ensure all breakout groups have a well-briefed facilitator

Each workgroup needs an appointed facilitator with clear process guidelines. Their job is to:

a. reiterate the outcomes the group need to achieve

b. get everyone's voice into the room within the first 3–4 minutes

c. use techniques like brainstorming, collective build, people stepping into the shoes of different stakeholder groups etc., to maximize creative thinking

d. manage time

e. return the group to core focus, if they get stuck or wander off track

f. ensure the group comes to a collective output which is summarized

If necessary, they could delegate one or more of these roles.

7. Ban reporting back from breakouts on their conversation

For many years I sat through large leadership gatherings where each small group would have one member feedback to the main plenary, and it became increasingly boring. I called it 'death by serial feedback!' I changed the process, which now included all members standing and jointly presenting their output, in a way that started a new live engagement and dialogue with all the other small groups. This included being clear about what they were asking other participants to commit to, and how they would take this proposal into action. This inter-group dialogue needs skilful facilitating to ensure the groups are co-creating better thinking and more energized commitment than the small groups did by themselves.

8. End with commitments not vague intentions

Agreement to a good idea is made with the cognitive brain, but real change is always embodied. If the change does not start in the room, it is very unlikely to happen when people are back at work, bombarded with emails, meetings and demands, and falling back into their past engrooved habits. Start being the change you want to see and beginning the actions right there in the room.

Example of a large team of teams event at GHD

In earlier chapters we have shared some of the story of GHD's journey to becoming a globally networked company, supported by an extensive team of team's journey. As part of this work with GHD, I, Peter, and colleagues facilitated several large leadership and partnership workshops. In 2023 at their annual gathering of the top 120 leaders, we radically redesigned their normal format. We said: 'There will be no platform, podium or presentations!' Instead, the large room was set up with 12 tables of 10 leaders. Each table was facilitated by one member of the top team who had been given brief training and guidance on how to facilitate their table team. Each table was selected to have a maximum diversity of countries and roles. In the middle of the circles of tables was a large theatre in the round, for real-time interchange between groups and the whole gathering.

The three-day gathering started with the song 'Surfing USA' (we were hosted in Huntingdon Beach California!). The music got louder and louder till everyone had taken their seats, and then suddenly stopped and the room went dark. Onto the screen came two important GHD clients saying what they appreciated about the work of GHD, and what they were going to need different from them over the next three years. This signalled that the conference was not going to be inward-looking, but instead, starting 'outside-in' and 'future-back'.

Many of the attendees were anxious as they had not been given the usual timetable agenda for the three days. So, we followed the client presentations by telling them the agenda was:

Day One: discovering how the organization could double the beneficial value they created in the world, within the next three years.

Day Two: to collectively work out the roadmap to achieve the 2027 vision and outcome.

Day Three: to start the transformation process live in the room and create clear joint commitments across the organization before everyone returns to their own countries and functions.

Despite much pre-scepticism of how this would work, the event was extremely engaging and high energy from start to finish. Transformation happened in the room, at personal, inter-personal, inter-team and function levels. It also created a lasting legacy of new ways of doing events both internally and externally.

Evaluation and evolution

As discussed in Chapter 7, evaluation of all development work should not just happen at the end of the process, but weave throughout the whole journey. When undertaking a complex journey it is important to check progress and also changing conditions at regular intervals. The map and plan of the journey is always different from what is encountered en route. Constant evaluation, feedback and 'after action reviews' of what has occurred produces valuable learning and course correction, so that the work can evolve and learn from its own unfolding.

In Chapter 7 we provide a number of evaluation tools and methods that can be used to evaluate:

- the quality of the 'inputs'
- the learning and development 'outputs'
- the 'outcomes' in changed decisions, processes, behaviours and actions
- the 'value creation' that this creates for all key stakeholder groups
- the 'ROI' return on investment of the process

Putting the different methods together

When designing a team of teams or organizational transformation journey (see Chapters 4 and 6), it is important to adapt and weave a number of these tools and methods into the process. So we end this chapter with a reflection on a three-year team of teams organizational transformation, written jointly by Alex Bristol the CEO, and Inge Simon and Peter Hawkins who were the organizational coaches.

Flying high: the story of Skyguide

Skyguide, the Swiss Air Navigation Services Provider (ANSP) is responsible, on behalf of the Swiss confederation, for ensuring safety in the Swiss civil and military airspace as well as delegated parts of Austria, Germany, France and Italy.

Alex Bristol spent six years at Skyguide as Chief Operating Officer before being appointed CEO. During this time, he gained a deep understanding of the organization's longstanding culture – recognizing both its strengths and areas where inefficiencies and shortcomings existed.

The majority of employees are Air Traffic Controllers (ATCs), highly skilled experts. Their sense of belonging within the organization had been challenged by the advent of the Virtual Centre, which enables location-independent air traffic control. As CEO, one of Alex's key challenges was to shift mindsets, encouraging employees to move beyond their traditional expertise and embrace a transformative approach to their roles and the organization's future.

In the inquiry phase of the Systemic Team Coaching work, Inge perceived a number of emerging challenges.

1 **Collective leadership:** The need to move from a hub-and-spoke to a more collective and distributive leadership.

2 **The complexity of the stakeholder landscape:** Skyguide, being 99.91 per cent owned by the Swiss state, works closely with the Swiss Federal Government, national air traffic controllers, regulators, airlines, unions and boards. Early in its journey, airline passengers were not considered stakeholders, as Skyguide did not interact with them directly. This oversight is, often referred to as the '13th fairy', is a term that refers to who you forget to include, sometimes at your peril.

3 **The need for organizational transformation:** The organization faced a critical need for transformation to address the challenges of managing increasing air traffic, raising work quality standards, and remaining within financial constraints while demonstrating that their services were competitively priced compared to other successful European providers.

4 **Developing leaders:** Inge identified key polarities that leaders need to recognize and learn to navigate effectively, such as: stability and flexibility; security and uncertainty; operational efficiency (run) and innovation (transform); innovation and regulation; command and control versus empowerment; sustainability and quick wins; safety and capacity; high quality delivery and cost-effectiveness; service excellence and efficiency cost savings and future investment; top-down leadership and bottom-up engagement; and high reliability and cost savings.

5 **The need to shift the relationship between the board and executive:** At the same time there were many changes in the board membership, with many board members leaving and new board members arriving, which presented both an opportunity and a challenge. There was a need to involve more executive members in the supervisory board meetings, rather than everything going through the CEO.

6 **A need for the CEO to adopt a different leadership style:** The CEO needed to adopt a different leadership style, transitioning into the role of an

orchestrator and coach. This approach involved encouraging the team to step up, work collaboratively across boundaries (horizontally integrating), and reduce their dependency on the CEO.

The CEO Alex Bristol takes up the story.

The organization was very good in a crisis, and there were many of them, but decisions, change management and projects took far too long and were inefficient. We were very siloed not just between departments, but even between the divisions within each department. What I saw happening was that managers, rather than resolving issues directly would report them upwards, assuming their boss or their bosses boss would sort it out.

This also happened in our Executive Board, with the previous CEO having bilateral meetings with each executive and then going away and making the final decision by himself, so there was never full team ownership to what was decided. Decision-making was very slow.

I started the change process two months before I formally took over. With my predecessor's agreement I met with the Executive Board without him and we worked through a 'Stop, Start, Continue' exercise. What we collectively agreed had to change for the company to move forward. We decided that we needed a more joined-up organization, quicker decision-making and collective team leadership. I started by partnering with Inge Simons to work with the Operations Team I was leading, and continued to work with her during my transition.

Soon after I stepped into the CEO role, we brought in Peter Hawkins alongside Inge to work with our top team. We had a two-and-a-half-day workshop, where we collectively worked together to look at the future challenges that were coming over the horizon, our complex range of stakeholders, and then to co-create a strategy and vision for the company for the next 3–5 years.

At a later workshop with Peter and Inge, we rehearsed presenting this strategy and vision, in pairs with every team member part of the presentation and everyone getting feedback from their peers. So, we had to not only own it, but also embody it. This was great preparation for Covid, as although every team member had to lead more by themselves, they had a felt sense of what the rest of the team thought and could represent the whole team.

When new members came on board, within their first weeks and months, we invited them to share observations of the team, which gave us a fresh perspective on existing dynamics and patterns of behaviour.

We employ 1,500 full-time equivalents but, with many part-time employees, the number is closer to 1,750. It was essential to get everyone on board with shaping what the future needed us to become. We needed new engagement architecture, that would overcome the silos and create a culture of leadership and engagement at all levels. Using a world cafe structure, we explored the current culture and what needed to shift to enable the employees to be full partners in the transformation, while honouring what we would take with us from our rich heritage.

We moved from having large meetings of the senior leadership, which were led by myself, to what we now call the 'Horizon Team', which comprises the 50 most influential leaders across the business – the ones who have the creativity, energy and influence to bring about change. This team meets three times a year. Meetings are set up with small teams on separate round tables, with each member of the top team at different tables, addressing current and future challenges for the organization. The top team increasingly took on leadership roles in these events, while the broader group became more actively involved in shaping the new culture needed to implement our strategy.

Every leader needs to be a storyteller and needed to realize that engaging, motivating and aligning their people was more important than being a technical expert.

Another idea from Peter we took up and have developed was to introduce a Shadow Executive Board, which we call the 'Mirror Board'. I wanted greater diversity of thinking coming into the Executive team, particularly generational diversity. I asked senior leaders to nominate individuals aged 30 or younger who demonstrated exceptional talent and potential for future leadership. Initially, I selected six candidates, but the group quickly recognized the need for someone with a strong financial background, so we added a seventh member. This group meets monthly, two or three days before the Executive Board convenes, to discuss two or three significant topics that the Executive Board is grappling with. Twice a year, they gather for a full day to review their progress and consider additional topics they believe the Executive Board should address. They often identify issues that we might overlook.

They present a paper outlining their findings to the Executive Board's deliberations. I make it a point to circle back to them, explaining what was decided, how the decision was reached and why. In 75 per cent of cases, the Executive Board's decision aligns closely with the proposals from the Mirror Board. They also attend live some of our top team meetings so we can co-create new thinking together.

We also have a leadership development day once a year when we bring together the top 200 leaders. We generally start with a presentation of a new theory or model, and then have the leaders apply this to their own work and practice using new approaches around their tables and commit to how they will use this back at work.

Because of the work with the top team, the Operational and Technical teams meet together twice a year, which is about 45 people, and work on what they can co-create and resolve together to take the organization forward.

We are very good when there is a crisis and we call a crisis meeting which brings together all the people who need to be around the table to address this, generate the learning and make the necessary changes happen. Our challenge is to have the same joined-up collaboration before it becomes a crisis.

Another forum we've established, drawing on our experience with Agile team working, is the PIPE meetings (Project Implementation Planning Events). These gatherings bring together the relevant stakeholders to collaboratively plan the next stage of a project. It would be beneficial if we could infuse these meetings with the same energy, collaboration, and generative spirit that characterized our crisis meetings.

When asked, 'What would you do differently if you were starting again?' Alex reflected:

I would begin the same way we did, but I would have introduced the Mirror board much earlier in the process. Additionally, in the second year, rather than relying on each Executive Board member to independently develop their teams as we did with the Executive team, I would have involved systemic team coaches like yourselves to work with each team and foster stronger connections between them.

Conclusion

In this chapter we have shared practical tools and methods for Systemic Team of Teams Coaching (STOTC), from robust scoping, contracting and inquiry to journey and network mapping and storytelling. These approaches help teams uncover hidden patterns, bridge silos and align around shared purpose. By fostering trust, agility and collaboration, coaches empower teams to balance stability with innovation and tackle challenges together.

The examples show how creative, participatory methods and forums can spark real transformation. Whether mapping networks, co-creating stories or surfacing insights, these tools turn complexity into opportunity. By helping teams connect, reflect and act, systemic team of teams coaches set the stage for lasting, meaningful change across organizations and ecosystems.

Back to one

But let us end how we began, with looking at a simple practice we can all do, to develop our systemic effectiveness, at whatever level or context we are working, even at home with our friends and family.

From grumble to gratitude

I, Peter, have developed a simple yet very challenging practice for leaders, coaches, systemic team coaches and systemic team of teams coaches: 'From Grumble to Gratitude' (Hawkins, 2025).

It begins each time someone you lead or coach discusses a problem in their work or life, or when you encounter something in your own life that you internally perceive as 'a problem'.

1   **Turn all problems into challenges:** When someone shares a problem, gently reframe it by replacing the word 'problem' with 'challenge'. This shifts the perspective from viewing it as something to be solved, to seeing it as an opportunity to be embraced. It encourages moving beyond isolated atomistic thinking to recognize the issue as part of a larger challenge and pattern that can only be addressed within its broader context.

2   **Always locate the challenge in a connection, not in an individual or a part:** Ensure that the connection includes your role in it. We can only truly understand a system by being connected to it, making any observation about the system inherently self-reflective and tied to our relationship with it. Moreover, we can only help a system we are part of, starting with the essential step of changing ourselves first.

3   **Treat the challenge as a generous lesson that life has given you:** Our most difficult colleagues, bosses, customers, clients etc. are also our biggest teachers. They are showing an aspect of life we have not yet found a way of fully connecting to, or owning as also part of ourselves.

4 **Find gratitude in your heart for the challenge and lesson life has provided:**
   This is easy to do when we like the challenge and/or feel confident in how
   we might respond, but extremely difficult when we resent the challenge,
   feel we are victimized by it or feel overwhelmed. If we can practise finding
   the gratitude in our heart, we find it is one of the most effective ways out
   of victimhood and overwhelm.

5 **Now do what is necessary to be done.**

PART FIVE

Going forward together

15

Going forward and looking back

Introduction

We started this book with the great challenges of our times. As a human species, we are facing a polycrisis with many challenges, including the climate emergency, global inequality, mass extinction of species, loss of biodiversity and the rapid increase in mental illness and distress. Unlike previous times of crisis and mass extinction in the Earth's history, this is the first to be caused by one species – humans. Behind the polycrisis is a metac crisis where all these great challenges are interdependent; we cannot address any one of them without addressing them all and the interconnections between them. All of them are symptoms of the failure of human consciousness to evolve in a way that is healthy for both the ecology and ourselves (Boulton, 2024; Hawkins, 2025; Lent, 2021; Whybrow et al, 2023).

In this final chapter we will review what we have learnt from this study and how creating and developing a flourishing team of teams can contribute to the 'great turning' of human consciousness that is needed (Macy, 2009; Macy and Johnstone, 2012) to create a regenerative transformation of our planet (Hawkins, 2021, 2025; Hutchins, 2021, 2024; Lent, 2021; Rifkin, 2009, 2022).

The need for global culture change

Peter Drucker is often quoted as saying 'Culture will eat your strategy for breakfast' and in our many years of working with change and development in organizations we have seen first-hand how true, and how often, this is the case. We are now witnessing how the strategy for sustainable global development, change and transformation – which is heroically spearheaded by: the

United Nations, with their sustainable development goals; many COP conferences; and many global bodies – is being eaten for breakfast, lunch and supper by our dominant world culture.

In Chapter 2, we explored how culture is many layered. The top layer includes the cultural norms of collective behaviours, habits, language and rituals. These emerge out of deeper patterns of feelings and emotions which in turn emerge from our unnoticed beliefs that frame how we make sense of the world (our epistemology) and how we understand the nature of our being (our ontology).

The dominant worldview of the last several hundred years was built on the scientific revolution. This began in the 16th century, and led to successive industrial revolutions, first with coal-fired steam engines which powered factories, trains and ships; then petrol engines took over, and this later led to aeroplanes and then rockets and satellites. The development of electricity enabled global communications, which led to the computer age and the current developments of the world wide web and artificial intelligence (Rifkin, 2022; Schwab, 2016). These have brought enormous benefits to our species in health, education, knowledge, travel, housing and power over the wider ecology.

The people and countries that first developed these scientific breakthroughs began to dominate the world, using the three 'C's of 'Capital, Colonization, and Carbon'. These dominating countries, which were mostly white western countries, no longer need to expand their empires, through large armies, or a more powerful navy, or air force. Instead, they use their strength in 'Capital' to exercise financial control. They can 'Colonize', not through human occupation, but through global trade. It is now the corporations that are the 'armies' which conquer by consumerization and economic and cultural colonization. Where past empires would impose their religion and beliefs through education, modern empires can seduce through marketing and consumerism, and cajole populations through the domination of markets, into their culture. The Cold War of the late 20th century was won by the US and the West because 'people preferred shopping malls, to the Gulags' (Harari, 2016, 2018).

This dominant culture of neo-liberal capitalism has many taken-for-granted beliefs (Harari, 2016; Hawkins, 2025; Lent, 2021; Rifkin, 2022) which include:

1 Humans are the peak of evolution.
2 Humans have a God-given right to rule and dominate the rest of the world.

3 Culture and nature are separate worlds.

4 The ecology and the rest of nature are there for humans to exploit and come without cost.

5 Evolution occurs through competition and the strongest win out.

6 Humans are fundamentally selfish.

7 World problems can be dealt with one at a time.

8 The answer to every major problem is technology.

9 Truth is arrived at through scientific empiricism, and what cannot be proved by science is, by definition, not true.

Already in the period 1949–1999 key pioneering writers and scholars were showing how the dominant human culture, built on the worldview listed above, could destroy not only our species but much of the beautiful ecology, of which we are just one small part. Selections of their writings should be on every school curriculum and every MBA and leadership training. Let us pay tribute to these early pioneers:

• Aldo Leopold (1949) *A Sand County Almanac*

• Rachel Carson (1962) *Silent Spring*

• Gregory Bateson (1972 and 1981) *Steps to the Ecology of Mind*, and *Mind and Nature*

• Arnie Naess (1987) *Self-realization: An ecological approach to being in the world*

• Lynn Margulis (1998) *Symbiotic Planet: A new look at evolution*

• Joanna Macy (1998) *World as Lover: World as self*

We have failed to listen to their warnings and take in their wisdom, but many have taken up their messages, and we have quoted many in this book.

They, and numerous others, have argued that we need to replace these 'epistemological errors' (Bateson, 1972) with new beliefs that are based on how the evolution of nature has brought about such a flourishing rich biodiversity of symbiotic ecologies.

We believe that the new worldview needs to transform the old beliefs by crossing them out and replacing them with new eco-centric and systemic awareness:

1 ~~Humans are the peak of evolution.~~

Humans are the youngest child of evolution and need to learn from their older brothers and sisters (Kimmerer, 2020).

2 ~~Humans have a given right to rule and dominate the rest of the world.~~

Humans can only flourish if they work in service of, and harmony with, the wider ecology.

3 ~~Culture and Nature are separate worlds.~~

Human culture is just one small part of nature.

4 ~~The ecology and the rest of nature are there for humans to exploit and come without cost.~~

Any species that exploits and destroys its ecology, diminishes its future and eventually destroys itself (Bateson, 1979).

5 ~~Evolution occurs through competition and the strongest win out.~~

Evolution evolves more through collaboration and symbiosis.

6 ~~Humans are fundamentally selfish.~~

Humans are fundamentally relational, collaborative and compassionate, it is culture, circumstances and fear that create selfishness.

7 ~~World problems can be dealt with one at a time.~~

The major challenges are all interconnected.

8 ~~The answer to every major problem is technology.~~

Technology can only solve technological problems, not positively change human consciousness or evolve human culture.

9 ~~Truth arrived out through scientific empiricism, and what cannot be proved by science is by definition not true.~~

Human science is another world belief that has brought both benefits and destruction in its wake.

The contribution of a Systemic Team of Teams Approach to global culture change

The Systemic Team of Teams Approach is, as we have shown in Chapter 3, a systemic way of looking at all levels of development from: individual coaching (Chapter 11), to team coaching (Chapter 10), to coaching connections between all parts of the organization (Chapter 9), to coaching the connections between the organization and all elements of their stakeholder world, to how organizations relate to the 'more-than-human world of the wider ecology (Chapter 6).

With this lens, leaders and those focussed on development (see Chapter 3), shift from focussing on individuals, problems and parts, to highlighting the flows that connect across the organization and the wider systemic levels of which the organization is just one small part.

Traditional approaches to individual, team and organizational development were built on neo-Darwinian and neo-liberal belief that the unit of flourishing and success and survival, was the individual, team, organization or species. But this is never the case. A child can only be healthy and flourish if their family is flourishing, the family can only flourish if their community is flourishing and has clean water and food, and the community can only flourish if its ecology is flourishing, the air is unpolluted and the climate allows for healthy living and production of food.

An ancient Chinese text attributed to Lao-Tse also looked at co-flourishing in the opposite direction:

If there is to be peace in the world,

There must be peace in the nations.

If there is to be peace in the nations,

There must be peace in the cities.

If there is to be peace in the cities,

There must be peace between neighbours.

If there is to be peace between neighbours,

There must be peace in the home.

If there is to be peace in the home,

There must be peace in the heart.

Health comes from the same root as the world whole. Healthy flourishing is always relational between any organism and all the systemic levels it is nested within. This realization has led us and others to develop the notion of 'Fractal flourishing', which combines fractal geometry, nested systemic thinking and the concepts of health and well-being (D'Arcy, 2015; Wilson, 1999).

Some of the key frameworks we have introduced throughout this book, that together build a systemic team of teams lens and approach, include:

- holarchy
- the fractal nature of holarchy, and two-way systemic nesting

- complex co-evolving systemic levels
- symbiosis and symbiogenesis
- networks and meshworks
- strategizing
- culture change
- organizational learning

The role of leadership

We believe that the role of an organizational leader is more akin to that of a conductor of an orchestra than an engineer, who builds an inanimate structure, or pulls levers to manage change. In a large orchestra, the musicians belong to different teams-violins, violas, cellos, double basses, brass, woodwind, tympani, etc., each with its team leader. Each team member needs to be in tune with their fellow team members while also listening to the music of the whole orchestra. Each team brings different expertise and plays a particular version of the overall score. All the teams need to be aligned, yet provide a differentiated contribution. They need to play distinct melodies simultaneously, co-creating a harmony that arises from their differences, and which is greater than the sum of the parts.

One CEO told Peter that his role was even more complicated, more like being the director of an opera theatre, with the need to create harmony, not just within the orchestra, but between the orchestra, the team of actors with their director, the scenery, props, lighting, the sales team, fundraising team, front of house, audiences, maintenance team – 'I could go on further', he added, but I, Peter, said, 'I have got the picture', or should I have said 'Opera'!

Harmony requires and emerges from differentiation. At times, it needs the creative tension and competition that emerges from all teams wanting to do their best. However, what is essential is each team remains more aligned with the overall purpose, than focussed solely on their own local success.

In Chapter 13, on ethical dilemmas, we show how the heart of 'systemic ethics' is to be in service of, and co-create value for, all systemic levels that the team is nested within. Unethical team functioning occurs when teams concentrate on their own success, in ways that are detrimental to these wider systems.

The future role of STOTA in bringing together the different development professions

In Chapter 3 we described the urgent need to overcome the fracturing and silos of the different professions who work to help individuals, teams, team of teams, and organizations and partnerships become future-fit. This book has been written with two very clear purposes:

1 To provide a well-researched and clearly defined development model and process for the intermediary level of development that conjoins Systemic Team Coaching and organizational development and transformation.

2 To offer a systemic approach that unifies all forms of development in organizations, from individual counselling and coaching; to team facilitation and team coaching; to coaching the connections across the organization and developing a team of teams; to organizational development and transformation including ways of teaming and partnering with the wider stakeholder and ecosystem partners; to shifting human consciousness and healing the split between the human and the 'more-than-human' world.

There is still much to be done to achieve both of these necessary but ambitious purposes, but we believe, and hope you now agree, that this book has made an important contribution on this journey, one that others will build on.

Our research (Chapter 8) and case studies (throughout the book), point to a several ways all forms of Systemic Team Coaching must evolve if they are to develop teams in ways that contribute meaningfully to transforming the wider organization. This contribution needs to be aligned to the regenerative journey of organizations towards becoming 'net-positive' and increasing the beneficial impact they co-create with and for all their stakeholders and the ecosystems within which they are nested.

The emerging agenda for team coaches and team of teams coaches

The emergent agenda for all those practising team facilitation and coaching ensures that:

1 The work has sponsorship and full engagement from the senior leadership.

2   The team development is linked, not only to the current business agenda, but the future changing needs of all stakeholders and ecosystem partners, including communities and the ecology.

3   The team's development is not just looking internally but continually exploring how the team can better partner and team with all the other teams in the organization. This particularly concerns those that are immediately above and beneath them, and those upstream and downstream in the value chain.

4   All teams need to also focus on how they team with all their stakeholders: investors, customers, suppliers, partner organizations, local communities and the ecology, on the journey to them becoming true ecosystem partners. The capacity to team well with customers and clients is increasingly becoming a competitive advantage.

5   You have the necessary training and development not only in team coaching, but in working systemically and in organizational development and transformation (see Chapters 6 and 12).

6   You have regular supervision from a Systemic Team Coaching supervisor (see Chapter 12 and the 'Recommended resources' section), preferably one who has worked organization wide using a Systemic Team of Teams Approach.

The agenda emerging for those who already, or wish to, coach multiple teams across an organization, both horizontally and vertically, include:

1   Incorporating all the above imperatives for systemic team coaches.

2   Ensuring you are well grounded in understanding organization's life cycles and transitions (see Chapter 5); organizational development and transformation (see Chapter 6); theories and models of organizational change (see Chapter 2); and that you know how to build from team coaching to inter-team coaching, to team of teams coaching, to organizational development (see Chapter 4).

3   Being able to build a partnership with multiple key sponsors at different levels and across different parts of the organization, thus avoiding being a 'go-between' (see Chapter 13).

4   Considering the increased complexity of the ethical dilemmas involved in this work (see Chapter 13).

5   Being able to create a team of suitable team of teams coaches, that are well inducted and aligned to the overall purpose of the organization and its transformational journey, not just to the teams they will be working with.

6   Ensuring the contracting with all members of this team of coaches are clear. This includes having a shared but differentiated approach that provides a common language and methods across all the teams being coached but is flexed for the different needs of individual teams. The contracting must also address all the requirements for working as an aligned team of team coaches, including attending team meetings and team supervision.

7   Having supervision collectively for the team of team coaches, which may also include internal team coaches, or leader representatives. This supervision should ideally be done by both the person leading the overall project and an experienced independent systemic team of teams supervisor (see Chapter 12).

The emerging agenda for the professions

From our research and case studies it is clear that organizations are increasingly requiring professional development practitioners, who can work across and between the various systemic levels of development: with individuals, teams, team of teams, organizations and between organizations and their stakeholders and ecosystem partners.

Currently the development professions, as we explored in Chapter 3, are fragmented, siloed, competing and all sub-optimal. In Chapter 3 we quoted Barbara Kellerman (2012: xiv) saying: 'the leadership industry has not in any major, meaningful, measurable way improved the human condition'. Twelve years later we believe some aspects of the different development professions have contributed to improvement, but the human population and the metacrisis of our times have grown even faster.

The time is ripe for professional bodies who all contribute to this agenda to come together. Coaches, team coaches, team of teams coaches and organizational development and transformation consultants, leadership development professionals, action researchers and strategy consultants, all need to align around a unifying purpose to help organizations, and those who work in them, to become truly 'future-fit'.

The emerging agenda for training organizations

You may remember the quote in Chapter 9, where the CEO who talked about how all their organization's challenges were not in the people or the parts, but in the connections, and asked: 'Where are the coaches and consultants who can coach the connections?' If we are to address the metacrisis of our times, it is crucial that all forms of development from personal and organizational, to national and societal, focus not just on the person or system they are working with, but also on all the parts and connections within that system and the wider systemic levels the person or system is nested within.

This requires all trainings to be systemic, supporting trainee developers whatever their primary focus, to develop 'systemic perceiving, thinking, doing and being' (see Chapter 12). The aim is not just to become expert technicians in the tools and methods of their craft, but to enable them to partner effectively across all levels of a system, to bring about the necessary regeneration and transformation. In the language of vertical development (see Chapter 12), this means to mature each person's worldview from that of an 'Expert-Technician', to 'Transforming', via the intermediate levels of 'Achieving' and 'Redefining'.

In the early stages of training, it is right that we learn the tools and methods and become proficient in them. But then we need all trainees to shift their focus from their own performance and process, to 'achieving' the purpose their craft and work are there to serve and the outcomes that are needed. This is not the outcome the coachee or team or organization necessarily want, but the one required for them to become future-fit, meeting the future needs of all their stakeholders and the necessity of organizations to become 'net-positive'.

Then the training needs to help trainees to become 'redefining'. Foundational to this is to see the deeper patterns through and beyond the presenting problems and symptoms; to see how these patterns are being played out across multiple systemic levels, and how different patterns are interconnected in a more complex meshwork of issues.

Only then can trainees across all development disciplines move beyond insight and action plans, to being 'Transforming': that is to work in partnership with coachees, teams, team of teams, organizations and wider systems, to enable embodied, relational, transformational change in the present moment.

Coach training needs to help future coaches move beyond both individualism and human-centrism, realizing they are never just coaching an individual. They may be coaching with and through an individual, for the coachee arrives with their team dynamics, organizational culture, wider societal beliefs, assumptions, mindsets and the ecology, coursing through every aspect of their being. Coach training needs to be grounded in the understanding that has emerged from the quantum and complexity sciences, and help future coaches perceive, think, do and be systemic. This involves deep training in reflective and preflective practice and lifetime commitment to learn through supervision. It requires all individual coaches to have basic training in Systemic Team Coaching and organizational development, as a very high percentage of the issues brought to coaching by executives include:

- How do I develop my team?
- How do I deal with conflict in my team, or with difficult team members?
- How do I manage difficult organizational politics or conflicting demands?

To ensure that coaches do not end up helping coaches address short-term symptoms, which may well make the wider systemic issues worse, wider training in team, team of teams and organizational development and transformation is essential.

Those who teach Systemic Team Coaching need to extend their training to ensure that each trainee knows how to be part of a team of team coaches; one that can carry out Systemic Team of Teams Coaching and organizational transformation. Trainings in organizational development need to address the skills in coaching, team coaching and team of teams coaching that are necessary to work with the key individuals, teams and connections within and beyond the organization.

We must move beyond specialisms to integrate the inter-disciplinary trainings that address development in, and across, all systemic levels, from the individual to the wider ecology.

Going forward

There is much to be done. The challenges of our time require that we all step up; that we all raise our sights from our local concerns and professional silos, to see the interconnected bigger picture. We must realize we are all part of the 'great work of our times'. Thomas Berry (1999) illuminates the nature of this great work very eloquently:

> The Great Work is an era of transition from a period of a culture that has been predominantly human-centred and self-destructive to a mode of existence that is life centred and Earth-centred.

To proceed into the future effectively, we must recognize our dependence on the Earth, as well as our potential to foster the flourishing of life.

Leaders, and all those involved in developing individual and collective leadership, share this great work of our times, which is to transform human consciousness so that our species is future-fit to thrive part of the Earth's living ecology (Hawkins, 2025). Our hope is that this book has made a small contribution to this great and urgent calling, and helped you and all those your work impacts, to better contribute and play your part.

If not now, when?
If not us, then who?
If not working together, then how?

RESEARCH PARTNERS AND PARTICIPATING ORGANIZATIONS

Seventy organizations took part in our research, some of which wish to be kept anonymous. The named organizations are:

Organization name	Location
Ace Up	USA
Guerbet	France
Hungarian Baptist Aid	Hungary
Kriminalvården (Swedish Prison and Probation Authority)	Sweden
Lesaffre China	China
MSF	Switzerland
Numeris	Canada
Peel Police	Canada
Renault	France
Servier	France
Terre des hommes	Lebanon
Terre des hommes	Global
The 4th Paradigm Technology Co. Ltd	China
Unilever	UK, Netherlands and Global
SITA FOR AIRCRAFT	The Netherlands
Brain Tumour Research	?
Leveros	UK and India
ASSA Insure Company	Brazil
Nestlé Centroamérica	Panama
Desert Snow	Central America
Kerzner international	UAE
Storm Communication	UAE

(continued)

(Continued)

Organization name	Location
Waimanalo Health Center	France
Rand Merchant Bank	South Africa
Hitachi Energy	Sweden
Mälarenergi	Sweden
Tangible SRL SB	Italy
Spark Centre	Canada
Marine Systems Technology	UK
ten23 health	Switzerland
ACCA	Global
Newzoo	Netherlands
Skyguide	Switzerland
HP Inc.	Global
GHD	Global
Pemberton Asset Management	UK
Fraport Twin Star Airport Management AD	Bulgaria
Sisma S.p.A.	Italy
CasAmica	Italy
IKEA Italia Retail srl	Italy
Aboca SPA	Italy
Promotica SPA	Italy
Cod' Crai Ovest	Italy
Standard Chartered Bank	Singapore
ABB	Global
Turbocharging Industries and Services India Private Limited	India
CSIRO	Australia
Alpine Shire Council	Australia
Schindler Lifts Australia Pty Ltd	Australia
Woven by Toyota	Japan
Straumann Group	USA

(continued)

(Continued)

Organization name	Location
Thermo Fisher	USA
Toast	USA
Datadog	France
British Army Leadership College	UK
Pemberton Asset Management	UK and global
Rand Merchant Bank and First Bank	South Africa
Singapore Civil Service	Singapore

Our panel of global research partners include:

Research Partners	Location
Bianca Soldatelli Aichinger	Portugal
Daniela Aneva	USA
Susana Azevedo	Portugal
Beata Barkoczi	Hungary
Houda Benjelloun	UAE
Dawn Bentley	UK
Ujjaval Buch	India
Mauricio Campos	Switzerland
Heather Clayton	Canada
Susan Douglas	USA
Madeliene Dunford	Kenya
Ilka Dunne	South Africa
Vlad Duțescu	Romania
Danela Ezekiel	UK
Tatiana Gupta	USA
Terry Hoffmann	USA
Tania Hodgkinson	Cypress
David Jarrett	UK
Christophe Mikolajczak	Belgium
Steve McInnes	Australia
Raffaella Napoli	Italy

(continued)

(Continued)

Research Partners	Location
Darine Najem	Lebanon
Terry Owen	USA
Madelien Perrier	France
Nick Pope	Australia
Smita Raghum	India
Fátima Ribeiro	Portugal
Selina Ryan	Australia
Luca Salvini	Italy
Ram S Ramanathan	India
Lucy Shenouda	Canada
Inge Simons	Switzerland
Jenny Sima	Sweden
Anders Troedsson	Sweden
Jean-François Vié	France
Salome Van Coller	South Africa
Anita Wang	China

GLOSSARY

account team a multidisciplinary and/or a multi-regional team brought together from across a company to focus on the relationship with one key customer or client organization.

action learning 'action learning couples the development of people in work organizations with action on their difficult problems... [it] makes the task the vehicle for learning and has three main components – people, who accept the responsibility for action on a particular task or issue; problems, or the tasks which are acted on; and the set of six or so colleagues who meet regularly to support and challenge each other to take action and to learn' (Pedler, 1997).

agile teaming is about quickly forming (and ending) teams as needed to achieve project-based commissions. They are helped by using Agile Methodology which help teams respond to unpredictability through incremental, iterative work cadences and empirical feedback.

Anthropocene a new geological epoch marked by a mass extinction of biodiversity driven by human activity, emphasizing humanity's profound impact on Earth's ecosystems and geology.

appreciative inquiry (AI) a strengths-based approach to organizational change, emphasizing what works well to envision and achieve a desired future through the four stages of 'Discovery, Dreaming, Design, and Delivery'.

coaching supervision 'the process by which a coach, with the help of a supervisor, can attend to understanding better both the client system and themselves as part of the client–coach system, and by so doing transform their work and develop their craft' (Hawkins and Smith, 2006). Supervision does this by also attending to transforming the relationship between the supervisor and coach and the relationship with the wider contexts in which the work is happening.

co-coaching where two or more coaches coach together bringing complementary skills and perspectives to team coaching.

collaborative leadership leadership that fosters alignment, accountability, and cohesion across multiple teams, enabling systemic collaboration while respecting individual team contexts.

culture as a systemic multi-layered system a view of culture comprising collective behaviours, feelings and beliefs, deeply influenced by historical and societal contexts.

ecosystemic partner an external stakeholder, where the relationship has developed in a partnership serving their wider joint ecosystem.

ecosystemic team coaching 'sees the team as co-evolving in dynamic relationship with its ever-changing ecosystem of interconnected teams, with which it co-creates shared value. Ecosystemic coaching focusses on the interplay between the team and other connected teams (inter-team coaching), its external partners (partnership coaching) and its wider stakeholder networks' (Hawkins, 2021).

ethical maturity expanding the breadth and depth of consideration that is brought to any issue or dilemma.

five disciplines of high-value creating teams a framework of team disciplines essential for team effectiveness developed by Peter Hawkins (2011b and 2021). They are purpose, clarifying, co-creating, connecting and core learning.

five keys of future-fit organizations these are purpose, stakeholder centric, partnering, learning and teaming.

fractal flourishing a concept emphasizing the interconnectedness of flourishing at systemic levels, from individuals to global ecosystems.

Hawkins' model of culture a multi-layered model that defines organizational culture through levels such as artefacts, patterns of behaviour, mindsets, emotional ground and motivational roots.

high-value creating team a team that co-creates beneficial value, with and for all their stakeholders.

high-value creating team of teams questionnaire a diagnostic tool to assess and improve the collaboration and value generation of interconnected teams.

Holacracy a system of organizational governance that replaces traditional hierarchical structures with a distributed authority model.

inquiry and sensemaking a stage in Systemic Team Coaching to understand current dynamics and align efforts with systemic goals.

lean process design based on maximizing customer value while minimizing waste.

learning team a group of people with a common purpose who take active responsibility for developing each other, themselves, their team and the wider organization in which they operate, through both action learning and unlearning.

meshwork a complex, interconnected structure where various elements or entities are woven together in a non-linear manner. It is characterized by overlapping connections and relationships, enabling flexibility and adaptability. In a meshwork, each node (or element) can influence and be influenced by multiple other nodes, creating a dynamic and resilient system.

metacrisis refers to deeply interconnected global challenges which transcend individual crises and amplify complexity, and which are all symptoms of the way humans think.

network a structured arrangement of interconnected nodes (which can represent individuals, organizations, systems, etc.) that communicate and exchange information or resources.

organizational learning methods and approaches developed to help whole organizations learn and develop in relation to the changing world they are within.

organizational life cycle the stages organizations go through – from inception, growth and maturity to potential decline – highlighting the need for adaptive strategies to ensure longevity and transformation.

polycrisis a state in which multiple crises interact simultaneously, amplifying their collective impact.

project team a team, with members often drawn from different teams, brought together for a specific, defined and time-limited task.

psychological safety a shared belief that team environments are safe for interpersonal risk-taking, fostering trust and openness.

requisite conflict the team having no more – or no less – conflict than currently exists in the system they lead or need to respond to.

requisite diversity having a level of diversity that is equal to the diversity in the stakeholder world they need to engage with.

scrum an agile team approach which emphasizes empirical feedback, team self-management and striving to build properly tested product innovations within short iterations.

systemic awareness understanding interconnections within systemic levels, recognizing impacts on and from larger systems.

systemic being involves cultivating the ability to be fully present and deeply attuned to the connections and patterns that exist across nested systems. This spans from the intrapersonal realm to the broader external world and unfolds over time, fostering a felt sense and holistic understanding of how these systems interact and evolve.

systemic doing focussed on systemic interventions, this approach emphasizes addressing relational patterns and wider systems rather than individual behaviours, to create systemic insights and transformative shifts.

systemic perceiving the ability to see, listen and sense the deeper patterns, flows and nested systemic levels, beyond what is present on the surface.

systemic supervision of team of teams coaches systemic supervision is the structured reflective practice of supporting coaches in addressing systemic complexities to enhance ethical practices, reflective capacity, professional growth, with consideration to whom and what ultimately needs to benefit from the supervision.

Systemic Team Coaching (STC) 'a process by which a team coach works with a whole team, both when they are together and when they are apart, in order to help them improve both their effectiveness and how they work together, and also how they develop their collective leadership to more effectively engage and co-create value with and for all their key stakeholder groups to jointly transform the wider business eco-system and create beneficial value for the wider ecology' (Hawkins, 2021).

Systemic Team of Teams Approach (STOTA) an integrative approach focussing on improving inter-team relationships and aligning efforts across systemic levels to ensure synergy, effectiveness and value creation across and beyond organizational boundaries.

Systemic Team of Teams Coaching (STOTC) Systemic Team of Teams Coaching is an organization and ecosystem-wide intervention, designed to foster effective collaboration and synergy among multiple teams, by focussing on partnering vertically, horizontally and transversally across the organization, as well as effectively teaming with stakeholders, beyond the organizational boundaries. It ensures that the team of teams function collectively and synergistically and are more effective than the sum of their parts through collaboration and partnering.

systemic thinking a cognitive approach that frames teams as interconnected parts of larger systems, emphasizing their collaborative purpose and dynamics. It considers broader contexts such as historical, social, ecological and relational influences on team behaviour and outcomes.

team-based culture an organizational culture that enables and supports empowered teams at all levels, effective agile teaming and a 'team of teams' approach.

Team Connect 360 a 360 feedback tool used in Systemic Team Coaching that maps to the Five Discipline Framework. It is used to gather 'outside-in feedback' from a variety of groups external to the team. It promotes deeper systemic insight and clarity around patterns and priorities.

team development any process carried out by a team, with or without assistance from outside, to develop their capability and capacity to work well together.

team KPIs Team Key Performance Indicators are measurable objectives that can only be achieved by the team members collaborating.

team maturity the developmental stage of a team characterized by its ability to self-organize, align around shared goals and sustain high-value creation while addressing conflicts constructively.

team of teams this model emphasizes that every team operates as part of a larger system, where success depends on both internal efficiency and external synergy with other teams, stakeholders and ecosystem partners.

Three Horizons a strategic framework (Sharpe, 2020) for balancing focus on current operations, near-term innovations and long-term foresight to ensure sustainable success and adaptability.

transformational team KPIs KPIs that are collectively created by the team, which the whole team fully own and are committed to and to which they hold each other mutually accountable; and which cannot be achieved by the way the team and it members currently operate; to be attained require the team to change its behaviours, ways of thinking and relating, its ways of partnering internally and externally, and its team processes.

virtual team a distributed group of people working together across distances to achieve a common purpose via technology.

RECOMMENDED RESOURCES

Further reading

This book builds on the earlier work on Systemic Team Coaching, which can be found in:

Hawkins, P (2021) *Leadership Team Coaching: Developing collective transformational leadership*, 4th edn, London: Kogan Page (This book contains sections on inter-team coaching and team of teams coaching.)

Hawkins, P (ed.) (2022) *Leadership Team Coaching in Practice: Case studies on creating highly effective teams*, 3rd edn, London: Kogan Page

A shorter introduction to Systemic Team Coaching is:

Leary-Joyce, J and Lines, H (2024) *Systemic Team Coaching*, London: Academy of Executive Coaching

Many blogs and articles on Systemic Team Coaching can be found on

https://renewalassociates.co.uk/resources/

and

https://www.systemicteamcoaching.com/

Other key books include:

Bushe, G R and Marshak, R J (2015) *Dialogic Organization Development: The theory and practice of transformational change*, Oakland, CA: Berrett-Koehler

Cooperrider, D L and Dutton, J E (eds) (1999) *Organizational Dimensions of Global Change: No limits to cooperation*, Thousand Oaks, CA: Sage Publications

Fussell, C (2017) *One Mission: How Leaders Build a Team of Teams* London: Macmillan

McChrystal, S, Collins, T, Silverman, D and Fussell, C (2015) *Team of Teams: New rules of engagement for a complex world*, New York: Penguin

Rod, A and Fridjhon, M (2016) *Creating Intelligent Teams: Leading with relationship systems intelligence*, Randburg: KR Publishing

Training and development programmes

Renewal Associates run training and development programmes in Systemic Team Coaching and Systemic Team of Teams Coaching, right around the world. Over 3,000 people right across the world have completed our trainings and many are part of local communities of practice.

These programmes come in three forms:

1 **In-house bespoke development programmes** for leaders, managers, HR, internal coaches and consultants.
2 **In-person trainings** that are held in many different centres around the world. These are run in partnership with Academy of Executive Coaching.
3 **Virtual trainings** that are run in partnership with Coaching.com and run every year, and people have attended from over 100 different countries.

There are three levels of training:

a. **Team Development Essentials.** This training provides the basic models, methods and tools to become team and systemic literate. It is available twice a year virtually and can be run in-house.
b. **Systemic Team Coaching Practitioner.** This training and development equips the practitioner to professionally coach teams systemically.
c. **Systemic Team Coaching Senior Practitioner.** This training and development deepens the practitioner Systemic Team Coaching and equips practitioners to professionally do Systemic Team of Teams Coaching and work with organizational transformation.

Details on all of these trainings are available on:

https://renewalassociates.co.uk/systemic-team-coaching/training-streams/

https://www.systemicteamcoaching.com/training-overview

Systemic Team Coaching supervision

Renewal Associates have a register of trained and accredited team coaching supervisors, including those who are experienced in Systemic Team of Teams Coaching.

For information on these supervisors write to:

admin@renewalassociates.co.uk

Information on our trainings in Team Coach Supervision can also be found on

https://renewalassociates.co.uk/training-and-qualifications/team-coach-supervision-training-programme/

McChrystal Group

Renewal Associates would like to acknowledge the work and support of the McChrystal Group who have pioneered work in both the concept of 'Team of Teams' and helping leaders in organizations apply it. They hold the registered trademark for utilizing the term 'Team of teams' in leadership development in the USA and help many organizations both in the USA and internationally. www.mcchrystalgroup.com

BIBLIOGRAPHY

Adizes, I (1990) *Managing Organizational Change: The new paradigm*, Santa Barbara, CA: Adizes Institute Publishing

American Medical Association (2020) Website. https://code-medical-ethics.ama-assn.org/ (archived at https://perma.cc/6AS9-D2JZ)

American Psychological Association (2017) Ethical Principles of Psychologists and Code of Conduct (2002, amended effective 1 June 2010, and 1 January 2017). www.apa.org/ethics/code/ (archived at https://perma.cc/7LEY-6MKU)

Amidon, E (2015) *The Open Path: Recognizing non-dual awareness*, Boulder, CO: Shambhala Publications

Anderson, M C (2001) Executive briefing: Case study on the return on investment of executive coaching. www.metrixglobal.net

Argyris, C and Schön, D A (1974) *Theory in Practice: Increasing professional effectiveness*, San Francisco, CA: Jossey-Bass

Argyris, C and Schön, D A (1978) *Organizational Learning: A theory of action perspective*, Reading, MA: Addison-Wesley

Assagioli, R (1993) *Psychosynthesis*, London: Aquarian/Thorsons

Barabási, A L (2002) *Linked: The new science of networks*, Cambridge, MA: Perseus Publishing

Bateson, G (1972) *Steps to an Ecology of Mind*, New York: Ballantine Books

Bateson, G (1978) The pattern which connects, *The CoEvolution Quarterly*, (Summer), 5–15

Bateson, G (1979) *Mind and Nature: A necessary unity*, New York: Dutton

Bateson, G (1991) *A Sacred Unity: Further steps to an ecology of mind*, New York: Harper Collins

Beckhard, R (1972) Optimizing team building effort, *Journal of Contemporary Business*, 1(3), 23–32

Berne, E (2010) *Games People Play: The psychology of human relationships*, London: Penguin Books

Berry, T (1999) *The Great Work: Our way into the future*, New York: Bell Tower

Bersin, J (2021) *HR Technology Market 2021: Trends, solutions, and future directions*, Bersin by Deloitte

Boehm, C (1999) *Hierarchy in the Forest: The evolution of egalitarian behaviour*, Cambridge, MA: Harvard University Press

Bohm, D and Nichol, L (1998) *On Dialogue* (1st edn), London: Routledge

Boulton, J (2024) *The Dao of Complexity: Making sense and making waves in turbulent times*, Berlin: De Gruyter

Bragg, S M (2009) *Why Mergers Fail: The management perspective*, AccountingTools Inc

Brahma Kumaris World Spiritual University (2023) www.brahmakumaris.uk/ (archived at https://perma.cc/VRW5-ZY5R)

Braks, A (2020) *Executive Coaching in Strategic Holistic Leadership: The drivers and dynamics of vertical development*, London: OpenUP, McGraw-Hill

Braks, A (2024) Being Purposeful: Is this to be purpose-driven or purpose-led? www.stageshift.coach/antoinette_braks (archived at https://perma.cc/ M45N-AS76)

Brassey, J, Hartenstein, L, Jeffery, B and Simon, P (2023) Working nine to thrive, McKinsey Health Institute, www.mckinsey.com/mhi/our-insights/working-nine-to-thrive (archived at https://perma.cc/DXZ2-GW7S)

Bridges, W (1991) *Managing Transitions: Making the most of change*, Reading, MA: Addison-Wesley

Brown, J, and Isaacs, D (2005) *The World Café: Shaping our futures through conversations that matter*, San Francisco: Berrett-Koehler Publishers

Bushe, G R (2013) Generative process, generative outcome: The transformational potential of appreciative inquiry, *The Appreciative Inquiry Practitioner*, 15(3), 8–14

Bushe, G R and Marshak, R J (2015) *Dialogic Organization Development: The theory and practice of transformational change*, Oakland, CA: Berrett-Koehler

Capra, F (1996) *The Web of Life: A new scientific understanding of living systems*, New York: Anchor Books

Capra, F and Luisi, P L (2016) *The Systems View of Life: A unifying vision*, Cambridge: Cambridge University Press

Carboni, I and Cross, R (2020) *Collaborative Practices of High-Performing Teams: Agility at the Point of Execution*, Connected Commons, July

Carr, C and Peters, J (2012) The experience and impact of team coaching: A dual case study, Doctoral dissertation, Middlesex University, Institute for Work Based Learning

Carroll, M and Shaw, E (2013) *Ethical maturity in the helping professions*, London: Jessica Kingsley

Carson, R (1962) *Silent Spring*, Boston: Houghton Mifflin

Carter, J, O'Connor, P and O'Donovan, E (2020) *The People Side of Agile: How to help your team deliver*, London: Kogan Page

Charmaz, K (2014) *Constructing Grounded Theory* (2nd edn), Los Angeles, CA: Sage

Cheng, F (2009) *Five Meditations on Beauty*, translated by J Emmons, New York: Penguin Books

Clerk, K, Harrison, T and Fenton, J (2016) Customer engagement and retention: An empirical study, *Journal of Business Research*, 69(2), 640–47

Collins, J C (2001) *Good To Great: Why some companies make the leap and others don't*, London: Random House

Collins, J C and Lazier, B (2020) *Beyond Entrepreneurship 2.0: Turning your business into an enduring company*, London: Random House

Cooperrider, D L and Dutton, J E (eds) (1999) *Organizational Dimensions of Global Change: No limits to cooperation*, Thousand Oaks, CA: Sage Publications

Cooperrider, D L and Godwin, L (2022) Our Earthshot moment: Net positive OD for the creation of a world of full spectrum flourishing, in One Giant Leap: How Organization Development and Change Can Help Organizations, Industries, and World-changing Megacommunities Lead the Net-Positive Earthshot, *The OD Review*, 54(1) (spring), 7–22

Cooperrider, D L and Srivastva, S (1987) Appreciative inquiry in organizational life, *Research in Organizational Change and Development*, 1, 129–69

Covey, S R (2013) *The 7 Habits of Highly Effective People: Powerful lessons in personal change* (25th anniversary edn), New York: Simon & Schuster

Cross, R, Parise, S and Weiss, L (2007) The role of networks in organizational change, *The McKinsey Quarterly*, 2, 28–35

D'Arcy, L (2015) Fractal perspectives on systems thinking: Exploring connectivity in growth, *Journal of Systemic Change*, 2(1), 15–29

Dartnall, E (2012) Supervisors' perceptions of the impact of supervision on therapeutic outcomes: A grounded theory study, Doctoral dissertation, City University, London

De Geus, A (1997) *The Living Company: Habits for survival in a turbulent business environment*, Cambridge, MA: Harvard Business School Press

de Mello, A (1982) *The Song of the Bird*, Garden City, NY: Image Books

De Meuse, K P, Dai, G and Lee, R J (2009) Evaluating the effectiveness of executive coaching: Beyond ROI? *Coaching: An International Journal of Theory, Research and Practice*, 2(2), 117–34

Denning, S (2011) Steve Jobs and why big companies die? www.forbes.com/sites/stevedenning/2011/11/19/peggy-noonan-on-steve-jobs-and-why-big-companies-die/ (archived at https://perma.cc/4J6K-XS5B)

Dethmer, J, Chapman, D and Warner Klemp, K (2015) *The 15 Commitments of Conscious Leadership: A new paradigm for sustainable success*, Conscious Leadership Group.

De Waal, F B M (2009, UK edn 2019) *The Age of Empathy: Nature's lessons for a kinder society*, London: Souvenir Press

Douglas, S, Page, A, Moltu, C, Kyron, M and Satterthwaite, T (2024) The connections matter: Bi-directional learning in program evaluation and practice-oriented research, *Administration and Policy in Mental Health and Mental Health Services Research*, 51, 318–35

Duțescu, V (2024) *Navigating the Shifting Sands* (Review of *Navigating the Shifting Sands*). EMCC Romania blog. https://www.emccromania.org/blog/ navigating-the-shifting-sands-psychological-safety (archived at https://perma. cc/629P-T7E6)

Edmondson, A C (2012) *Teaming: How organizations learn, innovate, and compete in the knowledge economy*, San Francisco, CA: Jossey-Bass

Elkington, J and Braun, S (2014) *The Breakthrough Challenge: 10 ways to connect today's profits with tomorrow's bottom line*, San Francisco, CA: Jossey-Bass

Emery, F E and Trist, E L (1965) The causal texture of organizational environments, *Human Relations*, 18(1), 21–32

Emery, F and Trist, E (1972) *Toward a Social Ecology: Contextual approaches to the human ecosystem*, New York: Plenum Press

Erdal, D (2011) *Beyond the Corporation: Humanity working*, London: Bodley Head

Forster, E M (1910) *Howards End*, London: Edward Arnold

Franklin, B (1732) *Poor Richard's Almanack*, Philadelphia, PA: Benjamin Franklin

Freeman, L C (1979) Centrality in social networks: Conceptual clarification, *Social Networks*, 1(3), 215–39

Frengos, T (2024) *Fifteen Pauses: The life changing silence and stillness of Japanese Ma*, Tom Frengos: Tokyo

Fussell, C (2017) *One Mission: How leaders build a team of teams*, London: Macmillan

Garcia, H and Miralles, F (2017) *IKIGAI: The Japanese secret to a long and happy life*, London: Penguin Books

Garratt, B (1987) *The Learning Organisation*, London: Fontana/Collins

Gergen, K J (1999) *An Invitation to Social Construction*, London: Sage Publications

Gergen, K J (2009) Social construction: Revolution in the making, in Gergen K J (ed.), *An Invitation to Social Construction* (pp 1–30), London: Sage

Gergen, K J, McNamee, S and Barrett, F J (2001) Toward transformative dialogue, *International Journal of Public Administration*, 24(7–8), 679–707

Gerstner, L V, Jr (2002) *Who Says Elephants Can't Dance?: Leading a great enterprise through dramatic change*, New York: Harper Business

Glaser, B G and Strauss, A L (1967) *The Discovery of Grounded Theory: Strategies for qualitative research*, Chicago, IL: Aldine Publishing

Goldsmith, M (2004) Coaching for behavioral change, *Leader to Leader*, 2004(31), 37–43

Goldsmith, M (2011) *Mojo: How to get it, how to keep it, how to get it back if you lose it*, London: Profile Books

Goldsmith, M (2013) Our 'pay for results' executive coaching approach. www. marshallgoldsmith.com/articles/our-pay-for results-executive-coaching-process/

Goldsmith, M and Reiter, M (2007) *What Got You Here Won't Get You There: How successful people become even more successful*, New York: Hyperion

Goleman, D (1998) *Working with Emotional Intelligence*, New York: Bantam Books

Goleman, D (2006) *Social Intelligence: The new science of human relationships*, New York: Bantam Books

Grant, A M (2012) ROI is a poor measure of coaching success: towards a more holistic approach using a well-being and engagement framework, *Coaching: An International Journal of Theory, Research and Practice*, 2012, 1–12, London: Routledge

Greiner, L E (1972) Evolution and revolution as organizations grow, *Harvard Business Review*, 50(4), 37–46

Greiner, L E (1998) Evolution and revolution as organizations grow, *Harvard Business Review*, 76(3), 55–65

Gumbel, P (2009, 8 June) Toyota at the tipping point, *Time*. http://content.time.com/time/magazine/article/0,9171,1902834,00.html

Gunderson, L H and Holling, C S (2002) *Panarchy: Understanding transformations in human and natural systems*, Washington, DC: Island Press

Hamel, G and Prahalad, C (1994) *Competing for the Future* (1st edn), Boston, MA: Harvard Business School Press

Hammer, M and Champy, J (1993) *Reengineering the Corporation: A manifesto for business revolution*, New York: Harper Business

Handy, C (1994) *The Empty Raincoat: Making sense of the future*, London: Hutchinson

Hanh Thich Nhat (1987) *Interbeing: Fourteen guidelines for engaged Buddhism*, London: Parallax Press

Harari, Y N (2016) *Homo Deus: A brief history of tomorrow*, London: Harvill Secker

Harari, Y N (2018) *21 Lessons for the 21st Century*, London: Jonathan Cape

Hastings, R and Meyer, E (2020) *No Rules Rules: Netflix and the culture of reinvention*, New York: Penguin Press

Hawkins, P (1986) Living the learning, PhD thesis, University of Bath Management School

Hawkins, P (1991) The spiritual dimension of the learning organisation, *Management Education and Development*, 22(3), 172–87

Hawkins, P (1994) The changing view of learning, in Burgoyne, J (ed.), *Towards the Learning Company*, London: McGraw-Hill

Hawkins, P (1997) Organizational culture: Sailing between evangelism and complexity, *Human Relations*, 50(4), 417–40

Hawkins, P (2004) A centennial tribute to Gregory Bateson 1904–1980 and his influence on the fields of organizational development and action research, *Action Research*, 2(4), 409–23

Hawkins, P (2005) *The Wise Fool's Guide to Leadership*, Winchester: O Books

Hawkins, P (2011a) Building emotional, ethical and cognitive capacities in coaches: a developmental model of supervision, in Passmore, J (ed.), *Supervision in Coaching*, London: Kogan Page

Hawkins, P (2011b) *Leadership Team Coaching: Developing collective transformational leadership* (1st edn) (2nd edn 2014, 3rd edn 2017), London: Kogan Page

Hawkins, P (2012) *Creating a Coaching Culture*, Maidenhead: Open University Press/McGraw-Hill

Hawkins, P (2015) Cracking the shell, *Coaching at Work*, 10(2), 42–45

Hawkins, P (2017) Tomorrow's leadership and the necessary revolution in today's leadership development, Henley Business School. www.henley.fi/en/news-events/catch-up-with-our-latest-research-tomorrows-leadership-and-the-necessary-revolution-in-todays-leadership-development/

Hawkins, P (2018) *A Systemic Primer*, Renewal Associates. www:renewalassociates.co.uk (archived at https://perma.cc/YQ5J-QDCX)

Hawkins, P (2019a) Resourcing: The neglected third leg of supervision, in Turner, E and Palmer, S (eds), *The Heart of Coaching Supervision: Working with reflection and self-care*, Abingdon: Routledge

Hawkins, P. (2019b) Systemic organizational learning and the coevolution of organizational culture, Chapter 10 in Örtenblad, A R (ed.), *The Handbook on the Learning Organization*, Oxford: Oxford University Press

Hawkins, P (2019c) Systemic team coaching, in Clutterbuck, D, Gannon, J, Hayes, S, Iordanou, I, Lowe, K and MacKie, D (eds), *The Practitioner's Handbook of Team Coaching*, London: Sage

Hawkins, P (2020a) We need to move beyond the high-performing teams. www.renewalassociates.co.uk/2020/07/we-need-to-move-beyond-high-performing-teams/

Hawkins, P (2020b) We are all in this together: Coronavirus, climate change, collaboration and consciousness change, 20 September. www.renewalassociates.co.uk/2020/09/we-are-all-in-this-together-corona-virus-climate-crisis-collaboration-and-consciousness-change-2/

Hawkins, P (2020c) Let the wider ecology do the coaching, 19 November. www.renewalassociates.co.uk/2020/11/let-the-wider-ecology-do-the-coaching/

Hawkins, P (2021) *Leadership Team Coaching: Developing collective transformational leadership* (4th edn), London: Kogan Page

Hawkins, P (2022a) Coaching the team leader, Chapter 31 in Underhill, P, Passmore, J and Goldsmith, M (eds), *Coach Me! Your personal board of directors* (pp 108–110), Hoboken, NJ: Wiley

Hawkins, P (ed.) (2022b) *Leadership Team Coaching in Practice: Case studies on creating highly effective teams* (3rd edn), London: Kogan Page

Hawkins, P (2023a) Is your inner team more than the sum of its parts? www.
renewalassociates.co.uk/Blogs (archived at https://perma.cc/29WT-VMN2)

Hawkins, P (2023b) Transforming David Kantor's four player model of team roles.
www.renewalassociates.co.uk/Blogs (archived at https://perma.cc/Q3EL-458R)

Hawkins, P (2023c) Transforming ourselves enabling others, and opening the seven
levels: A practice, in Curtis, M (ed.), *Cherishing the Earth: Nourishing the spirit*,
London: The Lindsey Press

Hawkins, P (2024a) The heart of systemic ethics. Ethical Edge Insights, 1, 5
December, Vanguard Insights. www.ethicaledgeinsights.com (archived at https://
perma.cc/LA8L-9SKH)

Hawkins, P (2024b) Is your team safe enough: Beyond psychological maturity.
www.renewalassociates.co.uk (archived at https://perma.cc/ZL35-R47T)

Hawkins, P (2025) *Beauty in Leadership and Coaching: And its role in
transforming human consciousness*, London: Routledge

Hawkins, P and Carr, C (2023) Ethics in team coaching, Chapter 10, in Smith,
W A, Passmore, J, Turner, E, Lai, Y L and Clutterbuck, D (eds), *The Ethical
Coaches' Handbook: A guide to developing ethical maturity in practice*,
London: Routledge

Hawkins, P and Hogan A (2022) Coaching the board: How coaching boards is
different from coaching executive teams, Chapter 15 in Hawkins, P (ed.),
Leadership Team Coaching in Practice, London: Kogan Page

Hawkins, P and McMahon, A (2020) *Supervision in the Helping Professions* (5th
edn), London: McGraw-Hill Open University Press

Hawkins, P and Presswell, D (2022) Using embodied interventions in team
coaching, in Hawkins, P (ed.), *Leadership Team Coaching in Practice*, London:
Kogan Page.

Hawkins, P. and Ryde, J. (2020) *Integrative Psychotherapy in Theory and Practice:
A relational, systemic and ecological approach*, London: Jessica Kingsley

Hawkins, P and Smith, N (2006) *Coaching, Mentoring and Organizational
Consultancy*, Maidenhead and New York: Open University Press

Hawkins, P and Smith, N (2013) *Coaching, Mentoring and Organizational
Consultancy: Supervision, skills and development* (2nd edn), Maidenhead: Open
University Press

Hawkins, P and Turner, E (2020) *Systemic Coaching: Delivering values beyond the
individual*, London: Routledge

Hay, J (2009) *Transactional Analysis For Trainers*, (2nd edn), Nottingham:
Sherwood Publishing

Hiatt, J M (2006) *ADKAR: A model for change in business, government and our
community*, Loveland, CO: Prosci

Hiatt, J and Creasey, T (2012) *Change Management: The people side of change*,
Loveland, CO: Prosci Research

Holling, C S and Gunderson, L H (2002) *Panarchy: Understanding transformations in human and natural systems*, Washington DC: Island Press

Hutchins, G (2012) *The Nature of Business: Redesigning for resilience*, Totnes, Devon: Green Books

Hutchins, G (2016) *Future-Fit*, New York: CreateSpace Independent Publishers

Hutchins, G (2021) *The Regenerative Business: How to align your business with nature for sustainable success*, Devon: Greenleaf Publishing

Hutchins, G (2024) *Nature Works: Activating regenerative leadership consciousness*, Kent: Wordzworth Publishing. https://wordzworth.com (archived at https://perma.cc/9RN8-69FD)

Hutchins, G and Storm, L (2019) *Regenerative Leadership: The DNA of life-affirming 21st century organizations*, Kent: Wordzworth Publishing. https://wordzworth.com (archived at https://perma.cc/UKV4-B4BG)

Ingold, T (2007) *Lines: A brief history*, London: Routledge

Ingold, T (2011) *Being Alive: Essays on movement; knowledge and connection*, London: Routledge

Ingold, T (2015) *The Life of Lines*, London: Routledge

International Coaching Federation (ICF) (2021). ICF Code of Ethics. Revised 25 June 2021. Available at: https://coachingfederation.org/about/icf-ethics (archived at https://perma.cc/KQ4A-FYT9)

Investment Office (2024) www.investmentoffice.com/Observations/Chart_Gallery/Average_Company_Liefspan_on_S_P_500_Index.html (archived at https://perma.cc/YXC2-YKJC)

IPCC Intergovernmental Panel on Climate Change (2021) Climate Change 2021: The physical science basis. Contribution of Working Group I to the Sixth Assessment Report of the Intergovernmental Panel on Climate Change. Cambridge University Press

Isaacs, W (1999) *Dialogue and the Art of Thinking Together*, New York: Doubleday

Isaacson, W (2011) *Steve Jobs: The exclusive biography*, New York: Simon and Schuster

Ismail, S, Malone, M S and Van Geest, Y (2014) *Exponential Organizations: Why new organizations are ten times better, faster, and cheaper than yours (and what to do about it)*, New York: Diversion Books

Jacobs, R W J (1997) *Real-time Strategic Change: How to involve an entire organization in fast and far-reaching change*, New York: Penguin

Johnson, B (1992) *Polarity Management: Identifying and managing unsolvable problems*, Arvada, CO: Whole Systems Enterprises

Jung, C (1966) *Collected Works* (2nd edn), London: Routledge

Kahane, A (2012) *Transformative Scenario Planning: Working together to change the future*, San Francisco, CA: Berrett-Koehler

Kahane, A (2019) *Facilitating Breakthrough: How to remove obstacles, bridge differences, and move forward together*, Oakland, CA: Berrett-Koehler

Kantor, D (2012) *Reading the Room: Group dynamics for coaches and leaders*, San Francisco, CA: Jossey-Bass

Karpman, S (1968) Fairy tales and script drama analysis, *Transactional Analysis Bulletin*, 7(26), 39–43

Katzenbach, J R and Smith, D K (2019) *The Wisdom of Teams: Creating the high-performance organization*, updated edn, Cambridge, MA: Harvard Business Review Press

Kauffman, S (1993) *The Origins of Order: Self-organization and selection in evolution*, New York: Oxford University Press

Kauffman, S A (1995) *At Home in the Universe: The search for the laws of self-organization and complexity*, New York: Oxford University Press

Keesing, R (1974) Review of the book 'Steps to an ecology of mind', by G Bateson, *American Anthropologist*, 76, 370–72. Doi.org/10.1525/aa.1974.76.2.02a00330 (archived at https://perma.cc/W6WE-TEST)

Kegan, R (1994) *In Over Our Heads: The mental demands of modern life*, Cambridge, MA: Harvard University Press

Kegan, R and Lahey, L L (2009) *Immunity to Change*, Cambridge, MA: Harvard Business Review Press

Kellerman, B (2012) *The End of Leadership*, New York: Harper Business

Kimmerer, R (2020) *Braiding Sweetgrass: Indigenous wisdom, scientific knowledge and the teachings of plants*, London: Penguin Books

Kirkpatrick, D L (1977) Evaluating training programmes: Evidence vs. proof, *Training and Development Journal*, 31(11), 9–12

Kirkpatrick, D L and Kirkpatrick, J D (1994) *Evaluating Training Programs*, San Francisco, CA: Berrett-Koehler

Kohlberg, L (1981) *Essays on Moral Development*, Vol. I: The Philosophy of Moral Development, San Francisco, CA: Harper & Row

Kotter, J P (1995) Leading change: Why transformation efforts fail, *Harvard Business Review*, March–April 1995, 59–67

Kübler-Ross, E and Kessler, D (2005) *On Grief and Grieving: Finding the meaning of grief through the five stages of loss*, New York: Scribner

Kuhn, T (1962 and 1970) *The Structure of Scientific Revolutions* (2nd edn), Chicago: University of Chicago Press

Laloux, F (2014) *Reinventing Organisations: A guide to creating organisations inspired by the next stage of human consciousness*, Belgium: Nelson Parker

Lawrence, M, Homer-Dixon, T, Janzwood, S, Rockström, J, Renn, O and Donges, J F (2024) Global polycrisis: The causal mechanisms of crisis entanglement, *Global Sustainability*, 7, e6

Leary-Joyce, J and Lines, H (2017 and 2nd edn 2024) *Systemic Team Coaching*, London: Academy of Executive Coaching

Lencioni, P (2002) *The Five Dysfunctions of a Team: A leadership fable*, San Francisco, CA: Jossey-Bass

Lent, J (2021) *The Web of Meaning*, London: Profile Books

Leopold, A (1949) *A Sand County Almanac with Essays on Conservation from Roun River*, New York: Oxford University Press, reproduced 1989

Lewin, K (June 1947) Frontiers in group dynamics: Concept, method and reality in social science; social equilibria and social change, *Human Relations*, 1, 5–41

Lewin, K and Lewin, G W (eds) (1948) *Resolving Social Conflicts: Selected papers on group dynamics (1935–1946)*, New York: Harper and Brothers

Lifton, R J (1993) *The Protean Self: Human resilience in an age of human fragmentation*, New York: Basic Books

Loevinger, J (1976) *Ego Development*, San Francisco, CA: Jossey-Bass

Lovelock, J (1979) *Gaia*, Oxford: Oxford University Press

Luetz, J M (2014) The positive drama triangle: A new perspective on the conflict triangle, *International Journal of Coaching in Organizations*, 12(1), 21–36

Macy, J (1998) *World as Lover, World as Self: Courage for global justice and ecological renewal*, Berkeley, CA: Parallax Press

Macy, J (2009) The great turning. 29 June. www.ecoliteracy.org/article/great-turning (archived at https://perma.cc/9W3H-UJP4)

Macy, J and Johnstone, C (2012) *Active Hope: How we face the mess we are in without going crazy*, Novato, CA: New World Library

Mann, C (2016) *Strategic Trends in the Use of Coaching*, 6th Ridler Report, London: Ridler & Co Ltd

Margulis, L (1998) *Symbiotic Planet : A new look at evolution*, New York: Basic Books

Marshak, R J and Bushe, G R (2009) The postmodern turn in organization development, *The Journal of Applied Behavioral Science*, 45(3), 201–27

Martin, R (2014) *Playing to Win: How strategy really works*, Cambridge, MA: Harvard Business Review Press

Mathews, F (2009) Invitation to Ontopoetics, in PAN *Philosophy Activism Nature*, 6

Maturana, H R and Varela, F J (1980) *Autopoiesis and Cognition: Realization of the living*, (2nd edn), Dordrecht: Springer Netherlands

McChrystal, S, Collins, T, Silverman, D and Fussell, C (2015) *Team of Teams: New rules of engagement for a complex world*, New York: Penguin

McGilchrist, I (2009) *The Master and his Emissary: The divided brain and the making of the western world*, New Haven, CT: Yale University Press

McGilchrist, I (2021) *The Matter with Things: Our brains, our delusions and the unmaking of the world, Vol I and II*, London: Perspectiva Press

McGovern, J, Lindermann, M, Vergara, M A, Murphy, S, Barker, L and Warrenfelz, R (2001) Maximizing the impact of executive coaching: Behavioral change, organizational outcomes and return on investment, *The Manchester Review*, 6(1), 1–9

McKinsey Quarterly. (2008) Enduring ideas: The 7-S Framework. 1 March. Available at: https://www.mckinsey.com/capabilities/strategy-and-corporate-finance/our-insights/enduring-ideas-the-7-s-framework (Accessed: 23 March 2025).

McKinsey and Company (2021) Mergers and Acquisitions: The lessons to learn. McKinsey M&A Insights. www.mckinsey.com (archived at https://perma.cc/ UXT5-TSHF)

McKinsey (2023) New leadership in an era of thriving organizations. McKinsey. www.mckinsey.com (archived at https://perma.cc/UXT5-TSHF)

McLuhan, M (1964) *Understanding Media: The extensions of man*, New York: McGraw-Hill

Mill, J S (1863) *Utilitarianism*, London: Parker, Son, and Bourn

Miller, H (1957) *Big Sur*, New York: New Directions

Minuchin, S (1974) *Families and Family Therapy*, Cambridge, MA: Harvard University Press

Morin, E (1999) The progress of knowledge has led to a regression of thought. https://footnotes2plato.com/2024/02/03/the-progress-of-knowledge-has-led-to-a-regression-of-thought-by-edgar-morin/ (archived at https://perma.cc/ GK8Q-N4DL)

Murray, W H (1951) *The Scottish Himalayan Expedition*, London: Dent

Naess, A (1987) Self-realization: An ecological approach to being in the world, *The Trumpeter,* 4(3), 35–42

Naess, A and Rothenberg, D (2011) *Ecology, Community and Lifestyle*, Cambridge: Cambridge University Press

Nooyi, I (2008) Discussion at the annual meeting of the World Economic Forum. https://2001-2009.state.gov/secretary/rm/2008/01/99627.htm (archived at https://perma.cc/MZ62-ASF8)

Oshry, B (1995, 2nd edn 2007) *Seeing Systems: Unlocking the mysteries of organizational life*, San Francisco, CA: Berrett-Koehler

Oshry, B (1999) *Leading Systems: Lessons from the power lab*, San Francisco, CA: Berrett-Koehler

Ouspensky, P D (1950) *In Search of the Miraculous: Fragments of an unknown teaching*, London: Routledge & Kegan Paul

Owen, H (2008) *Open Space Technology: A user's guide* (3rd edn), San Francisco, CA: Berrett-Koehler

Parker-Wilkins, V (2006) Business impact of executive coaching: Demonstrating monetary value, *Industrial and Commercial Training*, 38, 122

Parlett, M (2024) *Future sense: Five explorations of whole intelligence for a world that is waking-up*, Leicestershire: Matador Publishing

Pedler, M, Burgoyne, J G and Boydell, T (1991) *The Learning Company: A strategy for sustainable development*, London: McGraw-Hill

Perls, F (1969) *Ego, Hunger and Aggression: A revision of Freud's theory and method*, New York: Random House

Peters, J and Carr, C (2013a) *50 Terrific Tips for Teams: Proven strategies for building high performing teams*, Calgary, Alberta: InnerActive Leadership Associates,

Peters, J and Carr, C (2013b) *High Performance Team Coaching: A comprehensive system for leaders and coaches*, Calgary, Alberta: InnerActive Leadership Associates

Peters, T J and Waterman, R H (1982) *In Search of Excellence*, New York: Harper & Row

Petrie, N (2014) Vertical Leadership Development, Part 1: Developing Leaders for a Complex World. White Paper, Centre for Creative Leadership. http://insights. ccl.org/wp-content/uploads/2015/04/VerticalLeadersPart1.pdf

Philips, P P and Philips, J J (2007) *The Value of Learning: How organizations capture value and ROI and translate them into support, improvement and funds*, San Francisco, CA: John Wiley and Sons

Philips, P P, Philips, J J and Edwards, L A (2012) *Measuring the Success of Coaching: A step by step guide for measuring impact and calculating ROI*, Alexandria, VA: ASTD Press

Phillips, J J and Phillips, P P (2016) *Handbook of Training Evaluation and Measurement Methods*, London: Routledge

Pittinsky, T L (ed.) (2009) *Crossing the Divide: Intergroup leadership in a world of difference*, Cambridge, MA: Harvard Business Review Press

Polman, P and Winston, A (2021) *Net Positive: How courageous companies thrive by giving more than they take*, Cambridge, MA: Harvard Business Review Press

Porter, M E (1980) *Competitive Strategy: Techniques for analyzing industries and competitors*, New York: Free Press

Porter, M E (1985) *Competitive Advantage: Creating and Sustaining Superior Performance*, New York: Free Press

Porter, M E and Kramer, M R (2011) Shared value: How to re-invent capitalism and unleash a wave of innovation and growth, *Harvard Business Review*, January–February, 89(1/2), 62–77

Price, C and Toye, S (2017) *Accelerating Performance: How organizations can mobilize, execute, and transform with agility*, Hoboken, NJ: Wiley

Prigogine, I (1980) *From Being to Becoming: Time and complexity in the physical sciences*, San Francisco, CA: W H Freeman

Prigogine, I (1997) *The End of Certainty: Time, chaos, and the new laws of nature*, New York, NY: Free Press

Prigogine, I and Stengers, E (1984) *Order Out of Chaos*, New York: Bantam Books

Pritchett, P, Tichy, N M and Cohen, E (1998) *The Leadership Engine: Building leaders at every level*, Atlanta, GA: Pritchett & Hull Associates, Incorporated

Pross, A (2012) *What is Life: How chemistry becomes biology*, Oxford: Oxford University Press

Raihani, N (2021) *The Social Instinct: How cooperation shaped the world*, London: St Martin's Publishing Group

Revans, R W (1982) *The Origins and Growth of Action Learning*, London: Chartwell-Bratt, Bromley & Lund

Rifkin, J (2009) *The Empathic Civilization*, New York: Tarcher Perigee

Rifkin, J (2022) *The Age of Resilience: Reimagining existence on a rewilding earth*, London: Swift Press

Robertson, B J (2015) *Holacracy: The revolutionary management system that abolishes hierarchy*, London: Penguin/Random House

Roccas, S and Brewer, M (2002) Social identity complexity, *Personality and Social Psychology Review*, 6(2), 88–106

Rod, A and Fridjhon, M (2016) *Creating Intelligent Teams: Leading with relationship systems intelligence*, Randburg: KR Publishing

Rovelli, C (2022) *Helgoland: The strange and beautiful story of quantum physics*, London: Penguin

Rubin, I M, Plovnick, M S and Fry, R E (1978) *Task-orientated Team Development*, New York: McGraw-Hill

Rushkoff, D (2019) *Team Human*, New York: Norton

Scharmer, O (2009) *Theory U: Leading from the future as it emerges*, San Francisco, CA: Berrett-Koehler

Scharmer, O with Kaufer, K (2013) *Leading from the Emerging Future: From ego-system to eco-system economies*, San Francisco, CA: Berrett-Koehler

Schein, E H (1969 and 1988) *Process Consultation: Its role in organizational development*, London: Wesley

Schein, E H (1985) *Organizational Culture and Leadership*, San Francisco, CA: Jossey-Bass

Schein, E H (1992) *Organizational Culture and Leadership* (2nd edn), San Francisco, CA: Jossey-Bass

Schein, E H (1999) *Process Consultation Revisited: Building the helping relationship*, Lond: Addison-Wesley

Schein, E H (2003) On dialogue, culture, and organisational learning, *Reflections*, 4(4), 27–38

Schein, E H (2010) *Organizational culture and leadership* (4th edn), San Francisco, CA: Jossey-Bass

Schrödinger, E (1951) *Science and Humanism, Physics in our Time*, Cambridge: Cambridge University Press

Schwab, K (2016) *The Fourth Industrial Revolution*, Cologne/Geneva: World Economic Forum

Schwartz, R C (2023) *The Internal Family Systems Model and Therapy: A comprehensive guide to treatment* (2nd edn), New York, NY: The Guilford Press

Schweitzer, A (1987) *The Philosophy of Civilization*, Buffalo, New York: Prometheus Books

Schweitzer, A (2009) *Out of My Life and Thought: An autobiography* [*Aus meinem Leben und Denken*], translated by A B Lemke, Baltimore, MD: Johns Hopkins University Press (60th anniversary edn, pp 154–55)

Senge, P (1990 and 2006) *The Fifth Discipline: The art and practice of the learning organization*, New York: Doubleday

Senge, P (2008) *The Necessary Revolution: How individuals and organizations are working together to create a sustainable world*, New York: Doubleday

Senge, P, Kleiner, A, Ross, R, Roberts, C and Smith, B (1994) *The Fifth Discipline Field Book: Strategies and tools for building a learning organization*, New York: Doubleday

Sharpe, B (2020) *Three Horizons: The patterning of hope* (2nd edn), Axminster, Devon: Triarchy Press

Singer, P (2011) *Practical Ethics* (3rd edn), Cambridge: Cambridge University Press

Stacey, R (2010) *Complexity and Organizational Reality*, London: Routledge

Stacey, R D (2001) Complexity and the organization: A new perspective on organizations, in Van De Ven, P A A and Cummings, S G (eds), *The Handbook of Organizational Change and Innovation* (pp 233–50), Oxford: Oxford University Press

Stolorow, R D and Atwood, G E (1992) *Context of Being: The intersubjective foundations of psychological life*, Hilldale, NJ: The Analytic Press

Sustainable Solutions (2017) 'The Silo Effect': HR & Talent Predictions 2017–2020. https://sustainable-sos.livejournal.com/170764.html (archived at https://perma.cc/M96N-WD3B)

Suttie, J (2021) If humans evolved to cooperate, why is cooperation so hard? *Greater Good Magazine.* www.greatergood.berkeley.edu/article/item/if_humans_evolved_to_cooperate_why_is_cooperation_so_hard (archived at https://perma.cc/8ED5-KGZC)

Tichy, N M (1983) *Managing Strategic Change: Technical, political, and cultural dynamics*, New York: Wiley-Interscience

Tichy, N M (2002) *The Leadership Engine: How winning companies build leaders at every level*, New York: HarperCollins

Tooze, A (2022) Welcome to the world of the polycrisis, *Financial Times*, 28 October. www.ft.com/content/498398e7-11b1-494b-9cd3-6d669dc3de33 (archived at https://perma.cc/SRB7-7MAN)

Torbert, W R (2004) *Action Inquiry: The secret of timely and transforming leadership*, San Francisco, CA: Berrett-Koehler

Toynbee, A (1961 [1934]) *A Study of History: Vol 12, Reconsiderations*, Oxford: Oxford University Press

Turner, E and Passmore, J (2019) Mastering ethics, in Passmore, J, Underhill B and Goldsmith, M (eds), *Mastering Executive Coaching*, Abingdon: Routledge

Van Gennep, A (1909 [1977]) *Les rites de passage* (in French), Paris: Émile Nourry [*The Rites of Passage*], translated by M Vizedom and G Caffee, Hove, East Sussex: Psychology Press

Wack, P (1985a) Scenarios: Uncharted waters ahead, *Harvard Business Review*, 63(5), 72–89

Wack, P (1985b) The gentil bureaucrat: A scenario planning approach, in Crayton, W C T K, Rubino, D D P and Wack, P (eds), *Scenario Planning: A field guide to the future* (pp 81–97), London: Wiley

Waddock, S, Ansari, S and Haider, Z (2022) Responsibility and the role of business in society: A framework and future research directions, *Business and Society*, 61(5), 1001–21. https://doi.org/10.1177/00076503211022073

Wageman, R, Nunes, D A, Burruss, J A and Hackman, J R (2008) *Senior Leadership Teams: What it takes to make them great*, Boston, MA: Harvard Business Review Press

Wartzman, R (2011) *What Would Drucker Do Now? Solutions to today's toughest challenges from the father of modern management*, New York: McGraw-Hill Education

Weisbord, M and Janoff, S (2010) *Future Search: An action guide to finding common ground in organizations and communities*, San Francisco, CA: Berrett-Koehler Publishers

West, M A (2012) *Effective Teamwork: Practical lessons from organizational research* (3rd edn), Oxford: BPS Blackwell

West, M A (2013) Developing cultures of high-quality care, talk at the Kings Fund London, March, www.kingsfund.org.uk/audio-video/michael-west-developing-cultures-high-quality-care (archived at https://perma.cc/S3LQ-W44C)

West, M A and Dawson, J F (2012) *Employee Engagement and NHS Performance: Research report*, London: The King's Fund

West, M A, Guthrie, J P, Dawson, J F, Borrill, C S and Carter, M R (2006) Reducing patient mortality in hospitals: the role of human resource management, *Journal of Organizational Behaviour*, 27, 983–1002

Western, S (2013) *Leadership: A critical text*, London: Sage

Whitehead, A N (1929) *Process and Reality: An essay in cosmology*, London: G Allen & Unwin

Whybrow, A, Turner, E, McClean, J and Hawkins, P (2023) *Ecological and Climate-Conscious Coaching: A companion guide to evolving coaching practice*, London: Routledge

Wilson, E O (2012) *The Meaning of Human Existence*, New York: Liveright Publishing

Wilson, E O (2023) *The Diversity of Life*, Cambridge: Harvard University Press

Winnicott, D (1965) *Maturational Processes and the Facilitating Environment: Studies in the theory of emotional development*, London: Hogarth Press

Woese, C R and Goldenfield, N (2009) How the microbial world saved evolution from the Scylla of molecular biology and the Charybdis of the modern synthesis. *Microbiology and molecular biology reviews*, 73, 14–21

Yemiscigil, A, Born, D H and Ling, H (2023) What makes leadership development programs succeed? *Harvard Business Review*, 28 February. www.hks.harvard.edu/publications/what-makes-leadership-development-programs-succeed (archived at https://perma.cc/ENF7-4G6A)

Zaccaro, S J and DeChurch, L A (2012) Leadership forms and functions in multiteam systems, in Zaccaro, S J, Marks, M A and DeChurch, L A (eds), *Multiteam Systems: An organizational form for dynamic and complex environments* (pp 253–88), New York, NY: Taylor & Francis

INDEX

NB: page numbers in *italic* indicate figures or tables

Looking for another book?

Explore our award-winning
books from global business
experts in Human Resources,
Learning and Development

Scan the code to browse

www.koganpage.com/hr-learning-
development

Also from Kogan Page

www.koganpage.com

From 4 December 2025 the EU Responsible Person (GPSR) is:
eucomply oÜ, Pärnu mnt. 139b – 14, 11317 Tallinn, Estonia
www.eucompliancepartner.com

www.ingramcontent.com/pod-product-compliance
Lightning Source LLC
Chambersburg PA
CBHW040914210326
41597CB00030B/5077

9 781398 613959